The Eddy
by
Joe Paatalo

10,000 Lakes Publishing

© 2020 by Joe Paatalo.
10,000 Lakes Publishing
All rights reserved, including the right of reproduction in whole or in part by any means, electronic or mechanical, including photocopying, recording, or by any information storage and retrieval system, without written permission from the publisher.
Editing by Beth Lynne, Sean Bloomfield, and Colton Witte.
Interior Formatting by BZ Hercules.
Cover design and layout by Colton Witte.
Cover photo by Marilyn Beauchman.
ISBN: 978-0-9974768-4-2
Printed in the United States of America

For more information and copies of this book, visit 10kLP.com

For Dad, the best man I have ever known.

Acknowledgements

The author wishes to thank the following people for their inspiration and support: To all the kind teachers at Arlington High School, especially the Health and Environment folks who endured all my stories; to Toni McNaron and the College in the Schools folks at the University of Minnesota, all of whom have made me a better teacher; to Chris and Naomi Silver, the best friends a person could ever hope for; to Roy Erickson, John Eret and Ken Hanson, all great listeners and terrific road partners; to the wonderfully talented Judith Engstrom, my toughest critic and the person who made me a better writer; to the Paatalo and Nelson families, for all their love and understanding; to my incredible wife Lynn, for her unyielding faith, support, and love, for which I am forever grateful; to Sean Bloomfield and Colton Witte from 10,000 Lakes Publishing for their incredible support; and finally, to Toby from Como High School, wherever she may be.

Table of Contents

Prologue 1
Chapter 1 5
Chapter 2 11
Chapter 3 19
Chapter 4 31
Chapter 5 45
Chapter 6 57
Chapter 7 63
Chapter 8 71
Chapter 9 77
Chapter 10 85
Chapter 11 91
Chapter 12 99
Chapter 13 107
Chapter 14 115
Chapter 15 125
Chapter 16 141
Chapter 17 151
Chapter 18 157
Chapter 19 167
Chapter 20 175
Chapter 21 183
Chapter 22 191

Chapter 23 201
Chapter 24 211
Chapter 25 219
Chapter 26 227
Chapter 27 235
Chapter 28 237
Chapter 29 243
Chapter 30 251
Chapter 31 259
Chapter 32 263
Chapter 33 267
Chapter 34 275
Epilogue 281

The Eddy

Prologue

The young man steps into the river, spreads his feet for balance, and considers the conflicting currents he must cast across. There is easier water to fish, but he ignores it, instead focusing on the far bank where the water pools behind a boulder. Stripping line off his reel, he gauges the distance with a few false casts, and then launches his fly across the braided water so that it lands in the eddy behind the rock. A quick mend of his line and the fly hesitates for a moment before it is pulled under by the twisting current playing havoc with his fly line. For twenty minutes, he repeats this cast, each time trying to keep his fly afloat for as long as possible. He does not catch a fish, but it is not for lack of skill. When he accepts that a fish will not rise, he reels his line in and walks back to the bank where I am sitting.

"I think you've passed me by," I tell him.

He sits down next to me, smiles, and clips the grasshopper off his leader and places it in the hatband of his baseball cap. "I doubt it," he says, and rummages through his fly box for a new pattern. Looking at him, I notice the days of cutting and hauling logs for my cabin have made him lean and strong. He looks older, more confident than the person I hired in May. "Man, I know there's a fish in that eddy," he says. "I just need to keep the fly there longer."

I look out at the Fox River and smile. "Sure, it's a safe haven for the fish," I say, "but sooner or later, it has to venture out to feed. It can't stay there forever."

The young man chooses a heavy fly from his box, a Michigan Wiggler, and holds it up for me. "What do you think?" He ties it on, places a split shot six inches above the fly, and then sets his rod down and leans back on the bank. "So," he says, "did you finish your book?"

"Mostly," I say. "Just a few more lines, I think." We sit there silently for a while and watch the river. It is the end of August and the Upper Michigan summer is winding down. Up here, fall arrives quickly, often without notice. Soon I will wake to a hard frost and wonder how the summer slipped away.

"I bet it's a good story," he says, breaking the silence. He is lying with his hands behind his head, eyes closed. "Am I in it?"

I can't help but laugh. "It takes place fifteen years ago, but yeah, I suppose you are."

He smiles and swats at a fly buzzing around his head. "Gonna be tough leaving tomorrow," he says. He is close to finishing his degree down south, and I know he is worried about the future. "Will you be here next summer? There's still work to be done, and I can't fish streamers for shit."

He opens his eyes and looks at me. I know what he is asking, and for a moment, I feel my chest tighten and I have to look away. There is so much I wish I could say. I want to tell him things that can change his life. I want him to know that stories can save him if he listens. I want him to know that time and memory are circles. I want him to see that truth is organic and nothing is absolute: not this moment, not this summer, nothing. I want him to understand that love is not what he thinks it is and a hundred other things that are swimming in my head.

But instead, I say, "The place will always be here for you should you need it. And I'll be around." I leave it at that.

"Good," he says, satisfied. "Because you know I'll come back. I guarantee you."

I laugh and pull a couple of beers out of my vest and hand him one. "Of that I'm certain," I say.

He takes a beer, offers a toast to the summer, and then heads back to the river to figure out the puzzle. I am content to stay on the bank. I close my eyes and for a long time listen

The Eddy

to the river as it slides on by. In time, I find myself drifting with it, past the eddies, through the riffles, and finally into the deep, quiet water where mystery and memory meet.

Joe Paatalo

The Eddy

Chapter 1

The first time I lifted the Harley from Billy, I tried to kill myself by driving it through a Kansas twister. Not the easiest way to off yourself, I admit, but at the time, it seemed to make sense. For years, I tried to dismiss the act as a moment of temporary insanity, an impulsive act of teenage angst best left buried in the past. But some things don't rest that easily. They come back in ways you never see coming. I wish to be up front about what happened that night and in the months that followed, but truth, I've discovered, is an elusive thing. All I can say with any certainty is it was the start of a journey that's taken me years to understand. From my current vantage point, here's how I remember it.

It was a school night in the spring of my junior year. As usual, Billy and Mom were out drinking, trying to solve their relationship problems, and I was home alone, watching the weather channel, drinking some of Billy's beer. I was bored, surly, and generally pissed at the world. I was like that a lot then.

I was sitting on the couch with beer cans all around, watching tornado warnings scroll across the bottom of the TV screen. The radar was lit up with reds and yellows, and a talking head with plastic hair was pointing at the colors, loving the sound of his concerned voice. Out to the west of our house, tornados were popping up everywhere. On the screen, it looked like little bomb explosions on a map. In Kansas, you get used to this sort of thing, but this one had the look of something epic.

To this day, I'm not sure what triggered it. Maybe it was the weather. Maybe it was that smug look on the weatherman's face. Maybe it doesn't matter. All I know is whatever dam I'd built up over the years to hold back my rage and frustration suddenly burst that night. I remember sitting there, staring at the mess around me, awash in a flood of raw emotion. And it was too much. I couldn't take it anymore.

I got up, grabbed a six pack from the fridge for extra lubrication, and made my way out to the garage. I stuffed the beer in the saddle bags of Billy's Harley and then backed the bike out into the quiet cul de sac. For a while, I sat there, staring at the flickering lights from the house, breathing in the humid Kansas air. Around me, everything was the same, all suburban—perfect with spring green lawns and new minivans in the driveways—sour, homogenous milk. I wanted to puke.

Instead, I swallowed hard and hit the ignition. The bike roared to life, and the next thing I knew I was fishtailing down the street, leaving a world of anguish and a trail of rubber behind me. Two quick turns later and I was barreling down the Kansas turnpike at 90 miles an hour, heading straight for the beast—no premeditation, no weighing of choices, no consideration of consequences. Just me and speed, floating across the asphalt with a twisted sense of freedom.

I drove like that for twenty minutes until I neared the small community of Grotto, the epicenter of the storm. I eased off the throttle, and as I slowed, I could feel the pockets of warm air hitting my face, a sign of two fronts clashing. I pulled off the highway into the parking lot of a closed 76 station. My hands were stiff from white-knuckling the handlebars, and when I shut the bike down, I was aware of a shortness of breath, as if I couldn't get enough oxygen. I sat there breathing heavily, my heart pounding in my chest like it was too big for my body. Around me, the air was heavy and still, the sky green like the underside of a

The Eddy

cottonwood leaf. The few houses scattered about were dark and brooding, either empty or cut off from electricity. The whole scene felt as if I'd stepped into an old sepia-toned photograph, everything frozen except for me. I knew what I was about to do was crazy, but I didn't care. I wanted to feel something, anything other than mind-numbing misery.

I was pondering the insanity of all of this, close to losing my nerve, when I heard a siren wail in the distance. I had no idea where the next tornado would occur, so I turned south, crossed below the highway underpass, and drove slowly down the county road, out of town, scanning the horizon. I must have driven only five miles when, to my east, I saw a form on the outer edges of a cow pasture.

At first, it looked like a thick rope being spun from the sky, lowered by some cosmic cowboy. Oddly, it didn't scare me. More than anything, I was transfixed by its strange movements, its oddity more captivating than its danger. I remember thinking if it moved across the highway, I'd intercept it. Either I'd blow right through it, or it would lift me away from this world. I put my hand on the throttle, a twitch away from gassing it, when the trees to my east dipped as if taking a bow. There was a moment of silence, as if the world around me took a deep breath and held it. And then it exhaled.

It's difficult describing what happened next. What I remember, though, is feeling incredibly small and insignificant, like one of those tumbleweeds you see dancing across the road in an old Western. And like one of those weeds, the wind just lifted me off my bike and tossed me in a ditch. I landed on my back, unable to breathe, gasping for air. Above me, I could hear the train-roar of wind; I could see the chaos of flying debris. Frozen, breathless, I waited for the end.

And suddenly, I wanted to live. I never wanted to live so badly. Maybe I did all along; I don't know. But now I was praying out loud, promising a god I never acknowledged before all kinds of things if he'd give me another chance.

Then, as though someone turned the channel on that

old movie, the roar was gone. Over. There was a quick wave of hail, and then dead silence except for a ringing in my ears.

When I finally caught my breath, I stood up on unsteady legs and looked around. Shingles, corrugated metal, and farm implements littered the highway. A child's tricycle, from who knows where, was up in a tree. I stumbled around, close to tears, thinking the bike was lost for good, when I saw it, twenty yards away from me in a field, lying on its side. I walked over to it slowly, afraid to look, certain it was trashed.

But the bike wasn't even scratched. It was covered in mud and grass but looked fine once I cleaned it off. It was as if someone had lifted it gently out of the chaos and set it aside. How something so violent could perform a curious act like that was a mystery. When I pulled the bike back up to the road, it fired up as if nothing had happened. I remember saying a prayer of thanks as I gawked at the destruction around me.

Slowly, I took the bike back through town. A few people emerged from the silent houses in a daze, staring and pointing. The 76 sign from the gas station was buried in someone's roof. A little kid kept pointing at it, yelling for someone to look. There were cars turned over on front lawns, trees in places where they had no right to be. But the destruction was random. A whole section of the town seemed unscathed and then, right in the middle, it looked as if someone set off clusters of bombs.

Later, I found out dozens had been injured and one person killed—a young woman who was struck by a flying television, which to this day strikes me as an absurdly awful way to go. Why I survived was a mystery.

I didn't feel like hanging around the town gawking when it was all over. Ambulances were wailing in the distance, and I wanted no part of that shit show. So I cruised past the shell-shocked people, through the maze of debris scattered everywhere, and finally onto the turnpike that would take me home. It was clear to me now I was on a machine beyond my ability to control, so I kept the bike

The Eddy

steady at 55, afraid of anything faster. Before the storm, what happened to me didn't seem to matter, but it mattered now. As I drove, I remember feeling as if I'd crossed over some invisible border, and as tempting as it was to look back at the wreckage behind me, I knew it was best to keep my gaze forward.

On the way home, it started raining, but I didn't care. I was crying, which I hardly ever do. Nothing was clear anymore. How could I go home now? To what? I was embarrassed by what I had done, and the thought of returning to the house made me sick to my stomach. Even though I was soaked, muddy, and spent, I couldn't face that house. I just couldn't. I pulled off at my high school, parked in the lot, and sat under the eaves of the double-wide front doors, staring into the night sky, drinking the rest of Billy's beer. Each time I opened a new bottle, it exploded and foamed down the sleeve of my leather jacket and pooled at my elbow. I didn't care. My rage, which had been simmering for months, seemed spent, replaced by a low-grade misery. It was clear now I didn't want to die, but I felt stifled, trapped. All I was sure of was I hated Kansas; I hated Billy; I hated school; and I hated myself. And what was I left with? Layers and layers of guilt.

When there was nothing left of the beer, nothing left but to go home, I smashed the bottles on the concrete walkway and pissed on the school logo. It was the only satisfying act of the entire evening.

Joe Paatalo

Chapter 2

Billy never said anything about the bike, but I was sure he knew I'd taken it. We had settled into a quiet truce since our last knock-down, drag-out fight months earlier and hadn't spoken much since. If Mom suspected anything, she kept it to herself. She had her hands full with Billy and, I think, was trying to terminate the relationship. I was so wrapped in my own world, I hardly paid attention. I was glad every time they left the house and I didn't have to listen to them. I took the bike out a time or two after I tried to off myself, but I always felt so guilty, not because of Billy but because of what the bike reminded me of.

Billy was the third guy since my dad left and, while he wasn't the worst, he wasn't exactly keeper material. He cared more about Harleys than he did about a job, and he drank way too much. He was a wild child in the '70s, tattooed and rip-cord lean, at least in the old pictures Mom kept. But he had grown a bit soft, lost the bad boy edge that made guys like that sexy to women. I think Mom thought she could restore the roar, but women seem to do that a lot—think they can fix what's broken or find what's been lost. Never works, though. At least not that I've seen.

About the best thing I could say about Billy was he wasn't physically abusive, unlike my dad. When Billy got mad, his mouth turned foul, and he'd attack me where I felt most vulnerable. He was gifted that way, calling me creatively disgusting names that might have been funny had you read them in a bathroom stall. But directed toward me, they stung, especially when he picked up on the theme of a useless Indian. I didn't look Indian, outside of my long hair, but that didn't stop Billy. He knew my biological father claimed Choctaw blood, and while Mom insisted the only thing Indian about my dad was his fondness for the pipe—a reference to his love for weed—Billy found comfort in the ignorant stereotypes and used them like cheap weaponry.

The truth was I remember little about my father, other than he was violent and scared the shit out of me. He was never around, forever walking out the door and promising never to come back. By the time I was seven he made good on that promise and disappeared forever, which was fine with me. The only thing he left me was my name, Toby Casper. That and my jet-black hair. I never asked Mom about him, never cared to know anything. Like most of the things in my life at the time, I found it best not to look back.

Anyway, about the time Mom was preparing to give Billy his walking papers, he did about the only nice thing I ever remember—he gave me his backup Harley, one he had been working on. It was a cherry red 1985 FXW6 with 1,300 cc's, an Evo engine, and an electric start. It was a thing of beauty. It burned more oil than gas and tended to break down, but I loved it. If I couldn't escape suburban Kansas, at least I could leave it for a while. And I did. Every chance I could.

Mom wasn't too thrilled with the bike, but she was worried about me and wanted me to be happy. In the end, the bike bought Billy a few months, but by the time school let out, he was gone.

I found out on the last day of the school year. I came home and all his crap was gone. At first, I panicked, was afraid to look in the garage. I just knew the bastard had taken it back. What would I do all summer without the bike? But when I opened the garage door, it was there. I could've cried, I was so relieved. I called Mom at the hospital where she was working, and she said we'd talk about it when she got home. She also told me Billy left a note for me on the table.

In the kitchen, I poured myself a glass of milk, sat down, and opened the greasy envelope.

The Eddy

Dude, I left you the bike, so take care of it. It's worth five grand, at least. I know me and you didn't get along to good and for that I'm sorry. I never did get you. Guess I should of tried but I'm not to good at that. I know you got some stuff to figure out and I hope you do. Take care of your Mom. She's a good lady and loves you.

Billy

P.S. I know you took my bike a few times. I guess I'd have done it too if I was your age. Thanks for not taking it out in bad weather.

It was kind of hard to hate him after that, and I felt bad I didn't try to get to know him. True, he was an oaf, but most people have some good in them, I guess. When Mom came home that day, she seemed pretty bummed. Knowing you have to split and actually doing it are two different things. Just because you've done it a few times doesn't make it any easier. I knew she'd bounce back; she always did. She was still vibrant and pretty, with her short, spiky brown hair and young girl figure. Men always hit on her. That was never the problem. She just couldn't pick a normal guy to save her life.

That night, I made Mom some lasagna and opened a bottle of Cabernet she'd been saving. She let me have a glass and we toasted new beginnings. We talked for a long time about how change was a good thing, her resiliency and desperate optimism permeating everything she said. I didn't buy it. What was there to feel hopeful about? But I listened politely. And when she finished venting about her own mess, she started on me about getting some new friends. She couldn't understand why I didn't hang with anyone at school anymore and insisted it was unhealthy for me to spend so much time alone, farting around with bikes or reading in my room. She wanted me to tell her something *positive* about my life as a way of affirming my normalcy.

But what was I going to say to her? That I was gay, and my best friend turned on me because I made the horrible mistake of telling him? That he set me up, and for months I had to live with a series of foul notes slipped into my locker, notes that made me ashamed and embarrassed? Or should I have started with how I once got pinned on the ground in the parking lot and was forced to watch as six goons took turns pissing on my bike, and that the assistant principal's reaction to all of this was for me to see a counselor who could *straighten* me out? Or maybe I should have started with a real attention getter, that until recently, I thought I'd be better off dead.

No, Mom had her own problems. Besides, I knew what she'd do. She'd march into school in the fall and create a ruckus, which would only stir things up again. And I wanted no part of that. Some things were best left buried.

After our talk that evening, I promised Mom I'd change, become more social and positive. I hated like hell lying to her, but if it made her feel good and helped her move on, what harm could it do? Afterwards, I cleaned the kitchen, found an old movie she loved, *Roman Holiday*, and then got out of the house. It was dark when I pulled my bike out of the garage, the air heavy and smelling of rain. I found it comforting as I slipped away into the darkness, becoming just another shadow fading into the landscape.

And that was the way it went for the first half of the summer. Dinners with Mom in the evening after making pizzas all day at work, and long drives at night, out past the new developments to where the two-lane highways cut across the prairie. I loved the feel of the hot summer air through my hair and the smell of baking asphalt on the back roads. If I had any identity at all at the time, it came from the freedom of the highway. My own great fantasy, I guess—drive off into the sunset and go until the road ended. If I could've gotten away with disappearing, I'd have tried it. It was never far from my mind. But even then, I understood it wasn't an option. As much as I was drawn to the idea of cutting out, the thought of Mom trying to run me down and stressing her out made the notion lose its appeal.

So instead of fleeing, I settled for being mobile in Kansas, becoming a prairie rider who explored the outskirts of where the great suburban exodus ended. I spent most of my money on gas, riding for hours on end. In time, I discovered places like the rolling Flint Hills to the northeast. In the summer, they turned golden yellow, stretching out as far as the eye could see. It was like looking at an ocean of grass, solemn and lonely, stark and pretty at the same time. Occasionally, I'd find an old abandoned farm or barn, and I'd shut the bike off, walk around inside, listening to the wind blow through the structure, wondering about the people who used to live there—their dreams, their hopes, whether any of it ever came to anything.

Late at night, as I returned home, I always made a point to ride past Southview and flip it the bird. For me, it embodied everything I hated about where I lived. And try as I might, I could never ride far enough to get that school completely from my mind, even in the dog days of summer.

You see, Southview was one of those sparkling new high schools that exemplified the sprawl of suburbia. Moving outward from Kansas City, each successive suburb was more ostentatious than the last—bigger houses, obnoxious garages, strip malls with fancy facades, high schools the size of college campuses. Southview, at the far reaches of the city's grasp, had even more—the latest technology, the best gyms money could buy, huge classrooms with big windows. Everyone, including the teachers, was earnest, hard-working, and dull. In fact, they celebrated dull, made it a virtue. Everyone played at being different, but it was only a game. At best, they were a thousand flavors of vanilla. They had no clue what it meant to be different. They were the inhabitants of the outer rings, the last refuge for those who retreated from all things different. To them, I was the poster child of the world in decay they were running from—me and the few black kids from the city. And those poor black kids had it tough too. At least I could blend in if I had to. Their safest bet was to become white, which is what most of them did. No sagging pants or cockeyed hats at Southview. This rule was self-imposed.

But there was no conforming for me, no pretending, even if I wanted to. And sometimes I did want to. But I couldn't. So I settled on a quiet rebellion—leather, long hair, and a perpetual scowl that said '*Fuck with me and pay the price.*' After the initial fun of exposing me as a pervert, most people pretty much ignored me. Those who couldn't get enough of the fun, it took only one public fight to display two important things: I could fight, and if you took me on, you'd better knock me out because I wouldn't quit. I was gay, but I wasn't a pussy.

So most of my miserable days at Southview were spent in the corners of a classroom with my back to the wall. I took my notes, read the high school canon, listened to the merits of Creative Intelligence, and in general watched as my class prepared themselves for the University of Kansas or Saint Something or Other. In time, I was convinced they would take their rightful place on the plains, bitching about high taxes and gay marriage.

Looking back now, I realize my views were pretty skewed, but I was young, filled with endless angst, and I lacked any affiliation that might have kept me measured. Being attached to nothing, I filled that vacant space with what was most available – anger. And while anger wasn't the most efficient fuel, it sure took me places. The problem was, once I was there, it was difficult finding my way back.

In the summer, as I cruised past the school and drove the open spaces where the sprawl had yet to reach, I spent a lot of time wondering how I would survive my last year at Southview. Dropping out seemed tempting, but I wanted to go to college, to go somewhere away from all of this, and a G.E.D. wasn't going to cut it. I had the grades to graduate with distinction, so it made sense to tough it out. But when you're seventeen, nine months seems like a lot to bear, and I was consumed with dread, afraid I'd snap and hit the throttle next time. I was so concerned with all of this, I just

The Eddy

wasn't paying any attention to Mom, so I was shocked one day in early August when she told me we had to move.

At first, I was relieved. It was the best news I could hope for. Anywhere but here. But then Mom delivered the bad news. "We've got no money, Toby. I can't afford the house. I took a nursing job in St. Paul that pays more, but we're going to have to sell some stuff."

By stuff, she meant the bike. We were behind in the mortgage and all the savings were gone. I was so wrapped in my world, I never thought to wonder how Mom would make up Billy's meager contribution to the bills. Small as it was, it kept the wolf from the door. Mom never directly asked me to sell the bike, but I did. It got me five grand, just as Billy said, and I gave it all to Mom. She cried a bit and promised to buy me a new bike, but I'd never hold her to it. She was my mom.

It was late August when we packed the van and headed north. We'd sold almost everything, but we were still jammed into her Caravan. Mostly we had boxes of books, clothes, and photos. Not much for a new start. I figured since we were starting so lean, we should toss the books as well, but Mom refused. I think books kept her from feeling like white trash. She used to say, "Just because we're poor doesn't mean we're ignorant." Mom was well-educated, but money and men had never been kind to her.

The ride north was pretty depressing. As much as I hated Kansas and Southview, at least I knew what I was dealing with. I knew nothing about Minnesota other than Minneapolis had a few cool bands, the Mississippi River started somewhere in the state, and it got brutally cold in the winter. California or Florida would have been more my style, but apparently, the Twin Cities needed registered nurses and were paying well for experience. I was just along for the ride.

Mom was pretty upbeat about the whole thing. She kept saying, "You're gonna love it. The apartment's next to a lake. We're in the inner city where it's really diverse. There's so much to do. Blah, blah, blah."

Fine, I thought. But what about school? It was going to be a hell of a senior year.

Chapter 3

Phyllis Wheatley High was everything Southview was not. Built in the '50s, it was a cramped, crowded, two-story roach motel. Without air conditioning, air hung oppressively in the complex, the sole source of circulation coming from narrow windows that opened only partially in the classrooms. In the warmth of fall and spring, the school smelled of industrial cleansers and teenage sweat. The building had no way of exhaling. Wheatley was the armpit of the school district, in more ways than one.

In addition to its aesthetic and venting problems, Wheatley had other issues. Broken families, economic stress, marginalized kids, new immigrants—it all added up to some of the lowest test scores in the state. Hundreds of thousands of dollars had been poured into new programs and retaining stressed-out staff, but nothing seemed to work. The school was perennially on probation, teachers came and went, and no parent who paid any attention to his kid's education wanted him stigmatized by being there. So it made complete sense, based on the way my life was going, that I'd end up in a place like Wheatley.

Looking back, my first few days there were actually kind of funny. I walked around shell-shocked, mouth open half the time. The place was loud and chaotic, a cornucopia of languages and faces from all over the world, expressing themselves in ways both colorful and obscene. Sometimes I'd just stop in the hall, lean against a locker so I wouldn't get swept away, and I'd listen to all the noise. I remember thinking at the time the word *fuck* might be the most versatile word in the English language.

Unfortunately, along with all this diversity came the

economic reality of poverty—ninth grade girls with babies, kids who lived by themselves, bangers with more than one bullet scar. I knew my life had not been easy, but compared to some of these kids, I was lucky. It was clear a lot of them were never going to graduate, that they were there for the relatively safe environment and the free meal that came with it.

But to say Wheatley was all turmoil and lost causes would be unfair. There were plenty of academically motivated kids too. You just had to know where to look. The school had a number of advanced placement courses, including some that offered college credit, and the kids who figured out that education was their only way out took them with relish. Clearly, some students were not ready for the challenge, but no one who wanted the academic rigor was turned away. It was a shame most of these classes were filled with Asian and white kids. It was an unintended form of segregation. I never did figure out why most of the smart black kids stayed clear of these classes.

In all, I actually came to like Wheatley once I got used to it and started looking past its scruffy surface. The place had energy. It felt real. It also allowed me to move with some anonymity, which I liked.

Since I was up in credits, I chose a light schedule, something I could sleep through. Most of my classes—like *African American History, Sports and Economics, Minorities in Film*—were filled with black kids. The classes were shamefully easy, and many of the teachers spent the majority of their time trying to keep kids on task. The only advanced class I took was *Modern Fiction*, since I liked to read. It was the only advanced class with any black kids, and it was run by one odd, tough dude, Mr. Mitchell James.

James was in his late thirties and had been at the school for almost ten years. Word in the halls was he was fired from a rich suburban school for beating up a kid. Whether it was true was a matter of speculation and gossip, but it certainly didn't hurt his street cred. He was tall and lean with wide shoulders and had the posture and stance of

The Eddy

an athlete, the kind of guy who never locked his knees and looked as if he was ready to take a punch at any time. He kept his graying hair cropped, and he wore a goatee, also graying, that partially covered a nasty scar from his chin to the bottom of his jaw line. He might have been considered handsome if you looked at him quickly in a dimly lit place, but in the light, it was clear he was a bit too damaged. His nose was flat with a small knot in the middle, and his eyes were gray and often watery. He didn't smile that much, but when he did, it looked like he was laughing at some inside joke you couldn't possibly understand. Like most teachers at Wheatley, he dressed casually, usually in jeans and a flannel shirt. His one eccentricity was black high-top Chuck Taylors. He wore them nearly every day.

Unlike most teachers, James seldom raised his voice. He didn't need to. The smart kids liked him because he was creative and surprising, at times wildly erratic. Other kids hated him because he was demanding and sarcastic. You never slept in James' class. He tolerated a lot, but laziness was unforgivable. Lots of kids couldn't hack him and there was always a long line waiting to transfer out of his class. If you were black, he was especially tough on you. But even those kids came to grudgingly respect him. He'd rail against a kid for playing the race card, but at the end of the day, you might find him playing hoops with the same kid, talking about sports, Miles Davis, or some African American artist.

James occasionally got on my nerves, though, messed with my comfort zone. One day we were talking about James Baldwin and how he was an expatriate. James brought up the fact that he was gay and kept going on about how that was a double whammy for him. I guess I must have rolled my eyes or something.

"Casper, you got a problem with the gay thing?"

I was caught off guard. I usually didn't talk much in class. "Um... yeah, sort of. I mean, I don't care if he was gay. Why should that matter? Shouldn't the book stand on its own merit? His personal life was just that. Personal. Shouldn't matter." I was actually pleased with my response.

"Then I'm assuming the fact that he was black doesn't matter either?" He waited for a response, and I felt my face getting hot. I was kind of stuck.

"No. I guess not. Should it?"

"Depends on if you care who tells the story, Toby. Do you think it makes a difference where you get your news from?"

I wasn't quite sure where he was going. "Sure, it matters—people have agendas, I get that. I'm not sure what that has to do with being black or gay, though."

"If you wanted to understand something about civil rights, or what it was like being a minority and serving in a war, who would you want telling the story?"

Takeita Benson, a smart, talkative black girl who was quickly becoming my ally, jumped to my rescue. "I'd want the story from someone who understood it, from someone who was there. I don't want someone else telling my story."

James sat on the edge of his desk and shrugged his shoulders. "Yeah, me neither. Good point. Listen, guys, I'm not telling you what to think. I'm just trying to get you to think harder. You're smart enough to know that history has been told mostly by victors, the people in power. Whether it's black people, gay people, Native Americans, it doesn't matter; they deserve to have their stories told, through their eyes, their experiences."

Takeita had given me a chance to collect my thoughts. I wasn't quite ready to concede. "So a white guy can't tell a story truthfully about someone unlike him? Or a black woman?"

"Sure they can," James said. "And sometimes they can do it remarkably well. But perhaps there are limitations to what they tell. Look, I was going to give you guys a different assignment, but let's do this. For tomorrow, journal about this topic. Title it *Who deserves to tell the story*. Think it through. What are the limitations? Are there certain stories that can only be told through certain eyes? I'd like to hear what the rest of you have to say. No B.S. No short-cuts."

James used the remainder of the class to get back to

The Eddy

Baldwin and Paris, but I barely paid attention. I was jotting down notes for my journal assignment. When the bell rang, James stopped me before I could get to the hall.

"Hey, Toby, hold your ground, dude. If your argument holds up to scrutiny, then fine. If it doesn't, well, I guess that's what we call education." He smiled and his scar line seemed amplified by the tension.

I looked at him closely, not sure what to think. His next class was streaming through the door. Impulsively, I said, "Do you mind if I ask a personal question, Mr. James?"

He shrugged. "Go ahead."

"How did you end up here? I mean, I've heard some stories, and I was just wondering. You don't have to tell me; it's none of my business."

He grabbed a kid passing his desk and pulled his sagging pants up. The kid seemed annoyed but tolerated it. James gave him a light kick on the butt. "Tell you what, you tell my story, based on what you've heard. That's your assignment. I'll let you know how close you are."

He turned away from me and started on another kid who had headphones on. I didn't have a chance to respond. By the time I got out in the hall, I realized what he was doing and felt chumped. I thought of a few ways I should've responded instead of drifting away, but that's the way it usually goes. Seldom do you get a chance to make a good exit.

I never did the assignment, and James never asked for it. I guess he figured he made his point. In truth, I conceded because once I got past my pride, I believed it. I thought I was done being pushed by him until I got called into the counselor's office a few weeks later.

Ms. Stichcomb, an old, salty vet, delivered the bad news. "Here's your new schedule, Toby. I hope you know it's in your best interest."

I was dumbstruck. Instead of *Sports and Economics* and *African American History*, I now had *Environmental Biology, Macro-Economics* and *Student Aid*. I hardly knew what to say. I was livid.

"My mom," I stuttered. "She doesn't—she can't—"

"It's not your mother. It was Mr. James. He changed your schedule. And before you get too upset, I agreed with him. I approved it." She stared at me over the tops of those cheater glasses that older ladies wear. She was prepared for a protest.

"But I don't need it. I'm fine the way I am. This is bullshit."

"Before you get too worked up, I think you should talk to Mr. James. He said you might be upset." She watched to see my reaction. "But I will say this. You are eighteen, and technically, you don't need these classes, and if you decide to change them, I will do that. But you'll need to stick with them for a week. I'm pretty busy and won't be able to do anything for you right away."

I stormed out of there, but not before delivering a good exit line. "Oh, you'll see me again. I'll be sure to find room in *my* busy schedule." I guess every now and then, you can get a zinger off when you make an exit.

By the end of the day, I was in James' room, waiting for his last student to leave.

"Kind of figured you'd be here, Toby. You don't look so happy."

"I'm not." I had a right to be indignant. "I liked my schedule. It worked for me. I don't need or want those other classes."

He sat back in his chair and put his hands behind his head. "Need and want are two different things. You're wasting your time in those other classes. They're a waste of your skills. They're bullshit, and you know it."

I wasn't used to hearing teachers swear. It caught me off guard. He was staring at me with a bit of a smirk. I felt myself getting angry. "I know what I'm doing. I don't need someone holding my hand. I'm fine on my own."

He shrugged his shoulders. "Okay, you're a big boy; that's fine. But you're coasting. My guess is you aren't working in anyone's class, except maybe mine. You can get A's with your eyes closed. Big deal. But if you take biology

The Eddy

with Winiski and economics with Trudeau, you might find they open your world up. Might make you think more universally. But hey, it's up to you. Thought I might give you the push you needed. That's all."

Now I was at a loss for words. I was still pissed, but I didn't know what to say. I looked around his room, now quite familiar to me. There were posters of John Coltrane and Neil Young, as well as quotes from Springsteen, Sitting Bull, and W.E.B DuBois, scattered on the walls. Behind his desk was a picture of some guy fishing in the evening on a river. There was a quote on it by someone who likened it to religion. I'd never looked at it closely before.

"I don't get it. Why are you messing with me? I'm doing fine in your class. I'm not causing any problems. Do you see me as some sort of project or something?"

He opened a water bottle and took a long swig. "No, you're not a project. I just thought I'd challenge you, that's all. You know, push you down the road less traveled, that kind of thing. Don't want to do it? Fine. No big deal to me. Up to you."

I was glaring at him now. I made up my mind I wasn't going to give in. All I wanted was to remain anonymous and get out of there without too much sweat. I think he was reading my thoughts.

"Hey, I spoke to both teachers and they'll take you mid-quarter. No problem. They like me, trust my instincts. Again, up to you."

"And if I say no? What then? You gonna harass me, make things hard for me?"

He shook his head and smiled that scary smile. "Nope, I wouldn't do that. I might call you chickenshit and question your manhood, but that would be the end of it."

I couldn't help but laugh. "Jesus, James, you're really something." I was beginning to falter. "I really, *really* don't want to do this. I'm not afraid of failing, but I just don't want to."

"I never said anything about failing; that was you." He stood up and walked over to me, put his hand on my shoulder. I stiffened. "If I thought you were afraid of failure, we'd be having another conversation. Give it a shot for a couple weeks and we'll talk again. If you want to tell me then to shove it up my ass, I'll bend over. Okay? Got nothing to lose."

Yeah, I thought, easy for you to say. Once again, I lost my footing. I found myself asking about the curriculum, for Christ sakes. By the time I was ready to leave, I had agreed to a mountain of work.

"Oh, and one more thing," he said. "Your student aid hour is with me. I need some help correcting all these shitty essays I keep assigning."

I found myself laughing as I walked out the door. Geez, that guy really got under my skin.

Economics was all business. The class was mostly white kids, so I was surprised to see Takeita there. She laughed when she saw me. "James got you too, I see." She patted the seat next to her. "I'll help you. It ain't that bad once you get used to it. Trudeau ain't like James, which is probably good. You can only take that guy in doses."

Jerry Trudeau was young, highly organized, and almost anal about numbers. He reminded me of the teachers at Southview a lot, except he was more laid back. His class required me to read a lot, stuff I'd never been interested in, but I actually learned a fair amount. He gave us part of the hour every day to work, so not only did I catch on quickly, but I got to know Takeita pretty well, which wasn't bad.

Biology, with Ronda Winiski, was another thing altogether. It was crazy. Winiski was the antithesis of the Trudeaus of the world. Her class was chaotic, spontaneous, all over the place. For her, grades didn't seem to matter. She loved biology and she made you love it too. She had the biggest classroom in the school, connected to a lab, and every foot of space was used—equipment, microscopes, charts, and animals. Her room smelled like a zoo. She had ferrets, snakes, rats, hissing cockroaches, various birds, animal skeletons—you name it. Every day when she came to school, she had some kid helping her haul stuff into her room. Nothing ever seemed to go out. The first ten minutes of every class was dedicated to caring for the animals—feeding them, charting their diets, cleaning cages, playing with them. Every other day, some animal would escape, and we'd spend five minutes running around trying to catch it.

It wasn't an honors class; she didn't believe in that kind of segregation. She had a lot of special ed kids, the type with low attention spans and assorted behavior problems, the *med* crowd. But those kids all had a task. It was all hands-on. Everyone seemed to have their own individual lesson plan, including me. A girl and I were in charge of designing rain gardens for the school, places that would absorb run-off from the streets when it rained hard. I think the girl had a thing for me, but I played stupid. We'd spend the day researching designs and figuring the costs, studying golf courses, municipal projects, suburban housing. It was great. Winiski gave us a camera and we'd walk around the neighborhood looking for public spaces we could redesign so they'd be more eco-friendly.

Winiski was one of those people with a warm soul. Decency and patience emanated from her. She was in her forties but looked older. I don't think she cared a lick what she looked like, which was unusual for a woman. She was stout with long, coarse gray hair, which she was constantly swiping out of her eyes. She wore loose-fitting skirts, oversized blouses, and clogs every day. She was like this '60s throwback—unattached, real liberal, no makeup, peace, love and understanding, that kind of thing. The fact that she was best friends with James amazed me. They seemed so different. He was all ice and angles. She was warmth and curves. One day, after class, I asked her about him. "How'd he get that scar?"

"Hockey," she said. "He played for UMD, up in Duluth. That's where he went to school. He was one of the best hockey players in the state coming out of high school. His freshman year he took a skate across the face in practice, cut him to the bone, required almost thirty stitches."

"Did he keep playing after that?"

"Oh, yeah. He was awfully tough."

"Never went pro?"

"Stopped playing in the middle of his senior year. Got hurt really bad the summer before. That's another story. He tried to come back, but he lost his speed. I think they tried to convert him to a defenseman, or something like that. But he said he became a thug on the fourth line, so he quit." Winiski was trying to straighten her desk, but it was hopeless. "Why do you ask?"

"I don't know. He's an odd dude. Sometimes I like him, but sometimes I'm not so sure. Did he actually get fired for beating someone up?"

Winiski stopped what she was doing and looked hard at me. She hesitated but then said, "If I tell you, it stays here. Got it?"

"Sure," I said.

"I mean it." She made a fist and shook it at me. "I don't want it coming back."

"Geez, you're scaring me," I said. She looked about as frightening as a Dalmatian puppy.

"He coached hockey when he got out of college and took his first teaching job. With his reputation, he could've worked anywhere. Medicine Lake, this hockey school, hired him. He took them to the state tournament his first two years, but they didn't win. I guess some parents weren't too happy, not good enough for them. He drove the kids hard. Well, you know how he is, pretty intense. Anyway, as he tells it, he checked a kid hard in practice. He was trying to make a point. The kid got up and took a swipe at him. You can imagine how that turned out. One punch, a few teeth later, he was looking for a job."

I nodded. "So that was it? He never coached again?"

"Never wanted to. Said he never liked it all that much. Said his temper was too bad. A character flaw, he claimed."

"Jesus, did he ever say he regretted it?"

"Not that he ever admitted." Her frankness hung in

the air. "Now I'm holding you to secrecy. He'd be pissed if I told you."

"Yeah, don't worry. I hardly talk to anyone anyway."

"So I noticed," she said. "Why is that?"

I shrugged. "Don't have that much in common with most people. Kids talk a lot; I'd rather listen. Guess I don't have much to say."

She pushed her hair out of face and smiled. "I seriously doubt that."

Joe Paatalo

The Eddy

Chapter 4

Being James' student aide was not all bad. I sat in on his eleventh-grade American Lit class and corrected his tests and kept track of his grade book, which he hated to do. It was an easy gig. He spent five weeks teaching *Huck Finn* and, although I'd read that book in junior high, it was like he was reading a different text altogether. He talked a lot about censorship and the word *nigger*, which brought about an animated discussion. He managed to keep the class of mostly black kids steady, but it was challenging even for him. I could tell by how tired he looked at the end of the hour. Nothing like the *N*-word to get a reaction out of kids. Everyone seems to want to lay claim to that word in one way or another. If he was trying to make a point about the power of language, he sure was successful.

I think what saved him was his take on the character of Jim the slave. He insisted Jim's use of language was brilliant, and he referred to him as one of the great heroes of American literature. It got everyone thinking, including me, about what it meant to have courage in today's world. It was one of those ideas that stay with you for a long time.

I also was aware of another thing. Any book would've been easier to teach. *Any* book. But he chose that one. Either he believed in its power or he was a masochist of the first order. I thought it took guts to take it on, and I respected him for it.

I can't say the year was entirely smooth. I had only a few friends, mostly girls like Takeita, who seemed to like anyone in pants. I didn't mind it that much, since I never had that many friends. I was all right with that. I worked at a pizza place a few nights a week and tried to squirrel away some money for a new bike, but I wasn't saving much. I really missed not having a bike. Mom let me drive her van, but that wasn't exactly liberating. I still wore my leather jacket every day, still kept the long hair, although I was considering putting it into dreads. In general, I kept to myself.

On Saturdays, I'd go clubbing in Minneapolis at some of the music venues. Sometimes I'd take a few friends, but mostly I liked to go alone. I felt older, more confident by myself. Again, I liked the anonymity. I could talk to anyone, pretend to be anything.

Things were tolerable, and I got to thinking I'd get through the year just fine and move on to college somewhere far away, when everything took a dramatic turn, changing my life forever.

I liked sports, but I really hated gym. I was a decent athlete, could play hoops and hold my own, and had good hand-eye coordination. But I hated the locker rooms and all the bullshit that was talked about in there. I also hated showering with everybody. I was in good shape, had nothing to be embarrassed about, but it made me uncomfortable. I wasn't the only one. There were five or six of us who shut down early in class, so we weren't sweating the next hour. We'd just cool off, hang out, and chat for five minutes, and then reapply deodorant, something I'd been doing for years.

Apparently, Max Hedstrom, a Neanderthal football player, took notice and decided he didn't like it. A group of us were doing our usual thing at the end of the hour, just shooting the bull, when Max decided he hadn't filled his asshole quota for the day.

"Hey, queers, I gotcha something." He tossed a bottle of Old Spice at us and I caught it.

"What did you call us?" I asked. I could feel my pulse quicken.

"Fags," he said. "Or queers. Which do you prefer?" He stood there smirking; cocky the way athletes often are in their domain. But there was something different about him,

The Eddy

something about his smug face and sense of superiority that turned my stomach in knots. I think I knew all along I'd end up in a fight again, but part of me hoped all of that was behind me. But stupid people are like weeds; they pop up everywhere. I suppose if I'd been more disciplined, I could've looked past him, but my anger was on constant simmer then, ready to boil over at any moment. Unfortunately for Max, he made the mistake of turning up the heat.

It's a bit blurry thinking back on it now, but I remember looking at his fat head with its thick football neck and wanting to rip it from his body. There was a moment of hesitation as I tried to fight the impulse, but it was too late. I couldn't stop myself. I hurled the bottle of Old Spice at him as hard as I could and watched as it rocketed off the side of his face and smashed against the wall. I should've stopped there, but when Max dropped to his knees in pain, I pounced on him. In an instant, I knocked him on his back and started pounding on his face. He never had a chance. By the time someone pulled me off him, he was covered in blood. His nose was broken, and he was curled in a fetal position with his hands around his face. He might've been crying, but I don't remember. I was numb. The only thing I was fully aware of was my aching hands and the smell of cheap cologne.

Moments later, the school cop showed up and hauled me to the office, put me in a room, and told me to shut up and sit still until I calmed down, which was funny because I hadn't said a word and was actually fairly calm. Max was sent to the nurse, and I later heard he was threatening my life. Big deal. Guys like that are cowards. I was eventually sent to the assistant principal for my suspension.

Edward Dewey was this hulking black guy who had been second-in-charge forever. He had the crappy job of dealing with all the discipline problems. He sat behind his computer and silently read through my record before talking to me. The cop was outside the door in case I went off again.

"Looks here like you haven't had any trouble since coming here. What happened?" He seemed tired.

"Hedstrom called me a fag and I beat the shit out of him."

Dewey looked up from his screen and looked at me for the first time. "A moron calls you a name and you assault him. Names can't hurt you, son. Aren't you smart enough to know that?"

I had an impulse to argue with him, to bring up the word *nigger*, or *squaw*, or *kike*, but it wouldn't have helped me. I sat there and said nothing.

"Standard suspension for fighting is three days, more if he presses an assault charge, which he might. You'll have to come back with a parent. Can't be around school at all; otherwise, you'll get arrested."

He said it as if he were reading the ingredients on a soup can. He printed out the standard form for me to sign. "Any questions?"

"Yeah, can I get my homework from the teachers?"

"Nope. We'll get it. Someone can pick it up for you. You'll have to leave the property immediately."

I didn't want to leave without talking to Winiski or James. For some reason, I wanted them to know. "Can I go to my locker?" I asked.

"With an escort, then you need to leave." He called for a hall monitor to walk me to my locker. She was a young Asian woman who was still in college part-time, trying to get her teaching license. She seemed earnest, but she couldn't have been more than five feet tall. She carried a pack radio with her in case there was trouble. Instead of going to my locker, I went to James' class. She followed, thinking I was on my way to my locker. When I got to James' class, he was in the middle of teaching American Lit. I turned to my escort and said, "I need to talk to him. Now. It's important."

She seemed skeptical, then relented. Sometimes I think teaching is more about instincts than anything. I guess she had them because she didn't get caught up in

The Eddy

regulations. She waited in the hall as I intruded on James' class.

James was sitting behind his desk while his students were having group conferences. I whispered to him, "Mr. James, I really need to talk to you. Can I bother you for a moment? It's important."

There must have been something in my tone or my eyes because he dropped everything and stepped out in the hall with me.

"Ka, I'll take it from here," he told the monitor. She nodded at him and left.

"What's up, Toby?"

I didn't know where to begin. I felt sick to my stomach. "I can't talk here. I can't. Something's happened."

James led me down the hall and put me in an unoccupied computer lab. In a few minutes, he returned. "I got someone to cover for me. Let's take a walk." He handed me a sweatshirt. "Put this on; it's cold."

We walked out past the parking lot toward the athletic fields without saying a word. It was a gray November day. It felt like snow. I didn't know where to begin.

"I got suspended, Mr. James. I beat the shit out of Max Hedstrom for calling me a fag."

We walked further in silence. "But that's not it, is it?" He stopped and looked at me. His hands were in his pockets and I could see his breath.

"No."

I could feel the tears welling up. I fought them back as best I could. "I'm gay, Mr. James... I'm sorry, but..." I started sobbing. I couldn't help it. Everything I'd held inside for so long seemed to pour right out of me. I could barely catch my breath.

James put his hand on my shoulder and walked me over to the baseball dugout, out of the wind. He sat next to me silently, waiting for me to gain my composure. It took a while. Finally, he said, "That must've been hard. I'm sorry for your pain."

I wasn't ready to speak yet, so I just nodded.

"Toby, look at me." I wiped at my nose and eyes and looked at him. He was smiling. "There ain't a thing wrong with you. The world? Yeah, well, that's another story. It can be a fucked-up place. Don't you ever feel guilty or apologize for who you are. You got that? Ever."

"I'm not sorry I'm gay, Mr. James." I was looking at him through blurry eyes. "I'm not." The tears started to flow again. "I'm just so tired of being angry all the time."

He looked at me and nodded his head. "Takes a lot out of you, doesn't it?"

I looked away and felt the hot tears streaming down my face. James sat there and let me cry. He said nothing for a long time, staring out at the baseball field. Finally, he said, "You told anyone else? Your mom?"

I shook my head. "I've never said it out loud before, to be honest." I wiped at my eyes again and took a deep breath.

"Yeah? Well, this is a big day then, right? It's been a long time coming. You've been holding this in for so long, I'm surprised you didn't explode."

I laughed. "I think I just did."

James just nodded and we sat there, both of us staring out at the field, with its worn-out paths and deep trenches in the batter's box. It looked so abandoned. "What am I gonna do?" I asked. I honestly had no clue. "Where do I go now?"

James thought about this for a while. I guess he was trying to choose his words carefully. "I don't know," he finally said. "A lot depends on where you want to go. I really don't have any answers. But I know this much, you're not leaving this school. I'll hunt your ass down and drag you back. You've got a lot of support here, people who understand. I'll point 'em out to you."

"I'm not going anywhere," I said. And I meant it. "Got nowhere to go. I just don't know if I want to deal with the whole 'coming out' thing. I hate that term, you know. Makes me sound like I've been hiding." I thought about this for a while. Maybe, in a way, I had been hiding.

"Mr. James, the thing is, I just don't want to have to explain myself." My nose was running uncontrollably. I finally gave up and just wiped the snot on the sleeve of my sweatshirt.

"Then don't," he said. "You've got nothing to explain. It'd be like having to explain why you're left-handed. How you choose to deal with who you are is entirely up to you. So long as you let go of feeling you're somehow screwed up, because you're not. I do think you should tell your mom, though. She might surprise you."

"She's cool," I said. "I'm not sure why I never told anyone." I paused. "This sounds stupid, but I guess I didn't want to disappoint people. Can you believe that?"

James looked at me and shook his head. "Yeah, I can. Believe me."

I looked up at him and he was wearing this half grin. I had the sense he knew something about disappointing people, but he didn't say anything more.

"You know," I said, "I think I knew I was gay since I was eight. It was always there, like a birthmark or something. I never thought that much about it until someone pointed it out."

"And when someone pointed it out?" James still had that half grin on his face.

"Then I guess I *had* to look at it, and when you're told enough that it's ugly, you get sort of angry."

"Or worse," James said, "you start to believe it."

I nodded. "Yeah, maybe."

"Well, it's not true. We both know that."

"Thanks." I looked at him and tried to smile. "You know, I'm not sure why I told you, of all people. A lot of kids think you're an asshole."

He laughed. "A lot of kids are right. Listen, you've got a few days off. Call me if you want to talk. I'm divorced, got no kids, so I got time." He wrote his number on a piece of scratch paper from his pocket and put his hand on my shoulder. "And I'll expect you to wash that sweatshirt. It's disgusting."

We got up to leave. "How come you got divorced?" I asked.

He shook his head and looked back at the unsightly school. "C'mon, I'll give you a ride home. And I can't answer that question."

I put my hands in my pockets and started walking. "Can't or won't?"

"Can't." He shrugged his shoulders and fell into step with me. "Some things just don't offer up any answers."

With our heads down and the wind blowing in our faces, we walked silently back, through the rocky, unkempt outfield, past the battered asphalt track and finally to the teachers' parking lot where James kept his old truck. It was cold; the fall was giving up the fight, and soon there would be snow. But none of that mattered. For the second time in my memory, a dam inside me had burst. This time, though, it felt good.

When I told my mom, she cried. Not because I was gay, but because she missed it.

"I should've known; what kind of mother am I?" She was hugging me, bawling into my chest. We were sitting at the kitchen table and I was stroking her head.

"It's okay, Mom. It's fine. Really."

"Why didn't you tell me sooner? I could've helped you."

I didn't have an answer. "I guess I wasn't ready, but it had nothing to do with you, Mom. Nothing. You've been great."

"Are you sure you're okay?" She looked up at me and wiped her eyes.

I was smiling, trying to make her feel better. "It's fine. Honest. You've been busy, that's all." Dumb thing to say. She started howling again about being a bad mom. It took her forever to stop. Normally, my mom wasn't a crier, but when she cut loose, it was a gusher. I finally got her calmed down by telling her I was hungry. Cooking gave her something to

The Eddy

do, and it allowed me to change my shirt. As she prepared dinner, I sat in the kitchen keeping her company. She kept saying, "God, Toby, I never knew."

And that's the thing. Why should she have known? I had girls over to the apartment, girls who were friends. I didn't look gay, whatever that meant. I wasn't into clothes or fashion; I wasn't the least bit effeminate; I wasn't particularly bookish or cultivated or any of that stereotypical bullshit associated with being gay. I was just a guy. I liked football, riding motorcycles, and puttering with engines. Yeah, I enjoyed a good book and liked writing, but there was nothing overtly *gay* about me.

But most people have a need to categorize things, I guess. Categories reinforce beliefs. Either you are something or you aren't. But if you don't fit somewhere, like me, what then? And as hard as it was to admit, I was just as uncomfortable with blurred lines as anyone. I thought of this as I sat in bed that night, trying to put the day's events in order.

A few weeks earlier, I had taken Takeita with me to one of my favorite clubs in Minneapolis. It was in the heart of the Native American community. Parking was hard to come by, so we had to walk several blocks through a rough neighborhood. Along the way, we passed several intoxicated Native men, passed out in doorways. A couple of them accosted us for change and cigarettes. It made me uncomfortable, and I said to Takeita, "God, all these drunk Indians are so pathetic; it's sad. Can't they do something about this tragedy?"

Takeita turned on me and smacked her lips. "Boy, you sound like one of those dumbass liberals with good intentions who don't know shit."

She caught me off guard. "What does that mean?"

"You just like all those people who talk about the crisis in the black community without ever seeing the other side. You think just because you see all these sad souls that everyone is like that. You see drunk Indians because they're in your face. What about all the hardworking Indians raising their kids, going to work, volunteering their time? You don't see 'em, so they don't exist. Nothing as obvious as a drunk Indian or a single parent sister. That kind of attitude is as bad as the tight-ass conservatives who think everyone is playing with the same deck of cards."

And she was right. I told her so after I put up a lame argument. I think she was disappointed when I conceded so easily. She liked a fight. It was like foreplay to her. I think she really had a thing for me, was waiting for the time I got the courage up to make a move on her. I wondered how she would take it when I told her I was gay, if she'd still want to hang with me. Before I went to sleep, I had to laugh out loud. What was I thinking? Of course she would. She was fiery and strong-willed, but she wasn't a hypocrite.

I never called James while I was out. I actually was feeling surprisingly good. When I got back to school, there were rumors swirling about how I kicked the shit out of Hedstrom. I didn't say much, but my cred went way up. Being suspended at Wheatley was a rite of passage, and apparently, it did me more good than harm. Everyone wanted to talk to me, but I played it cool. No big deal. If anyone thought I was gay, they sure didn't say anything. If they brought it up, I already decided I'd say it didn't matter one way or another. I wouldn't deny it, but I wouldn't make an issue out of it like it really mattered, that somehow my sexual orientation defined me, because it didn't. It was a part of who I was, sure, but I wasn't going to have some coming out party for someone else's satisfaction.

James must have told Winiski because she was really attentive to me when I got back. She kept checking on me, asking if I was okay. I said I was great, and I meant it. In truth, nothing around me changed all that much. I was different, but everything else was the same. I actually got to wondering how my notions of Southview might have been different had I been more honest with myself. Every now and then, I thought about Billy and his bike and the night I decided to drive through a tornado. It made me cringe.

A week after I got back, Takeita invited me to a party

The Eddy

and I went without hesitation. She was well connected and when she said a party would be cooking, you could pretty much guarantee people would be talking about it Monday. When I picked her up, I should've known something was up. She was decked out, dressed in tight jeans and a low-cut top. When she got in the van, her perfume made me dizzy. She was gorgeous, no doubt about it.

"Wow," I said. "You are so hot. Everybody gonna be lookin' at you tonight, girl."

She popped a breath mint and said, "Hope I don't make you jealous." She pulled the visor mirror down and applied some shiny lip gloss. She turned toward me and pursed her lips. "Tell me these aren't delicious."

Right then I knew it. I should have stopped the van and let her know, but for some reason, I couldn't find the words. When we got to the party, she was instantly out on the dance floor, and she dragged me with her. I wasn't much of a dancer, but it must have made for an interesting sight—a long-haired white dude in a leather jacket with this hot black chick dancing provocatively all around him. I could feel the eyes on me; I could feel the envy from all the guys. Even though I couldn't dance a lick, I stayed out there as long as I could. I needed time to think.

Eventually, we got off the floor, and Takeita got us something cold to drink. "C'mon, let's go cool off." She handed me something with Amaretto in it, and I almost puked.

She pulled me into the garage. We were standing between two old Cadillacs, and I could see my breath. She pushed me against one of the cars and gave me a long, deep kiss, pressing her body against mine. I didn't want to insult her, so I tried to return the gesture as best I could. I couldn't push her away, so I tried to slide down the car like I was melting or something. As I was slipping away from her embrace, I caught some of my hair on the molding of the car. I must have slipped on some old oil on the floor because my feet gave way and a big clump of hair ripped free from my head. I ended up on my butt, howling in pain.

"Oh my God! Are you okay?" she screeched.

I was holding the back of my head, feeling the bald spot. Takeita looked up at the chunk of hair hanging from the car and burst out laughing. I couldn't help but laugh too, but mine was more out of relief.

"Oh my God! I'm *so* going to hang this from my rearview mirror." She was holding my hair in her hands. I was still on the ground rubbing my head. "You are so smooth, Toby. No wonder all the girls like you." She was still laughing.

"Yeah, but wait till they find out I'm gay." That shut her up.

She opened her mouth to say something and then covered it with her hand. "Oh my God, oh my God," she kept saying. "You're serious!"

There was silence as she registered this, and then she burst out laughing again. It wasn't what I expected.

"You asshole!" She was still laughing. She gave me her hand and helped me up. "You could've saved me a lot of trouble. You know how hard it is to look this good?"

She brushed me off and then did something I'll never forget. She stood for a moment just looking at me and then put her hands to my face and kissed me again, this time softly. I'm not sure why, but it was maybe the sweetest thing I'd ever experienced. When she pulled away, I had tears in my eyes.

"I should've known," she said softly, "because I'm way too hard to resist."

And she was. She was so pretty. "You're the first guy who actually listened to me, really heard what I was saying."

She backed away and leaned on the other car and took a deep breath. "Toby, do you think it's too much to ask to find someone who likes you because of your personality, for *any* other reason other than the fact you give him a hard-on?" She wasn't joking now. "Is it?"

"I don't know," I said. I could see her eyes were watery. "But when guys see you, it's what they think of first. You don't exactly make it easy on them."

The Eddy

She looked down at the way she was dressed. "Yeah, maybe." She sighed. "Oh, man, you were going to get so lucky tonight."

"I'm really flattered..." I shrugged. "You know, there are plenty of guys in there who would love to hook up with you." She didn't care for the comment.

"Don't go thinking I'm desperate or easy. Because I'm not. People might think so because of the way I talk and dress, but I'm not. I just like the attention. My mom taught me right. I'm not like that."

I asked her if she wanted to go back inside and party, but what she really wanted was to talk. We left the party, bought a huge bag of chips and a couple of Slurpees, and parked next to a lake telling stories and laughing long into the night. She gave me all kinds of advice on romance, especially how not to lead girls on.

At one point, she said, "Here's the thing, Toby. You're a good-looking guy. You've got the tough exterior, like you don't wanna let anyone near you. You know, the leather, the long hair, Mr. Aloof. You probably got a tattoo somewhere too. It heats girls up. Plus, they won't miss the fact that you're tall and have that cute jawline."

I denied this vigorously, but she just waved me off.

"Boy, ain't no way girls gonna ignore you, so if you like them, you best be straight with them. In a manner of speaking, of course."

She moved on to how hard it was to take all the tough classes at Wheatley, and that a lot of the black kids thought she was a sell-out. I told her the world was full of idiots. We decided that gay guys and black chicks had a lot in common, that half of our existence seemed to be about trying to carve a small place out of the world where we wouldn't be judged and could be who we wanted to be. She ended the night by asking me if I knew any straight guys who could talk and weren't driven by what was in their pants.

"Not under the age of fifty," I said.

"Hmmm," she said before getting out of the car. "I'll have to think about that."

Joe Paatalo

The Eddy

Chapter 5

It was sometime around early December I started noticing a few changes in James. He was always intense, always hard-working, but I began to notice his irritability had ratcheted up. Mostly it was little things, like refusing to give directions for a third time or making a big deal out of being a minute late to his class. Most kids didn't notice it or would shrug it off by saying he was in a bad mood that day, but I saw him more than anyone; I knew something wasn't quite right. Just before winter break, I saw him almost snap.

Wheatley had this strange holiday tradition. The last day before break, the student body gathered for an hour-long assembly in the gym. The choir and the band dressed in a wild assortment of ethnic and cultural clothes, anything that expressed their heritage—traditional Hmong dresses, Somali *macawis* and *guntiinos*, and Mexican fancy dresses. They played a funky assortment of jazz and blues Christmas songs; some I didn't recognize. They were actually quite good. The black girls in the choir belted out a few soulful holiday numbers, and many of the students in the bleachers stood to dance and sing. It was one of the only occasions where the community showed up in force to watch.

Anyway, the highlight was the last twenty minutes where Santa came out with two large bags and tossed colored pencils, packets of pens, Snicker bars, and suckers into the stands. The candy alone must have cost at least five hundred bucks.

In the past, Santa was played by Mr. Jackson, the principal. He was a tall, skinny black guy, and I guess he did the role with relish. But somehow James had lost some fishing bet to him that year and had to do it. He was not happy. During 5th hour, I helped him get the costume on, and he was the surliest Santa I'd ever seen, and I should know; my mom used to drag me to the malls at Christmas for pictures when I was a kid.

James went through the routine, tossing his gifts, trying to be jolly, which for him wasn't easy. He looked pretty funny out there with the suit and his Chuck Taylors. I gave him credit for trying.

When it was all over, the students bolted for the exits, high on the prospect of two weeks off. I saw James slink down the hall back to his room, carrying his beard in his hand. I had to go to my locker, so I didn't see what happened, but as I was preparing to head out, I was almost bowled over by two black kids sprinting for the door. Twenty feet behind them was a crazed Santa in pursuit, high stepping in his Chucks. His eyes were wide and his face beet red. He went out the door after them and, when I ran to take a look, I saw the two kids split. Santa never hesitated. He chose one and kept running. The last I saw of him he was heading east on Maryland, a busy street, keeping pace with a frightened kid.

I hung around for a while trying to figure out what happened. The short version was the kids were talking smack, swearing and grabbing their crotches. When James told them to knock it off, one of them said, "Fuck you, Santa."

Apparently, it didn't sit too well with James, and when he demanded they come to the office with him, they flipped him off. After that, the chase was on. One kid in the hall was laughing so hard, he could barely tell the story. "Dude," he kept saying to anyone who would listen, "Santa went off like a linebacker. He was gonna kill 'em. Thought he was gonna rupture a hamstring."

When James finally came back, he was pouring sweat. I didn't see the kid, so no one knew what happened. Jackson came out of his office and grabbed James by the arm and led him into his office. I could hear Jackson say, "Jesus Christ, Mitch, that's the last time I ever make a bet with you."

There was some animated discussion, each man toe

to toe. The last thing I heard James say over his shoulder as he stormed past the kids outside the office was, "Find someone else to teach those bullshit classes, because I won't."

I watched him march down the hall back to his classroom. He was still clutching the beard in his hand. As he rounded the corner, I saw him whip it against the wall and keep walking. I waited for a few minutes and retrieved it. He had promised to give me a ride home, since Mom needed the van. I seriously considered walking, but it was pretty cold. I waited a while and then knocked on his door.

He was sitting at his desk in his t-shirt and shorts. His red tights and Santa regalia were spread out on the floor. He was still sweating. I tossed the beard on the pile. "You okay?"

He rubbed his eyes and grunted. "I'm fine. Just great. No big deal." He dismissed the whole thing with a wave of his hand, but I could tell he was still seething.

"Not exactly the way to go out on the holidays," I said.

He shrugged. "It isn't the kids so much. I'm supposed to teach sports lit to a group of athletes, mostly black, to keep them eligible, give 'em an English credit. I won't do it. Jackson's pissed."

"Why not?"

"Why not do it? C'mon." His voice went up an octave. I was sorry I asked. "I'm not going to pander; I don't care what their reading level is. It's an insult to say the only thing they can or will read is something about sports. It's a joke. That's not education. If I were a parent of one of 'em, I'd be outraged. Wouldn't you?"

I didn't know what to say. "I guess."

"Yeah, well, that's the problem with education, this school." He was on a roll. "No one's got the guts to maintain standards. No one's got the political will to say failure is a part of life. So we push the kids through and say we're educating them, and they walk away with nothing—no skills, can't read or write. Kids can't pass a minimum standard test and yet they're on the "B" honor roll. What a joke. Just like those two assholes in the hall. No one else is going to stop them. Everyone walks right by and pretends not to hear them. No one will hold them accountable for being pricks. But I will. I'll quit before I walk past that. To hell with everyone else."

I stood there feeling uncomfortable.

"Ah, forget it, Toby. It's not your concern. I'm just venting." He threw his arms up as if in temporary surrender. "Let's get out of here."

We didn't talk any more until we were in his truck. The cool air must have been good for him because he seemed to calm down.

"What are you doing for your break?" I asked.

He smiled. "Montana and Wyoming. Gonna fly fish for ten days."

"Isn't it a bit cold for that?" I envisioned someone bundled in a parka waving a stick while standing in a river.

"Nah, best time of the year. Chinook winds come through and it's perfect. No one else out there. I'm all alone. If it gets too cold, I'll just kick back and read."

The thought must have been pleasant. He kept smiling, and the scar on his chin seemed to glisten. I didn't want to say anything, to disturb his reverie, so I shut up. When he pulled up to my apartment, he said, "Hey, I almost forgot. You're pretty good with engines, right?"

I nodded. "Not bad."

"Want to make some Christmas cash? Come by my place tonight if you can get the van; otherwise, give me a call." He wrote his address on a scrap of paper. "I'll pay you some money up front. I got something right up your alley."

James lived on Portland Avenue, close to the St. Paul Cathedral. It was one of the oldest, wealthiest neighborhoods in the city. All the houses were grand, many constructed just after the turn of the century when the town was still under the influence of James J. Hill, the railroad baron. The area reeked of class and history, not the kind of place I associated with James. After all, he drove one of the

The Eddy

ugliest trucks I have ever seen, an early '90s powder blue Ford 150 4x4 with a maroon topper. This seemed way out of his league.

I located the house, an elegant brick two-story with an old-fashioned light pole in front of it, a tribute to a more refined era. The windows of the house were lit up, and I could see an enormous Christmas tree near a fireplace. The tree was aglow with hundreds of pale-yellow lights, and the bows of the tree were packed with elaborate ornaments. A fire was throwing additional light into the room, and a table was set with linens and huge wine goblets. It looked like a Budweiser commercial. I almost expected the Clydesdales to come around the corner at any moment. I never knew anyone who actually lived like this.

I walked around to the back garage where James told me to meet him. The garage was actually an old carriage house with two large barn doors and a tiny entryway on the side. I knocked, and when I entered, I was taken aback again. James was sitting in the corner of the garage on an old car bench seat, with all his fishing gear on the floor in front of him. He was sipping a beer, happily cleaning his fly line. On the other side of the garage was a black '69 Chevelle SuperSport, its body in mint condition. The hood, however, was open, and the guts of the engine were strewn about.

"How do you like it?" he asked.

"The car or the garage?"

"The garage. It's my home."

I looked around some more. The difference between the grand house and James' residence was shocking. There was a beat-up Old Town canoe hanging from his ceiling, its wooden ribs facing downward. On one wall of the garage was a dizzying array of fly fishing and camping gear. On another wall, an 8x8 bulletin board with photographs, some old and some new, all pinned and overlapping. Next to the Chevelle was a workbench strewn with tools, and above it was a built-in bookshelf with perhaps five hundred books. In the loft above the chaotic ground floor, I could see a bed and what I later found out was a fly-tying table. The whole place smelled of old canvas, wool, and motor oil. If the place had a focal point, which was debatable, it seemed to come from the car. "I like what you've done to your digs," I said. "It's really you..." I trailed off. "Uh, how long have you been living here?"

James opened another beer and offered me a coke. "Almost two years, I guess. My ex-wife Maggie lives in the *big* house."

I nodded and opened the soda. "Looks like she got the best of it."

"Yeah, well, it was all hers to begin with. Let me show you the car."

He led me over to the car. The Chevelle wasn't hard to appreciate. On the outside. It was cherry-perfect: original black grille, new slicks with original rims, top-of-the-line paint job. On the inside, however, it was stripped. He was waiting for replacement seats but had installed a top-of-the-line sound system. It served as the music source for his home.

The engine block was another story. He had a battery for power, but that was it. The engine, a 396 four-barrel and everything that went with it, was scattered around the garage.

"I need to get the engine back in, but that's not the issue. I've got all the parts, but I can't seem to make them work. Thought maybe you could have a go at it. I'm having someone drop the engine in tomorrow before I go; I just need someone to put it all together. Think you can do that?"

It looked a bit daunting. "You got all the tools?"

"I think so, but if you need something, let Maggie know. She'll pick it up or have it delivered."

"And manuals?"

"Got 'em all. Didn't do me much good, though. Look, I don't expect it done anytime soon. I've had it for six years and finally figured I'd had enough. I need to get it running or get rid of it."

"Don't do that," I said. "We can make her go."

"Well, maybe you can. I can't. I'm out of patience. I

should've started with the engine, but I got carried away with the body. Tell you what, I'll give you two hundred bucks up front and then twelve bucks an hour. Keep track of your time. What do you say?"

I didn't need to think about it. "Sure, but I'm not so sure it's the best use of your money. Someone else could do it quicker, probably even better."

James took a swig of beer and shook his head. "I know, but it would defeat the reason I got it. I wanted to do the whole project myself, but I didn't know my limitations. A man has got to know his limitations. So I've decided to compromise my integrity by having you do it. Next best thing."

"Okay," I said. It looked like fun, and I immediately thought of the new bike it could get me. "I hope I don't mess it up, though."

"Look at her, Toby. Do you think you could do any more damage?"

I laughed. "No, I guess not. And hey, thanks for the opportunity."

We shook hands and sat down on the car bench he used for a couch. I drank another Coke and he opened another beer.

"So what does your ex-wife do?" I asked. "That house is really something."

"She's a tax lawyer like her daddy. The house was a gift when she graduated from law school. She does very well for herself. Tonight, she's having a Christmas party with all the lawyers at her office."

I tried to imagine what that would be like. "Are you going?"

James laughed and almost choked on his beer. "Hell, no. I'd rather have my nuts roasted." He began puttering with his fishing gear again. "Don't get me wrong, Maggie's a doll. I just hate the company she keeps."

He stopped what he was doing and looked at me. "I know what you're going to ask. Don't bother. Life happens, that's all."

"How come you live here, next to her, in a garage?"

James shrugged. "It's a carriage house. And I just haven't gotten around to moving yet, that's all. Besides, it's cheap. She gave it to me. I can fix it up and rent it out, make some money. I've got plans for it."

"Kind of like your car?" I grinned.

"Wow, and you thought I was the asshole." He chuckled. "Here, take these before I forget." He threw a set of keys at me. "If you need anything while I'm away, just let Maggie know. You can leave a note in the mailbox if she's not home. She knows about you, so she'll be expecting you."

He finished his beer and handed me an envelope with two hundred bucks cash. "Maybe this will help a bit for Christmas."

I left his place feeling elated. I now had money to buy Mom something for Christmas and enough left over to add to my savings, which was pretty paltry. But the best part was I had a job that would pay me more than the six fifty I made at the Pizza Shack, and it would allow me to work on my own terms.

Out in front of the big house, as I crossed the street to where my van was parked, the snow began to fall. Big, fat, puffy flakes danced in the air, illuminated in their descent by the streetlamps. I stuck my tongue out and lunged at a few, but I couldn't seem to catch any. Before getting into the van, I turned back to the house to where the expensive cars of the lawyers were parked, each one worth a college education. I tried hard to not let it spoil my mood.

I kept my job at the Shack but cut back on my hours to work on James' car. It took me two days to figure out where he kept everything. I finally got frustrated and asked Takeita to help me get organized. James had no sense of organization whatsoever, and if you're wrenching on motors, there is nothing worse than not being able to find a tool or a part when you need it.

Takeita was a great help, except she'd get easily distracted, either by some piece of gear or some obscure

The Eddy

book. She wasn't bad with engines, though, and she helped me organize the chaos. Part of James' problem was he ordered some of the wrong parts. We had to make a list of what we needed, which took time.

"Hey, doesn't this thing even have air conditioning?" Takeita was looking at the engine schemata in the manual. "Seems like it should."

"Nah, none of 'em had it. They're muscle cars, meant to go fast. A.C. doesn't go with the high RPM'S. Burns the engine out."

"Black car; must get hot in the summer."

I was messing with the fuel line and started laughing. "You don't quite get it. These things aren't meant for comfort, necessarily. They're not Cadillacs. They're built for speed and show. They're like bikes, in a way. You don't ride them because you want it easy; you ride them because you want the thrill."

"Gimme a Lexus or an Acura anytime," she said.

"Yeah, they're nice, but I couldn't work on them. At least not without a computer. I wouldn't know where to start. Besides, this car has a Muncie four-speed. You really feel like you're driving in this thing."

I gave up on the fuel line. I could see it was the wrong size. "What I don't get is how he got so many of the parts messed up. I mean, he's not an idiot. Add a 3/8-inch fuel line to the list." I wiped my hands clean and gave up for the day.

"Maybe he's just not mechanical," Takeita said. "Maybe he's *just* an English teacher."

I went over to the fridge and grabbed a few Cokes. "I'm not so sure he's all of that either. I mean, he's good and all at what he does, but half the time he's pissed. I'm not sure whether he actually likes what he's doing. I don't mind being around him, but he puts me on edge sometimes. Winiski, now there's a great teacher. A natural. James? He's like one of these wrong parts. He just doesn't quite fit."

Takeita thought about this for a minute. "Maybe he doesn't have to fit. The guy does a lot more good than harm. He creeps me out sometimes, but I got a good shot at a scholarship, and I don't think I'd be there without him, or someone like him. I write ten times better now than I did two years ago." She laughed. "I still remember when he threw my first paper in the trash and said it was a waste of paper and his time. I was so pissed. He told me I was too smart to write crap like that."

"Really? What did you do?"

"I tried to drop his class; told him he didn't like black kids. And you know what he did? He hounded me every day until I came back. In the lunchroom, in the halls, in other teachers' classes. I told my mom he was harassing me. Know what she said? She told me to get my ass back in his class and prove something. So I did."

I nodded. "Yeah, that says a lot about you. And your mom." I looked around. "Could you live like this?"

Takeita crushed her can and threw it in a recycling bin. "If it made me happy, I don't see why not. It's better than a lot of places. He's surrounded by all the stuff he likes, and he doesn't have to share a bathroom."

We changed the subject, talked about college and getting out of town. She told me about some guy she liked who was in junior college. He was white and I teased her about that. When she left, I took the list of things over to the house and left them in the mailbox with my phone number. I was surprised when James' ex called me two days later and told me the parts were in.

It was bone-chilling that Saturday when I stopped by the house. James' ex-wife was in sweatpants with a fleece pullover. She was sipping a cup of tea when I rang the bell. She invited me in and, after I took my boots off, I stood next to the fire to thaw out. "My van's heater doesn't work too well." I was still shivering. "I'm not used to this kind of cold."

She poured a glass of hot cider and handed it to me. "I've lived my whole life here and still can't get used to it. Mitch has told me a lot about you."

I took a swig of cider. I felt its sweet, sour warmth all the way down to my gut. I wondered how much he had said. "You guys talk much?"

The Eddy

"A bit," she said. We sat down at her dining table. "Not like we used to, but we're still friends."

"Must seem weird, him living out there like that."

She laughed. "That's what everybody says. It wasn't supposed to be for this long, but it's okay. Not the easiest when I have a date over, but..." She trailed off, still smiling. "Are you going to finish the car?"

"I'd like to. It'll take a while, but if I have all the right parts, I think I can do it."

She was looking at me intently. I wouldn't have called her pretty, but she was cute. She had sandy hair and subtle freckles. Her eyes were green, and she wore glasses. She was tiny, maybe five-foot-three. She looked as if she had just gotten out of bed.

"I hope you can," she said. "He's had that thing for years. Maybe if he finishes it, he'll be ready to move on."

I took another sip of cider. It had a cinnamon flavor to it. "This is really good," I said. She offered me some more, but I declined. "Do you want him to move?"

She embraced her tea with both hands and took a drink. "I just want him to be happy, that's all. He's a good guy. He deserves that."

"Were you guys married long?"

"Ten years, Toby. That's a long time, isn't it?" She leaned back in her chair. "I'm not sure what Mitch told you, but we met in college, while he was playing hockey. It seems like a long time ago. He was really good, very athletic. A bit of a bad boy. Every girl on campus knew who he was."

I nodded. "Yeah, I know how that works."

"Well, you don't often come across jocks who can talk about Faulkner. Very seductive." She laughed. "Anyway, we made a good pair for a while." She looked out the kitchen window and seemed ready to say something, but she changed her mind.

"So I've got all the parts for you. If you need anything else, tools, you name it, let me know."

I finished the cider and got up to leave. "Thanks, Mrs.—"

"Maggie. Just call me Maggie. The stuff is in a box by the back door." She got up to walk me out. "Don't let Mitch push you around. Take your time and do it right. Sometimes he forgets to be nice. And if you need anything to eat or drink, let yourself in and have at it. I've got leftovers I'll never be able to eat. Don't knock. Make yourself at home."

I put my boots on and was halfway to the door when I turned around. "Can you tell me how he got hurt in college? I mean, after he was cut?"

"In the summer, you mean?" She slowly shook her head. "I only know the facts. But that doesn't mean I know the story, not sure anyone does. If he tells you, promise me you'll let me in on it." She gave me a weary smile.

"Sure," I said. There was silence for a moment. "Is he okay? I mean, I'm not sure if he talks to you, but sometimes I wonder."

She took a deep breath and chuckled. "You know what he used to tell me when I tried to get him to open up? He used to say, 'The difference between men and women is that most men lead lives of quiet desperation, while most women can't keep their desperation quiet.' Used to piss me off something fierce. But that's who he is. That's who he will always be. It's nice you're worried about him, but trust me, it goes nowhere."

I nodded, not sure what to say.

"Thanks for helping him, Toby. He doesn't take help very well, so it says a lot about you. And make sure he pays you. He sometimes forgets the details."

I said goodbye and went to the garage to work on the engine. For a long time, I thought about his line. I finally decided it was more bullshit than clever.

Chapter 6

James got back the day before school was scheduled to begin. He called me late at night as I was getting ready to rack out. I'd made considerable progress on the car, but it didn't really show yet. I thought he might be disappointed, but he wasn't. He seemed to be in a good mood.

"I see all the new parts. Thanks for sorting that out."

"Takeita helped me. A lot. I think we got most of what we need."

"Do I owe her?" he asked.

"No. Unless you want to give her something for cleaning up your place. How was your trip?"

"God, it was great. Really good." He sounded like he meant it. "How long do you think it'll be before we get her running?"

"I'm not sure. Depends on my time, but I'll check in with you tomorrow. Do you have some pictures or something?"

"Of the trip? Sure. If you're interested. I'll bring 'em tomorrow. And hey, thanks again."

The pictures were mostly of trout. They didn't seem that big to me, at least compared to the bass back home. But he thought they were special. Back in Kansas, people measured fish in pounds; James kept talking about inches, as if 20 was a magical number. I didn't mention that. I had to admit they were pretty, especially the rainbows.

"Did you bring any back?" I asked.

"No, no, I don't eat them; I let them go. They are tasty, though."

Well, that made no sense to me. "You go all the way out there and don't bring any back? And they're good to eat?

What's up with that?"

He smiled. "They're too precious to eat. If I want to eat fish, I'll get some farmed catfish or salmon. Sometimes it's important not to take, to just be a participant."

I flipped through the other pictures, not really sure what he was talking about. The ones I really liked were of the mountains and the river. He had a bunch of rocks and bugs too, but they didn't do much for me. "Sure is pretty country. Nothing like I've ever seen."

"You need to take a road trip sometime, Toby. See the country. Get out there and *smell* the world."

"I'd like to smell Florida or California," I said, "somewhere I can ride my bike year-round."

He shook his head. "Too damn many people. See the country without all of the strip malls and housing divisions. See where the wheat and corn are grown. Get out of your car, somewhere off the beaten path."

I thought about this for a moment. "Yeah, well, I'm all for going somewhere, and I guess I'm not too particular at the moment. Seen my share of wheat, though."

James pointed at the pictures. "If you like any of those, let me know; I'll make you a copy."

I shrugged. I didn't want to hurt his feelings. "I like this one." I handed him a picture of a river with the sun going down in the distance.

"Good choice. I'll get it done for you."

We were between classes and the bell rang. He sighed and started getting ready for American Lit. "Come by and work on the car any night you're free. I'll be sure to pay you every other Friday, okay?"

It sounded good to me. I'd already made almost five hundred bucks. "I'll be by tomorrow. I've got the right fuel line now and need to get that in to see if I'm getting gas."

He was going to say something, but someone dumped a bag of Doritos on the floor. Normally, he might have been angry because there was a no-food policy in his room, but he just bent over and helped pick them up. He hardly scolded the kid.

The Eddy

After school that day, I helped Winiski clean her lab in preparation for the second semester. She offered me ten bucks to help, but I felt weird taking anything from her and refused it. I got Takeita to help me. She was never in much of a hurry to get home. We were messing with the ferrets when Takeita couldn't take it anymore.

"Hey, guess what, Toby. I got a letter of acceptance from Vanderbilt." She broke into a huge smile, flashing those brilliant white teeth, and then she started dancing.

Winiski heard the news and screamed from the other side of the room and bounded over to her and started dancing too. Watching Winiski shake her ass was a spectacle. They hugged each other. And then Takeita hugged me. And then Winiski hugged me too, although I'm not sure why.

"To hell with the lab," Winiski said. "I'm taking you guys over to Snuffy's for a celebration burger and malt. Grab your coats!"

I sat in the back of Winiski's station wagon while the women chattered like chipmunks. *What are you going to do for a computer? Are you staying in the dorms? I heard the nursing program is first-rate. You're going to need some new clothes.* And on and on. It didn't stop at the malt shop either. I sat there, munching fries, getting more depressed by the minute.

When they finally stopped to take a breath, Winiski looked at me. "Aren't you excited, Toby?"

"You bet," I said and stuffed more fries in my mouth. I didn't want to put a damper on the occasion.

"Your time will come," Takeita said. "How many apps do you have out?"

I wiped some ketchup from my chin and felt sheepish. "Uh, none yet."

"None?" Winiski's eyes bugged. "Toby, you've got to get on it. How many letters of rec do you have?"

I didn't say anything. I just looked at her.

"Oh, good God. Okay, I'll get started on one, and I'll get James to crank one out. I'm making an appointment with the counselor tomorrow so you can start applying. What did you get on your ACTs?"

I swallowed some raspberry malt. "I took it last year. I got a 27, I think."

Takeita's eyes widened. "A 27? My God, Toby. I got in with a 23. And I had to take it twice. What's your G.P.A.?"

I shrugged. "Not sure. Pretty good. A 3.5, maybe better. School was a lot tougher in Kansas than here."

Winiski pushed her plate away and leaned toward me. "Honey, what have you been doing? I've heard you talking about college, and I just assumed you were working toward it. What's going on?"

I didn't know what to say. I'd been meaning to do something but hadn't gotten around to it.

Winiski read my mind. "This isn't about procrastination. It's something else."

"Can't we just celebrate Takeita's good news?" I asked.

Winiski scooped some chocolate malt with her spoon, took a bite, and pointed the utensil at me. "We're gonna talk. Tomorrow. Got it?"

"Sure," I said, and turned toward Takeita, ready to change the subject. "Tell me more about Vanderbilt, about Tennessee."

She lit up again and started jabbering away. I smiled and pretended I was excited, but I don't think I heard a word she said.

True to her word, Winiski cornered me the next day in the hall after school and steered me into her room. She sat me down at a table and pulled a chair up next to me.

"Okay, let's talk turkey."

"Turkey? Nobody says that anymore, Ms. Winiski." I laughed at her, but she was having none of it.

"Talk to me, Toby. What's going on? Why haven't you applied anywhere yet? Why are you dragging your feet?"

"I've been meaning to apply. I just haven't." She kept looking at me, waiting for more.

The Eddy

"Okay, look. You talked to James, I know. It's just... For the first time in my life, I feel good about who I am. I used to be really angry. I'm not so much anymore. Sometimes I'm just afraid I'll step back. I might end up somewhere that brings everything back." I stared at the floor. "I can't go back. I just can't."

Winiski put her hand on mine and smiled. "You won't go back, Toby. You're too strong. And I understand how you feel. I really do."

I fought back a tear and closed my eyes. "I've never told anyone before, but I tried to kill myself once. Sort of. I kind of botched it." I tried to laugh. "It was pretty bad. I was a little out of my head, I guess."

"Honey, we all have baggage. But it's in the past, and you can't change it. Remind yourself of it if you need to, but don't let it haunt you. Trust me. I have enough baggage to make Samsonite jealous." She patted my hand.

"Who's Samsonite?" I asked.

She looked at me for a moment and burst out laughing. "He was just a guy with really long hair who liked luggage." She wiped at her eyes. "Listen, what do you want to do? Where do you want to go?"

I thought about it and then said, "I was just thinking I'd stay close to Mom and go to a junior college or something."

"And that's what you want? Really?"

"Well, no, not exactly."

"You think your mom wants you to stay close?"

"She just wants me to be happy. She's seen enough of my misery."

"Then let's apply where you want and see what comes of it. What do you want to study?"

"I was thinking maybe engineering. Or maybe writing. I don't know."

Winiski stood up. "All right, let's go."

I looked at her, puzzled.

"Right now. Let's go. Stichcomb's waiting for you. She's got an hour. Let's not waste it."

She grabbed my arm. There was no protesting. For the next hour, the three of us sat in the counselors' suite, filling out forms and talking about colleges. By the time I left the building, my head was swimming with ideas. I actually envisioned myself somewhere like San Diego State, driving around campus on my motorcycle, hanging out at the beach. It made me laugh, but why not, I thought, *Why the hell not?*

The Eddy

Chapter 7

By the middle of February, I was well into my final semester and the end felt close. I took a calculus class that took up the bulk of my study time, but other than that, it was pretty easy. I still had Winiski, and it was still my favorite class. I actually started to think about a career in environmental science. I didn't have James anymore, but I still saw him a few nights a week when I went to work on his car.

The Chevelle was starting to come together. I had the ignition in, the fuel line set, and most of the carburetor rebuilt. I was having some problems with the electrical system, though. It was a little more complicated than I thought. I kept burning out fuses and couldn't figure out why.

I went over to the garage on a Friday night near the end of February to see if I could solve the problem. Normally, James was out most of the weekends fishing or something, but he was here that night. I was glad to see him. It had been a while since we'd really talked. He was sitting on the bench when I came in. Most of the lights were out and Bob Dylan's "Blood on the Tracks" was playing from his car. As soon as I walked over to him, I could see something was wrong. He was holding a cold beer can next to his eye. When he set it down, I could see a huge welt on the side of his face with a gash in the middle of it.

"Geez, what happened to you?" I stepped closer to have a look. I could see it was bad.

"Broke up a fight between two girls this afternoon. Got a little crazy. I pinned one girl on the ground. I was holding her down when the crowd surged on us and a bunch of kids started kicking. One of the fuckers caught me square."

He reached up and touched his swollen face and winced. "Real typical. They're like sharks. As soon as they see a fight, they come running, looking for blood. This time, they got mine." He grabbed his beer and took a long pull and then returned it to his face.

"Did you see who did it?" I asked.

He shook his head. "Doesn't matter. And no, I didn't."

"Damn," I said. "I never even heard about it. What did you do?"

James grunted and took another beer from the fridge. He seemed a little drunk. "What do you think I did? I waited for back-up. By the time someone came, everyone scattered. I went down to the office, filled out assault and workman's comp forms, and then went home. Jackson told me to get stitches, but I just came here."

I looked closer at the gash. "I think you need stitches," I said. "It doesn't look so good."

"I've had worse. It's no big deal. Got a headache, though." He tried to smile. "Thing is, nothing will happen. And do you know what started it? Some girl called another girl a whore or a bitch. It was some stupid fight over some worthless thug. A *he said she said* kind of thing. Next thing you know, the gangs are involved." He leaned back on the bench and took a deep breath. "Fucking savages. Gutless. They just started kicking and didn't care who got hurt. They wanted blood and they got mine."

"What will Jackson do?" I asked.

"What he always does. He'll make some sort of announcement and the staff will have a meeting about gangs, and we'll all be warned to be on the look-out, and then everyone will close his door. Look, I don't want to talk about it—I got something for you. Been meaning to give it to you." He got up on unsteady legs, walked across the garage, and grabbed a framed picture. "Here, this is for you."

It was a framed 8x10 of the picture of the river and the sunset. Across the picture, he'd written *Take the First Step.*

The Eddy

"It's really nice," I said, and meant it. "I'd forgotten about it."

"Well, I didn't." He plopped back down on the couch. He didn't look so good. "Look, I've talked to Ronda. It's good you're applying to school." His voice suddenly changed. "Hey, look at me."

I stood there, wondering if I should go get Maggie. I thought maybe he had a concussion. I started toward the door, but he stopped me.

"Look at me," he repeated. He stuck his hand in front of his face. "Put your hand in front of your face like this. Real close. Do it."

He was scaring me a bit, but I did it.

"What do you see?" he asked.

My hand was two inches from my face. "Uh, nothing. It's all blurry."

"Can you see your fingers?" He was starting to slur his words.

"No, not really," I said.

"Exactly. Now move your hand away from your face about a foot. What do you see?"

I did it. "I see my hand." I had no idea what this was about.

"Do you see all your fingers? Do you see all the lines in your hand?"

I nodded. "Yeah."

"Exactly. Get my point? Sometimes you need to back away from things to see them clearly. If they're too close, it's all a blur. You need to get away, gain some perspective. If you're too close to the shit, you don't see it clearly. Do I need to spell it out for you?"

I shook my head. He looked like he was ready to drift off. "Take my advice. It's free," he mumbled. I watched him close his eyes and then slipped out to get Maggie.

Maggie was having dinner with some guy when I knocked on the door. She was nicely dressed, with a green skirt, high boots, and a festive plum sweater. She looked pretty, prettier than I had previously thought. The guy was clean-cut, older, who was impeccably groomed. He had on chinos, loafers, and a turtleneck. His aftershave reminded me of old wool.

"I'm sorry to interrupt your dinner," I said after Maggie introduced me to her date. "I'm a little concerned about Mr. James. I think he may have gotten a concussion at school today. He got kicked in the head."

"Let me guess," Maggie said. "He didn't go to the hospital."

She got up to get her coat. I stood there looking at the guy. I just kind of nodded and he did the same. I'm not sure what he was thinking, but it crossed my mind that I probably had more in common with a billy goat than this dude.

"We may have to take a rain check on the play," Maggie said when she returned with her coat. She kissed the guy on the forehead. "I'll be right back."

When we got out to the garage, James was slumped on the couch, his eyes barely open. "Hey, Mag, you're looking sweet," he mumbled. He didn't move.

"Let me have a look," she said and turned on the overhead light. James groaned and covered his eyes. "Shit, Mitch. You need at least four or five stitches." She put her hand on his face. "You're hot, still swelling." She looked over at a bottle of Dewar's next to the couch. I hadn't noticed it before. "And you're drunk."

Maggie turned to me. "Help me get him in the house. He'll never go the hospital, so I won't even try. He might have a concussion, so I'll put him on the couch and wake him every few hours."

We got him on his feet, but he pushed us both away. "I can walk."

I wasn't so sure, so I kept an arm on his shoulder and guided him to the house. He kept his head down, looking at his feet as if he were unsure of where they were taking him. Maggie followed behind and didn't say anything.

When I got him to the kitchen, James looked up at Maggie's date. "Oh, hey, Dick. Good to see you."

The Eddy

"Don," was all the man said.

"Put him on the couch by the fireplace, Toby," Maggie said. I heard her say a few things to Don, some sort of apology, and then I heard him leave. She came back and helped me prop up James' head on a pillow. She took his tennis shoes off and covered him with a comforter. He was asleep before she even finished.

We walked back into the kitchen and Maggie grabbed her wine glass off the table and took a drink. "I think he's more drunk than hurt," she said. "I'll keep an eye on him tonight. Thanks for letting me know."

"Sorry about your date," I said. "Not much of a Friday night, I guess."

"It's okay. I was rather tired anyway. Were you going to work on the car?"

"I planned on it. It's Friday and I was hoping to collect from Mr. James. No big deal, though."

Maggie shook her head. "The hell it isn't." She grabbed her purse. "What's he owe you?"

"No, please. I'm sorry I mentioned it, really."

"Take this." She handed me two one-hundred-dollar bills. "I insist. Be a gentleman and take it."

I reluctantly put it in my pocket. "Thanks, Maggie. You didn't have to do that."

"I know," she said. "Listen, I appreciate your helping Mitch. I worry about him. Keep me posted, okay?"

She took a sip of wine and looked over at the lump on the couch. "Mitch told me about how you're applying to school. Good for you. So that you know, my firm supports a number of college students in the metro area. We help them with their expenses. No guarantee, but we might be able to help you. When you get accepted, let me know first thing. We still have some money."

I didn't know what to say. "That would be incredible. I never thought—I just figured I'd have work full time—nobody..."

"We'll just see what happens, okay?" She lifted her glass as a toast and then heard James moan in the other room. She sighed. "I better go check on the bastard."

I said goodbye and decided not to work on the car. I went back out to the garage to shut out the lights. Before I left, I grabbed a pink paperback from the bookshelf, *Zen and the Art of Motorcycle Maintenance*. I had no idea what it was about, but I liked the title.

By the end of March, I had solved most of the electrical problems on the Chevelle. I was able to start her up and, man, she sounded good. I had had issues with the Muncie four-speed, but I was getting close to getting it figured out. As soon as I did, we'd be able to roll her out. I told James to go ahead and order a new interior and we'd put it in together.

A few days before spring break, I got two interesting pieces of news. The first was that I could graduate if I wanted to. Mrs. Stichcomb told me when I stopped by her office for some information on more schools. I was kind of in shock. All I had to do was finish the quarter that ended in two days and I was done. I walked out of school in a daze.

The second piece of news hit me when I got home. There were two letters for me, one from Boise State, the other from the University of Oregon. Both of them had accepted me. I poured myself a glass of milk and sat at the table for a while, wondering what to do. I was excited, but I decided to sit on the news for a while. I'd even keep it from Mom. I didn't want anyone jumping to conclusions. I still wasn't sure that a local junior college wasn't the answer.

When Mom got home, I took the van and went for a long ride to think things through. Everything seemed to be changing, including the weather. In Minnesota, March is the cruelest month. The novelty of snow and crisp mornings wears off sometime in January, and it gets to feeling like a marathon. March rolls around and teases with a few warm days and melting snow, and then turns mean and drops a foot of snow or gets brutally cold for a stretch. I was ready for it to be over.

It was mild and drizzly when I took the van out,

The Eddy

heading east of the Cities on the interstate toward the Wisconsin border. I drove out past the river town of Hudson, Wisconsin on the St. Croix River and just kept driving east. The landscape was rolling and pretty, still fairly stark from the winter, but patches of green grass were beginning to poke out from the rotting snow. I turned south past the River Falls exit and followed a country road, thinking about the future, wondering if I had it in me to head west. There were a number of good small colleges out this way, and I began to think maybe I should seriously consider staying in this region. It was close to my mom, not far from the big city if I needed that.

I watched the fields rolling past me. I noticed the occasional deer or a flock of turkey feeding on old corn, and every now and then, a hawk would swoop down from a tree or a pole and hover in the air, floating in the currents.

As it started to get dark, I decided to turn north back to the freeway. I was on another county highway, going maybe 60, wondering about the weather in Oregon, when the van seemed to let go of the road. The next thing I knew, I was sliding sideways across the blacktop at more than 50 miles an hour. I tried to jerk the nose of the vehicle back into my lane, but it only increased my spin. I was more passenger than driver. Instinctively, I laid on the brakes, but it didn't seem to matter. I was heading for the ditch, and I was going to roll. I thought of my mom, I thought of James, and I wondered if dying hurt. At the last moment, I grabbed the steering wheel as hard as I could and said a quick prayer as I went off the road.

But I never made the ditch. The van's tires grabbed some gravel and the vehicle jerked violently back toward the road. It felt for a moment like I was on two wheels, and then everything came to a stop in the middle of the highway. I was still clinging to the wheel, facing the wrong direction, when a truck pulled up beside me. A guy was gesturing for me to roll down the window.

"Nice save, kid. You okay? Need any help?"

I could hardly speak. My hands were shaking, and I

thought I might puke.

"Hey, you okay?" The guy looked like a farmer. He had a John Deere hat on his head.

"Yeah. Yeah, I think so."

"Saw the whole thing. Thought you was gonna roll. These roads get awful slick at night. Gotta keep 'er slow. Four-wheel helps, gives you that extra purchase."

"No shit." I tried to smile.

"I got my flashers on, so you can turn around. You'll be fine. Just scares the hell out of you."

"No shit," I said again. "Thanks."

He nodded and backed away to give me some room. I slowly turned the van around and waved at him as I passed by. I drove slowly for about a mile and then pulled over and got out of the van, thinking I might vomit. The minute my feet hit the pavement, I slipped and landed on my ass. Everything was glazed ice. I crawled up next to the van and sat there, still shaking. Something sour shot up from my gut and I retched all over the ground. I watched it steam on the frozen shoulder as I wiped my mouth on my shirt sleeve. "Holy Christ," I kept saying. "Holy Jesus Christ."

It took me an hour and a half to get home. Cars kept zipping past me on the freeway, but I didn't care. When I got back to the apartment, I went straight to my mom and gave her a big hug.

"How was your drive?" she asked.

I pulled away from her and grinned. "Guess what, Mom? I got accepted to Boise State and the University of Oregon. Looks like I'm heading west!"

Chapter 8

I decided not to pull out of school until the end of the year. I found it ironic that, once I was set free, I didn't want to go. Part of it had to do with Winiski and James, but I actually enjoyed the friends I'd made and didn't want to miss out on the last few months of festivities. For some strange reason, I'd become popular. People wanted to hang with me at lunch; I was invited to all the parties; kids I didn't know gave me high fives in the hall. I'd developed a reputation as a badass, which was odd because I'd only had one fight. Maybe it was my hair or the way I dressed, but I think my reputation was cemented more by the fact that I hung out with Takeita, the finest chick in school. I didn't take any of it seriously, but Takeita loved it and kissed me in the hall all the time just to see what everyone's reaction would be. Takeita was a walking wet dream for all the boys, so I played it up occasionally by grinding away at her at the lockers. It was easy because Takeita was a natural actress.

Most of the people I cared about knew I was gay, and I think they took pleasure in seeing Takeita and me go at it in the halls. The truth is, I really didn't experience much homophobia at school. When I did, it was usually in the locker room, and it wasn't directed at me.

I'd discovered most homophobes don't know anyone gay, not really. Some people just need a reason to hate, I guess, because it defines their position in the world. The thing is, there was more homophobia at Southview, where almost everyone was white and dressed essentially the same. At Wheatley, you learned tolerance because you needed it to survive. Without it, you were isolated. Without it, you had to be ready to fight at all times. Sure, tolerance could be taught it in the classroom, but the real lessons took place in the lunchrooms and crowded halls. But for all of its problems, there was something to say about schools like Wheatley. Sure, there were gangs and a lot of apathy, but the kids who made it through sure knew a lot about surviving.

I spent most of spring break finishing up the Chevelle. James had gone west again, this time to fish in the Black Hills, so I spent most days at his place. I was determined to get the car finished by the time he got back. I was still struggling with the four-speed, so I hired a mechanic named Chuck to help me out. It ran me a little over two hundred bucks, but it was worth it. The guy helped me put in the old bucket seat after he adjusted the tranny, and he took the Chevelle out to see how she ran. I was standing in the driveway when he came back twenty minutes later with a big grin on his face.

"Damn, listen to this!" He revved the engine. It was like music. "Think he'd sell this to me?"

I was smiling ear to ear. "Not likely. God, it's gorgeous, ain't it?" Outside, with the late afternoon sun lighting it up, it looked even better than I imagined it would. It was a showpiece.

Maggie heard the engine rev and came out to have a look. Her eyes widened and she put her hand over her mouth in astonishment. Chuck had his arm hanging out the window and I was leaning against the hood, grinning like an idiot, watching her reaction.

"Toby, it's incredible," Maggie said. "I thought I'd never see the day."

Chuck revved the engine again and we all started laughing. I could hardly contain my joy. "Wait till James sees this. He's gonna flip," I said.

Maggie insisted on a ride, so we threw the old backseat in without bothering to fasten it down. It wasn't safe, but we didn't care. I took the keys from Chuck and took Maggie out. We drove around the Cathedral and through downtown St. Paul. We watched as people stopped to stare at the car, this sleek black thing of beauty. It was only 50

The Eddy

degrees out, but we kept the windows rolled down, listening to the engine hum. James had some Allman Brothers in the CD deck, so I punched the music in and turned it up. I looked in the rearview mirror at Maggie. She was still smiling.

"I feel like I'm in high school again," she shouted from the back.

"Yeah, it's not too bad," I said, although I was not sure she heard me.

After an hour or so, we returned to the house and Maggie invited me in. I parked the Chevelle in the garage and wiped down the sides. When I got up to the house, Maggie was holding a small glass of wine in her hand. "Let's have a toast," she said.

I took the offering and we clinked glasses. "Here's to you, Toby, and your amazing job."

"Well, I had help," I said. "But damn, I can't believe I did it. I really did it."

Maggie slowly shook her head. "Yes, you did, and I can't wait to see the smile on Mitch's face. I'll give you a call before he gets back so you can be here to see his reaction." She took another sip of wine. "He will be so amazed."

We talked about the car for a while, and Maggie told me about how he first got it and how, whenever they had an argument, he'd go out there for hours puttering away on it. "He'd come back in more frustrated than when he went out. He was such an inept mechanic, but that didn't keep him from tearing it up all the time, trying something new. Finally, he gave up on the engine altogether and worked on the body exclusively." She laughed and then sighed. "God, it's been at least seven years that thing has been sitting out there."

Maggie walked over to the window and looked out at the garage. "I sometimes saw that thing as a metaphor for our relationship. You know, everything fine on the outside, but a mess on the inside where it matters." She turned back to me and I could see her eyes were watering. "We used to have these ugly fights, Toby. Mostly about children. The longer he taught, the less he wanted kids. He finally refused to even talk about it. That's when he bought the Chevelle. If I ever mentioned kids, he'd tune me out and go work on that thing."

"That's too bad. I think you'd be a great mom."

She looked at me and tears started streaming down her face. I was afraid I'd said the wrong thing.

"That's very sweet of you to say so." She grabbed a dish towel from the kitchen counter and wiped her eyes. "He would've been a good dad, you know. He was just afraid, that's all." She trailed off. "Anyway, this is a big deal. I know it's just a car, but I worry about him not moving on. It's been over two years since we split. He's been stuck in neutral. He hasn't had a date, hasn't made any plans. Maybe this will be the impetus he needs." She smiled and looked out at the garage again. She was silent for some time.

"Hey," I said, trying to jar her away from some rusted memory. "If you don't mind, I'd rather you *didn't* call me when he gets back. You guys should just—well, here." I threw the keys on the table. "Just tell James to give me a call."

Maggie looked at the keys on the table and her eyes started welling again. She came over to where I was sitting and gave me another hug. She held me for almost a minute, and I sat there with my right arm around her back, letting her hold me. When she finally pulled away, her face was streaked with tears, but she was no longer crying.

"Thank you, Toby. I owe you."

"For what? Fixing the car was a lot of fun. It was good for me, and I made some money."

She smiled. "I'm sorry I cried. It must seem strange to you. It's all ancient history."

"It's okay, Maggie." I stood up to leave. "I left some tools out there and some other stuff, so I'll be around. You haven't seen the last of me."

Maggie's eyes suddenly lit up. "Oh my God, forgive me for not asking. I'm so sorry. Have you heard about college yet? What's the story?"

I smiled and shook my head. "That's okay, not yet.

But I think soon. I'll call you first thing when I hear."

She apologized profusely for not asking me earlier and then made me promise all over again to call her when I heard so we could talk about scholarship money. I figured there would be a better time to talk about it, so I just gave her a hug and cut out.

The sun was down when I got outside. The temperature had dropped, and the air was still. A low fog rose from the warm pavement, and the lights from all the houses cast a soft yellow pall down the street. I walked out past my van and kept going down Portland Avenue, past the row houses and turn-of-the-century homes with their wraparound porches and three-tone paint schemes. It felt good to move. The smell of spring was heavy in the moist air. Within a few weeks, everything would change. The old elms lining the neighborhood streets would bud and burst into a canopy of green almost overnight. People would emerge from their houses, stay out a little later, cut their grass, and plant their flower gardens. Everything would be fresh and new, alive with energy and possibility, the way spring should be.

But tonight, the world was still in transition, and I was happy to be alone with my thoughts, walking quietly into the fog.

Joe Paatalo

Chapter 9

I didn't see James until he called me the following Tuesday. He'd been absent on Monday, so I figured he'd gotten in late on Sunday from the Black Hills. He invited me over to his place and said he had some money for me. I went over after work at The Shack.

"Check it out," he said when I walked in the door. The car doors were open and the new interior, black leather bucket seats, and rear bench looked stunning. He'd added a custom silver racing wheel and a black eight-ball for the stick shift.

"I couldn't wait. I called in yesterday and spent the day doing this. What do you think?"

I sat down in the driver's seat and took in the smell of new leather. "Wow. It just keeps getting better. Did you take her out?"

"First thing when I got back. Man, it brought back some memories. I used to have one of these when I was in high school. I took it to college with me." He chuckled softly. It seemed to come from some distant, pleasant place. "I used to carry all my hockey gear in the trunk, along with a few cases of beer. In college, I remember this one girl, Sophie was her name. A real stunner, just gorgeous. We used to ride around a lot, hang out down by the big lake. Anyway, she couldn't stand the smell of the car. Sometimes we'd get in the back seat and... you know... My gear used to stink so bad from all the sweat that it permeated the whole car. Man, she used to say it ruined the mood."

James started laughing. "I used to make her grab the beer from the trunk, just so she'd get another good whiff. She was a bit of a priss. She finally told me I had to clean the trunk and air out the car or she wouldn't go out with me. Dropped her like that." He snapped his fingers to emphasize the point and laughed out loud. "It's all about priorities, Toby. You remember that."

"Sure," I said. I was surprised at how happy he seemed, unusual for him. "Whatever happened to that car?" I asked.

His smile disappeared. "Sold it and bought a Toyota truck, not sure why. Anyway, you did a great job. You should be proud."

I got out of the car and took another long look at her. "I am. I learned a lot. Thanks for the opportunity."

"And hey, I've got something for you." He handed me an envelope. "There's a thousand bucks in there, five from me and five from Maggie. A little college stash."

I could hardly believe it. It was a lot more than I expected. "Wow, thanks. I was actually thinking about a used bike."

"Well, you never know." James slapped me on the back. "So what's the story with college? Hear anything?"

I stuffed the money in my front pocket. "Uh, yeah... The University of Oregon. And Boise State. I haven't decided which."

"Well, God damn." He slapped me on the back again. "A Duck or a Bronco. Good for you." He was smiling ear to ear. He seemed genuinely happy for me. "Maggie's not home, but I'll tell her. She's trying to get some money lined up for you at work." He went over to the fridge and grabbed a couple Cokes and tossed me one. "Looks like the times they are a-changin'."

We sat and drank the sodas, talking and laughing about college and some of his exploits. I was happy to soak it all in, excited by the future in a way I'd never felt before. I'd grown accustomed to living with dread, and for the first time I could remember, I wasn't so afraid of the future.

Toward the end of the evening, after we'd played out the conversation, we went back to the car and opened up the hood so I could show him exactly what I'd done. I rambled on for a while, pointing out the new fuel lines and the gear ratios. When I looked up at him, I noticed he wasn't listening. He was looking down at his tennis shoes with a half-smile on his face, lost in some distant thought. I closed the hood and looked at him. "Hey, you were drifting on me," I said.

He raised his eyebrows and smiled. "Was I? Sorry."

"No problem." I went over to his workbench by the bulletin board to wipe my hands off on a rag. "Hey, is this your dad?" I was looking at the wall of pictures. They seemed to cover at least four decades. There were photos of mountains and streams and fish of all colors and sizes. There were hunting pictures as well, of dead birds and wild-eyed Labradors with their tongues lolling out. James walked over to the wall and looked at the photo I was pointing to, a picture of a handsome man in a tight t-shirt standing next to a woman in a wheelchair.

"Yeah, that's Dad and Mom."

"Handsome guy," I said. The photo was in color but had faded into a sepia yellow.

James nodded. "Yeah, I guess he was handsome. Never really thought about that before… He died my freshman year in college."

"Oh," I said, not sure how to respond. "And your mom?"

"Died when I was seven. M.S."

I looked at James. He was staring intently at the photo. "I'm sorry," I said.

James shrugged. "Life, that's all."

"I never knew my dad," I said. "Not really. What was he like, your dad?"

James took a deep breath and looked away. For a while, he didn't say anything, and I was sorry I asked. "He was a tough guy," he finally said. "Worked the mines in Red Rock in Northern Minnesota where I grew up. He was a marine in Korea, doted on my mom until she died and raised me and my younger sister, Jan, by himself. Never remarried. He collapsed at work after a double shift. Forty-five years old. Heart attack... He was a hard-working guy, my dad. Never missed a day of work and never complained." He looked back at the photo. "I'm sorry you didn't know your father, Toby."

"I'm not. He was an asshole. I never think about him." I looked at more of the photos. His father was in a lot of them. "You think about him much?" I asked.

James walked over to his car seat couch and sat down. He poured himself a splash of scotch. He didn't answer me.

"Can I ask a personal question, Mr. James?" I pulled up a stool and sat down across from him.

"Sure. I guess."

"Are you happy?"

He looked surprised. "What do you mean?"

"I mean, are you happy? Because sometimes I'm not sure how to read you. I was just wondering, that's all."

"I'm not sure what you mean by happy, Toby, but does it matter?"

I was taken aback. "*Does it matter?* Of course it matters. It means everything—doesn't it?"

James looked back at the photos and raised his cup. "Well, I'm happy now. Here's to a happy moment. One of the best I've had in a long time."

I wasn't about to let him off the hook. "But are you happy?" I insisted.

He put his feet up on his makeshift coffee table and squinted at me. "Geez, I don't know. Shit, Toby. Yeah, I guess so," he said, "but, if you pressed me hard enough, I really don't know what that means."

"It means happy. Everyone knows what that means. Little kids know what that means."

He nodded. "Yeah, that's true. They do know what it means. I think the definition gets a little hazy when you get older. When you're a kid, a dry ass, a line drive single, or being tucked in at night equals happiness. I'll grant you that. And I'm still partial to a dry ass. But I'm not so sure it really matters."

The Eddy

I thought about this for a moment and then said, "But it has to matter; I mean, it matters to me. I remember how I felt for a long time, and I know how I feel now. There's a real difference."

James smiled, leaned in close, and looked me in the eye. "Then it matters to you. Nothing else needs to be said."

I kept shaking my head. "I don't get it. Isn't that what life is supposed to be about?"

He raised his eyebrows. "Happiness? I don't think so, Toby. If it were, we'd all be self-serving bastards. It's overrated... To be honest with you, I'm not sure we're meant to be happy."

I found this depressing and let him know it.

"Look," he said, "this is a great night. Don't think too much. And don't worry about me. If that's what you're doing. My life is punctuated by moments of joy. Like this, tonight. Like when I was fishing Rapid Creek last week in South Dakota and caught a 22-inch brown on a midge and 6x, which means absolutely nothing to you. It's all I have a right to, really, and that's enough." He tossed back the rest of his drink. "I'll see Maggie and get things started for you tomorrow," he said as a way of dismissal. He stood up and put his hand on my shoulder and gave it a squeeze. "It's spring. Let's call it a night and be happy for that."

It was near the end of April when word started circulating that Wheatley might get reconstituted in the fall. It was doublespeak for saying all the teachers would be fired or reassigned to another school. Apparently, Wheatley's test scores had fallen for the fourth straight year and something had to be done. I didn't understand the politics, so I asked Winiski about it.

"It means we've failed to make what's called Adequate Yearly Progress. According to a federal mandate, we either had to make it or something drastic would be done."

"Just based on test scores?" It seemed insane. Half the kids never took the tests seriously.

"No, it's more than that, although that's a big part of it. School attendance, graduation rates, especially for minority students, all factor into it."

"But what happens to you? To all the good teachers?"

"Don't worry about me," Winiski said. She was sitting behind her desk, searching for something among a stack of papers. Looking at the piles, I thought she might be there all night. She wiped the hair from her eyes "If anything, I'll have to reapply for my job, and so will all the teachers. It's a pain in the ass, but whoever really wants to be here will most likely be back. It's called bureaucracy."

"And this is supposed to be good for the school?"

"It is what it is, Toby. I try not to get too worked up about it. I've been teaching for twenty years, and God willing, I'll teach another ten. Things come and go; it all cycles through."

"I don't know. It seems unfair. Why do the teachers take the brunt of it? I mean, this is the best school I've been in. I don't care what the numbers say."

Winiski gave up trying to find what she was looking for and stood up and stretched. She looked tired. "I'm glad to hear that. I think Wheatley does some things well. But on any given day, we have twenty percent of our student population gone; we can't seem to get our African-American students to graduate, much less take a challenging class; and we've dismissed or suspended almost four hundred kids this year alone. You've managed to do well because you're bright and motivated. You've got a good mother and a few teachers in your corner who helped you get through the rough patches. But you're an exception to the rule, kiddo. I'm not saying this is right. I'm just saying it's not a surprise. And teachers take the brunt because they're in the trenches where the battle is fought. It's that simple."

I was surprised at her nonchalance and told her.

"It's not about the system, Toby. It's about the kids. I teach kids; that's all I worry about. I'm done trying to teach adults; most of them are too far gone." Winiski started walking back to her lab.

The Eddy

"What does James think of all this?"

Winiski stopped, turned around, and looked at me. "Geez, you have a lot of questions... James is his own person. I love him like a brother. But he's had a group of parents riding him for a few years, mostly about curriculum, about teaching Huck Finn and all that crap dealing with the word *nigger*. It's just a few vocal zealots, but zealots are always dangerous. They'll be out to get him moved now, but it shouldn't go anywhere. He'll be fine."

I nodded. "I just can't imagine what this place would be like if you guys weren't here."

"Honey," she said, "we're all replaceable. We lose good people all the time and the world keeps spinning as if they were never here. Our legacy is with kids like you, because it sure as hell isn't locked into this place." She turned away and went into the lab.

I left Winiski feeling a little down. I'm not sure I understood her attitude. For that matter, I wasn't sure I wanted to. After I left her room, I strolled the halls, in no hurry to get home. The building was mostly empty, except for a few custodians casually walking their brooms down the halls, leaving little piles of refuse behind – discarded assignments, candy wrappers, broken shells of writing utensils. Without people, the place was depressing. The lockers, old and sagging, were covered with graffiti; the walls, once painted bright and suggestive colors were now faded and chipped. If the place had any life, any magic to transform and inspire, it came from the likes of people like Winiski and James. Without them the place had no soul, and I couldn't help but wonder what might have happened to me had they not been there. I might have been fine. But survival sometimes is as much about being in the right place at the right time as anything. That and maybe a little bit of luck. I already knew that all too well. It was tenuous stuff, and the balance could shift easily.

As I left the building that day, I thought about what it would be like to be a teacher, to be in a position to tilt the odds favorably. It was an appealing thought. But as I approached the apartment, I dismissed the thought completely. There was no way in hell I could do it. The price was too high.

The Eddy

Chapter 10

I suppose it was too much to hope for, to glide into the end of the year on a positive note and then drift into summer. It was the second week of May, the weather was warm and tempting, and attendance was on the downswing. You could tell by walking the halls between classes. There seemed to be more room, less chaos.

James was serving parking lot duty before school that week, which required him to be outside to make sure nothing happened as the kids arrived. It was easy duty. He usually just stood on the curb, chatted with kids, and reminded people to slow down. I normally walked to school and, since the weather was nice, I'd been leaving a bit early so I could hang with James outside before the day started. I seldom got a chance to talk with him since I'd finished working on the car.

It was a Friday, and we were talking about cars or fishing, I don't remember, when it happened. An old Buick, packed with a group of black kids I didn't recognize, pulled up beside us and stopped. The driver had his window down and said something to me. I couldn't hear what it was, but James did. James pointed at the kid to pull over and park, but the kid let fly a big green gob of spit that hit me right in the chest. I stood there dazed as the car peeled away. James, on the other hand, bolted into action. He took after the car in a full sprint.

The driver hit the gas when he saw James in his rear-view mirror and tried to make a hasty exit out of the lot, but there were too many cars coming in, making it impossible to exit in a hurry. James caught up to the Buick, and its doors flew open and kids scattered. The driver, not sure what to do, rolled up his window, as if that somehow could protect him. I heard James yell at the kid to roll it down, but the kid refused. James stepped back and kicked the door, putting a nice crater into the side. That got the kid's attention. He rolled down the window.

I heard the kid swear; he might have threatened James, and there was some exchange. The next thing I saw was James reaching into the car and grabbing the kid's head and slamming it into the steering wheel. By that time, there was a crowd around the car. The school police officer was soon on the scene and then everyone was being pushed back toward the school. That was the last I saw.

I went to first period trying to figure out what happened. I'm sure I'd been verbally attacked, but I honestly didn't hear what was said. I looked down at my chest. My leather jacket had a drying chunk of mucus on it. I'd forgotten to wipe it off. I got a pass to go to the bathroom and decided to walk by the office to see what was up. There were a number of cops milling about, but I didn't see James. The only thing I heard clearly in passing was that the kid driving the car was not a student at Wheatley.

On the way back to class, I took a peek outside. The Buick was still out there, parked in one of the spots reserved for the police. It had a helluva dent in the driver's door. I'm not sure whether it was another impulsive act on my part or a gesture of solidarity, but I took another detour, this time out to the parking lot, and I let loose with my best Chuck Norris on the Buick's passenger door. Those old American cars are pretty solid, but my kick was almost as good as James'. For good measure, I left a juicy snag on the windshield as a calling card.

I looked for James at the end of the day, but there was a sub in his room, which wasn't a good sign. I really didn't think much of it until the next day when I was having breakfast and reading the paper. On the second page of the Metro section was the headline: "Teacher Assaults Student." And there, beside the four-paragraph article, was a picture of Mitchell James. The photo was horrible. He looked like a thug. It was either a driver's license photo or an old yearbook shot. Either way, he looked guilty.

The article said the kid James assaulted was a student at another school, and that he was taken to the hospital with a broken nose and face contusions. Nothing was mentioned of what the kid was doing at Wheatley or what he'd done. I called Takeita right away, figuring she'd know more, but I couldn't reach her. I called James, but he didn't answer either. Finally, I took the van and headed over to the garage.

There were five cars parked in front of Maggie's place, including Winiski's. I thought better of going in and parked the van in the first space I could find. I was sitting there for about fifteen minutes, thinking I had no business being there, when Maggie came out of the house and waved to me. I sheepishly got out of the van, regretting my decision to butt in.

"I'm sorry. I shouldn't be here." I was standing on the sidewalk, ready to make an about-face.

"Don't be silly. I saw you pull up; I was waiting for you to come in. Join the party."

Winiski, Jackson, Trudeau, and a few people I didn't recognize were sitting in the living room. James was slouched in a loveseat with a cup of coffee in his hand. He looked hung over. Everyone nodded at me or said hi when I came in, except for James. A newspaper was spread out on the coffee table, open to the Metro section. I glanced at it but didn't say anything.

"We were just talking about yesterday, Toby. In fact, we were getting close to wrapping up," Maggie said. "Can I get you something to drink?"

"I'll get it." I waved Maggie off. "I'm sorry to intrude. I was just concerned. It seems like it all started because of me."

"Bullshit," James said. I nodded and slid out to the kitchen for some coffee. I stayed in there while the conversation started to heat up. After a while, I came back and stood in the doorway.

Jackson, who had been sitting on the couch, not saying anything, just twisting his hands together, finally spoke up. "For Christ sakes, Mitch, you took out a black kid! What were you thinking?"

"What the hell does that have to do with it?" Winiski interjected.

Jackson was pissed. "Are you kidding? It's got everything to do with it. Don't be simple. Everything we do in that school is about race, like it or not. I've got the Board breathing down my ass about suspensions, test scores, No Child, and shit you people aren't even aware of. And now, more bad press." He stood up. "Jesus, Mitch, why the hell couldn't you have punched a white kid, or maybe even a Latino? That would've been different, at least."

James looked up from his coffee and gave Jackson a little crooked smile. "I'll make a note of that for next time. Do you have a gender preference?"

I saw Maggie roll her eyes. Jackson glared at him. "Listen to me." He pointed his finger at James. "You're already temporarily suspended. There might not be a next time. This might be it. I keep going to bat for you, but I don't have much clout these days." He started heading for the door.

"Nice of you to come by, Ed." James still had that distant grin on his face.

Jackson turned around. "You better lean on the union for this one. I come over this morning to see what I can do to help, and you sit there making smart-ass comments. All these people here?" He pointed around the room. "They seem to care about what happens to you. More than you care yourself. Go ahead and piss away fourteen years. I'm done; I don't have time for this."

"Of course you don't," James snapped back. "It might require you to take an unpopular stand."

Jackson bristled, the tendons on his neck stretching his skin taut. "You are an arrogant asshole. You make the world far too simple. You're on your own."

James let out a short, sarcastic laugh. "I've always

The Eddy

been on my own, Ed—By the way, does this mean you don't want to go fishing with me next weekend?"

"Fuck off, Mitch." Jackson slammed the door.

Winiski stood up to leave. She was shaking her head in disgust. "Call me if you need anything, Mitch." She gave Maggie a hug and made her way to the door. "And Ed's right, Mitch. You are an asshole." She left without waiting for a response.

The meeting, or whatever it was, was clearly over. Everyone got up to leave. James sat there, leaning forward in his chair with his hands wrapped around his coffee cup and that faraway look on his face. Trudeau got up, didn't say anything, and gave James a pat on the shoulder before leaving.

When the room had cleared, Mitch got up and walked past Maggie and me. We heard the back door close behind him.

Maggie sighed and shook her head. "You all right?"

"Me? Yeah. Sure. I mean, I'm not exactly sure what happened."

"You mean just now or yesterday?"

"Both, I guess. I think the whole thing started with Takeita and me. You know, goofing in the halls. How did it get to this? And what happens now?"

"Depends on what the kid decides. He might go after the district. He'll most likely go after Mitch. Depending on the police report, it might even be criminal, but I doubt it. Mitch said he thought the kid was reaching for a weapon, so obviously, that changes everything. Turns out he didn't have one, though."

She went over to the refrigerator and pulled out a diet soda. "The union will cover everything for Mitch, but he has a bit of a history. I'd say he's got better than a 50-50 shot at keeping his job."

"Does he want to keep it?"

"Yeah, I'm pretty sure he does. I know him, despite what you saw. For reasons I've never understood completely, he's not about to walk away."

Joe Paatalo

She opened the can, and the liquid exploded down the sides and onto the floor. "Shit," she said quietly.

I grabbed a dish rag and began cleaning the mess.

Chapter 11

James was out for the rest of the school year, and there was a fair amount of speculation about his status. Everyone knew about the car incident, but in some versions, there was a gun in the car, and in others, he had gone ballistic on an innocent kid. The versions seemed to fall along racial lines, which didn't work in his favor. No one seemed too concerned about how it started. The stories just began and ended with a kid's smashed face. It's amazing how stories evolve and take on their own life. If James were around, I got the feeling there would be a lesson plan in all of it. The whole thing struck me as absurd the more I thought about it, and the more I thought about it, the less sure I was about what had happened. And I was there.

It was about this time I made up my mind to attend Oregon. It was a tough call, but finally I decided I wanted to be close to the ocean. The biking season would be longer than in Idaho, so it seemed to make the most sense. I called Maggie to let her know, and she asked me to come by to talk about college finances. I asked her about James, and she said she'd fill me in. I went over the following Saturday, eager to hear what she had for me.

"First year of tuition completely paid for." Maggie handed me a manila envelope with the agreement. She was smiling broadly. "You're responsible for room and board. If you maintain a 'B' average, you can apply for renewal. Congratulations."

I took the envelope and sat down at the kitchen table. Until now, everything was an abstraction. Now it was real. It was a little scary. "I don't know how to thank you, Maggie. I didn't think this would ever happen, to be honest. I'm kind of at a loss on what to do next."

She sat down next to me. "I think it's time you took a trip. Go get the lay of the land, figure out your housing situation. Maybe look for a part-time job."

I nodded. "Yeah, maybe. I've got a little money. I need to save some for transportation... But yeah, maybe I should."

"Go out and talk to Mitch. I haven't spoken to him for a few days, but he's planning on heading west soon. You might be able to catch a ride with him." My expression must have surprised her. She laughed. "He's not that bad. I just thought it might be worth checking out. Save some money. Anyway, he'll want to know what you're doing. Go talk to him. His truck is here, so I know he's out there. Packing, I think."

James was out in the driveway loading his truck. It was sunny and warm, and he was wearing cargo shorts, a black t-shirt, and his high-tops. He saw me and waved. "Grab yourself a soda, Toby. And grab me a beer if you don't mind."

We sat down on his tailgate to soak in the sun. He opened up his beer and nodded at the manila envelope I was holding. "Maggie get you some money?"

"Full tuition for the first year." I raised the envelope high. "A sweet deal, eh?"

"Well, good for you. I knew Mag would come through. And what school?"

"Oregon. Seemed like the best fit."

James took a swig of beer and smiled. "Damn good choice. You'll love it out there. Some real nice water too."

"I don't know about that, but it's close enough to the ocean. I've never seen the ocean... So what's the story with you, Mr. James? Has this thing been resolved?"

He ran his hand through his short hair and looked up into the sky. "Hardly. Maybe soon... I don't know. They're making me see a counselor for anger." He chuckled. "The union thinks it looks proactive."

"What do you think?"

"Well, I was angry at first." He laughed again. "But I'm over it. No big deal. But no sessions this summer. I'm out of

The Eddy

here tomorrow and won't be back for a while."

"Heading west?"

He held up his beer. "To the mountains or bust."

"How long?"

"As long as I can."

I looked at his knees, dangling from the tailgate. Both had long, nasty scars. It made me wince to look at them. "Hockey?" I asked, pointing at them with my Coke can.

He looked down at his legs and shrugged. "Something like that."

"So," I said, not sure how to broach the subject. "You think I could go with you? On this trip?"

He frowned and gave me a puzzled look. "Are you serious?"

I shrugged my shoulders. "Sure."

"Toby, I'm going fishing. I camp or sleep in my truck. I get lost and like it. I pee and poop outdoors. Not exactly your style. Trust me." He took another drink. "Really, you'd hate it."

"Do you go all the way to the coast?"

"The co—" He stopped in mid-sentence. "Well, I don't know. Maybe, but I don't know... Look, you'd hate it. Trust me. Besides, you're graduating in a few days. I'm leaving tomorrow."

"I wasn't planning on attending. You could drop me off in Oregon. I have to go out there anyway."

"You're kidding, right?" He looked at me and cocked his head. "You can't be serious. Really?"

"Why not? I mean, I might not be the greatest company, but I'd like to go. It would be fun."

James put his hands over his eyes and rubbed them. "Toby, you're a great kid. I'm excited for you. But this isn't something you'd enjoy. Trust me."

I looked into the back of his truck, at all the gear, and thought about his adventure. "Look, Mr. James, if you don't want me to go, just say so. I'm okay with that. I understand. Just say so, and I'll let it go. But—I'm all for trying something, you know, *lighting out*. If you'd rather travel alone, I get it."

He looked at me for a long time. "Toby, it's not that. I spend my time fishing and wandering around. I'm afraid you'd get bored. I just don't think you'd like—I just don't think you'd like the pace, if you know what I mean."

I wasn't sure what to say. I looked at his shoes, the ubiquitous Chuck Taylors. "How come you always wear those?" I pointed at his shoes.

James shrugged. "You know, nobody ever asked me that. You'd think someone would, but nobody ever does... When I was in college, I worked at a sporting goods store in Duluth. The place burned down, and all the merchandise was lost, or most of it, anyway. They had about twenty pairs of these, all size twelve, that were damaged by the smoke. I took them all. Thing is, I take a size eleven. But hey, what can I say? When I buy shoes now, I usually buy them in twelves. Guess I've gotten used to big shoes." He dangled his feet out from the gate of the truck. "Always liked them. No ankle support, though. Used to wear 'em as wading boots."

"Makes sense," I said, not knowing what the hell I was talking about. "Well, I guess I should be moving on." I got up to leave.

James groaned and rolled his eyes. "Ahhh... Hold on, Toby. Are you really serious, or are you just blowing smoke up my ass?"

I turned and looked at him. He had his head cocked and was squinting at me. "I'm serious. It would be fun. I'd like to learn how to fish."

"Do you have any gear? Have you ever camped?'

"Nope. No gear, never camped. But I could buy some stuff. I've got some money. And I think I have a fishing pole."

James laughed. "First off, we call them fly rods. Never say 'fishing pole.' We ain't going to Mayberry. Second, you'd need some camping clothes and some hiking boots. You wouldn't know what to look for." James looked at the back of his truck and squinted again at the sky. "What about your mom?" he asked.

"Mom? She's excited about my going to school, but

The Eddy

she's worried about the money." I waved the envelope. "She'll be relieved to see this."

"But what about cutting out with me? If I were to agree."

I laughed. "Mr. James, I've been on my own, for the most part, for a few years. I love my mom, but she—well, it's like I've been eighteen for a long time, if you know what I mean."

"Yeah, maybe so, but she's your mom, and I'm not doing anything without her say-so."

"And are you saying I can go?"

James drained the rest of his beer and stood up stiffly. "Here's the deal. If it doesn't work out, we'll get you on a bus or something, okay?"

"Sure." I was grinning, and James couldn't help but laugh.

"Jesus. All right, here's what you do. Throw all your stuff in a garbage bag, including lots of underwear. Grab a few books and anything else you'll want. Your mom will have to send extra clothes for you when you get to Eugene because I don't want to pack too heavy. I'll pick up all your camping clothes, and I'll supply everything else, so pack light. I'll put it in a travel bag when you get here tomorrow. Eight a.m. sharp. With your mom."

"Really? That's it?"

"Sure. Why not?"

"Wow," I said, trying to let it sink in. "Thanks, Mr. James."

"Look, if you change your mind or have any questions, call me tonight. I imagine you'll have a lot to do, so you best get cranking... And one more thing. Don't call me Mr. James anymore. You're done with school. Just call me Mitch."

"Mitch," I said, giving it a shot. I wasn't sure I could do it. "Can I just call you James?"

He squatted down like a catcher to stretch his knees and grunted. "I don't care, as long as you drop the *mister*. Sounds too much like work." He stood up and grimaced, then offered me his hand. "Looks like we're partners," he said.

I gave his hand a vigorous shake. "Looks like we're partners," I repeated.

He looked over at Maggie's house and shook his head. "See you in the morning," he said, and turned to go back to packing.

Before leaving, I stopped in to tell Maggie I was heading out with James. She must have thought it was funny because she laughed pretty hard. "Well, I promise you, it'll be memorable," she said. "I hope you like to fish."

"Well, I guess I'll find out," I said.

"And oh, by the way, a quick piece of advice. Never mess with his tunes. Trust me. He's anal about music."

"Should I bring my own stuff?" I asked.

"Not unless you want them dumped along the side of some gravel road."

"No hip-hop, then?"

"Not unless you want to be dumped along some gravel road."

Mom and I were at the garage by 7:30. James took my garbage bag and rifled through it, mumbling under his breath. While he finished repacking my gear, I submitted my paperwork to Maggie and introduced my mom to her. They hugged and seemed to hit it off. I was a bit embarrassed, but I suffered through it. Mom could make friends with anyone, especially another woman who'd been divorced. I let them chat, filled my thermos with coffee from the kitchen, and waited patiently for the goodbyes.

When James had the truck packed, he asked me to wait outside and went into the house to talk to my mom. Ten minutes later, he came out of the house and said, "Let's hit it."

My mom gave me a long hug and cried a little, and then Maggie hugged me and offered me some more advice. James sat in the truck with his arm out the window, waiting. Finally, he'd had enough. "Hey, I've got a schedule to keep, ladies."

The Eddy

Maggie rolled her eyes. "Who are you kidding?" She gave my arm a squeeze and then she and Mom went into the house for some more coffee. I almost felt sorry for Maggie.

I jumped into the ugly truck, put on my seatbelt, and looked at James. "Let's hit it," I said.

He grinned, put the truck in reverse, and slowly backed down the driveway. When he got to the bottom, he stopped, raised his coffee cup, and said, "Let's go find some joy."

Joe Paatalo

Chapter 12

"Now, there are a few rules we need to get straight, just so we don't have any issues."

We were cruising at seventy miles per hour on Highway 35 on our way to I 90 and South Dakota. The land undulated before me with farmsteads scattered every few miles. The corn crops had been in for a while, and I could see miles of hypnotizing rows of twelve-inch plants. We hadn't said much since leaving. James said that was part of the foreplay of a trip; you had to ease into it slowly. Now, after an hour and a half, he seemed ready to talk.

"I'm listening," I said.

"I always go the speed limit. Not because I'm afraid of a ticket, but because I'm not in a hurry. Used to drive Maggie nuts, but she's a lawyer and they see all time as money.

"Next, I like to get off the main highways, take a few detours. You can't experience the country on the interstates. You just can't. Occasionally, I get misdirected, but I *never* get lost. There's a difference."

"Smell the country?" I said.

"Something like that. Next, I like to drink beer at night. I like a few cold ones around a campfire. To be honest, I don't care if you have one or two, but you won't be getting drunk, okay?"

I nodded. Sounded reasonable to me.

"Also, occasionally, not often, but occasionally, I'll go into a small town to a watering hole to watch a ballgame or something. If you want to go, that's fine, but you can stay at camp if you'd like."

I felt like asking him what *something* was, but I

thought better of it.

"Now this part's important. If you ever want to go off on your own, while we're camping or fishing, whatever, you need to let me know where you'll be so nobody gets worried. If you say you'll be back at two o'clock or something, be back by two. This has nothing to do with your age; it's just what partners do."

"Sounds fair," I said. "Anything else?"

"Yeah, nothing personal, but don't mess with my music. I'm rather particular about that."

"Yeah, Maggie warned me about that. She said I should be sure to grab a lot of hip-hop and rap."

James' eyes widened and he looked at me. I was grinning. "Yeah, she would say that. None of that pollution in my truck."

"Can I ask you why that is? Just curious."

"Because I hate that misogynist shit. Because it's not music. Because I don't have the time to wade through it to find the one percent that actually has something to say."

"I could point some out to you. You know, save you the time."

"No thanks."

"So we listen to Dylan all the time?"

"Nothing wrong with Dylan. Never gets old. Hand me my CDs." He pointed down to a huge nylon zippered case.

He rifled through the catalog and found what he was looking for. "Give this a shot. The guy can write."

He popped in James McMurtry, a singer songwriter from Texas or some such place. The truck we were riding in may have been a piece of shit, but the stereo was fabulous. For the next forty-five minutes, I listened to McMurtry spin stories. Pretty poetic stuff if you didn't mind dysfunction. It was enough to make the time pass.

When we reached Mitchell, South Dakota, James pulled into a huge outdoor retailer. I'd never been in one of those places and was surprised at the size of the place and all the gear. I had no idea where to start. I found myself wandering toward all the stuffed animals on display in the

The Eddy

center of the store. Pheasants, grouse, bighorn sheep, deer, coyotes, bobcats—they were all there. It seemed rather morbid to me. James walked right past it and went straight to the shoe department. I followed, not sure what else to do.

"What size do you wear?" he asked.

"Ten and a half."

He grabbed a pair of lightweight Gore-Tex hiking boots off the shelf, checked out the padding, and then had the salesperson grab a size eleven for me. I tried them on. They were a little loose. "Great," he told the clerk. "We'll take them."

We bought polarized sunglasses, wool socks and liners, a good sharp knife, some nylon t-shirts, and a pair of loose-fitting nylon cargo pants. An hour later, we finally made it to the fly-fishing section. James spent a half hour buying all kinds of odd materials for tying flies—chenille, tinsel, beads, feathers, rubber legs, yarn. It looked like he was outfitting a first-grade arts and crafts event. By the time we paid for everything, the total was almost five hundred bucks.

"What do I owe you?" I asked as we headed back to the truck.

"We'll worry about that later." He threw me the box with the boots in it. "Put these on with the new socks. Don't forget the liners; they wick moisture away and keep you from getting blisters. You need to wear the boots every day so they break in."

They were actually quite comfortable. They ran a hundred and twenty bucks, more than twice what I ever paid for a pair of shoes.

"Look, I know they're expensive," James said. "But there a few things outdoorsmen never compromise on—boots, rain gear, and tents. If any of those fail you, you're in deep trouble. Either buy high-quality gear or wait until you can afford it. Trust me. I've learned the hard way."

I slipped on my new polarized sunglasses, which ran thirty-five bucks. "What about sunglasses?"

"I love the good ones, but I'm always breaking or

losing them. So I buy middle of the road. They're important, though. You'll see why later." He turned off the interstate at the edge of town.

"We going to the Corn Palace?" I asked, looking at a thirty-foot corn cob protruding from a billboard.

He took a back road and started heading south. "Hardly. I've got a friend who owns a thousand acres about an hour from here. He lets me hunt pheasants every year. Thought we might make camp there for the evening."

It was only 2:30 in the afternoon. We traveled down the blacktop for a while and turned onto a gravel road and started crisscrossing the countryside. I was completely lost. Every now and then, James would point out some pheasants along the road, pecking at gravel. He kept talking about how pretty they were, and I got the feeling he'd be perfectly content to drive these roads all day looking for birds.

Finally, we pulled onto a farmer's road in a field and James put the truck in four-wheel to navigate the rutted roads. Just as the road was ready to take a dip down toward a little river, James cut across a knoll to a hill with a grove of trees and parked the rig. We got out and surveyed the land. We could see for several miles, out across the newly planted fields, down to the little stream and the scrub oak that lined its banks. The wind was blowing hard. I could smell the freshly spread manure.

"So, this is what you mean by *smelling* the world," I said.

He was grinning, as happy as could be. "Ah, it's the smell of life. Ain't this great?"

I looked around. It was pretty, in a farmer's sort of way. But it was nothing to write home about. "Yeah, sure. It's nice."

"I've hunted here for ten years. Over there." He pointed to a spot near the river. "I must have gotten up a hundred roosters two years ago. It had just snowed and was so cold, I couldn't feel my hands. And boom! They just erupted at the end of that field. They came in waves, bird after bird. Must have lasted for five minutes. And you know

The Eddy

what? I never hit a single bird. Missed 'em all... It was great." He started laughing at the memory. "I watched 'em sail over that river like a squadron of planes. Beautiful. I had Bonzer with me, this great lab. He kept looking at me like I was the sorriest hunter he'd ever seen. Never forget that."

"Wow," I said, not quite getting it.

James ignored me and went to the cab of the truck, rummaged around a bit, and then the Allman Brothers started blasting "Blue Sky." He took a beer out of his cooler, opened it, and started dancing, right there in the field. It was the damnedest thing I've ever seen—a grown man, in the middle of some field in South Dakota, dancing with a beer in his hand, belting out the lyrics to an Allman Brothers song. And while he wasn't much of a dancer for style, I had to give him points for enthusiasm.

When the song ended, he was sweating and grinning. He turned the music off and sat on the hood of the truck and I joined him. I didn't say anything for a while, figuring it was a personal cleansing ritual or something. Finally, he looked at me and said, "So?"

"So you dance like you have a corn cob up your ass. But I liked it. Feeling better now?"

"Much. Thank you." He was still smiling. "This is a great place," he said. "It's just the way it should be. Let's unpack."

I looked around again. He seemed to be seeing a different landscape. I shrugged and began unpacking.

We pitched our tent right there on the hill under some enormous cottonwoods and set up a small collapsible table with two of those cheap nylon folding chairs. It made for a comfortable little camp. James took some frozen meat out of the cooler and placed it on the dashboard of the truck to thaw.

"Elk steaks tonight, with fried potatoes and onions. A little pistachio pudding for dessert, and we're talking South Dakota gourmet. You'll love it, Toby, trust me."

It did sound good. James grabbed a cold beer and an outdoor magazine and said he was going to read. He blew up his inflatable mattress and placed it under a cottonwood tree and was dozing within minutes.

I wasn't tired, so I took my shirt off, put my mattress on the hood of the truck, and relaxed. It seemed like an odd place to be, but the longer I sat there, the more I liked it. The wind was blowing stiffly; there were no bugs; even the smell of manure was tolerable. I tried to imagine what it would be like living out here. It was a lot like Kansas in some ways, flat and windy. Lonely too. The thing about the plains is they make you feel exposed. You can see the weather coming from a long way off, kind of like a roundhouse punch you can't avoid. You just brace yourself and hope it doesn't hurt too bad. Ever since the tornado, I'd been paranoid about weather. And I'd never liked the idea of being exposed. I could appreciate the beauty and starkness of places like this, but I could never live out here. No place to hide.

After James' nap, he built a small fire, and we took a walk down to the little stream while the flames burned down. Near the thicker cover by the river, we flushed a few pheasants. They exploded out from the switch grass and made me jump. They crapped as they took flight, startled by the unexpected intrusion.

"You know, they're not even indigenous," James said, admiring the birds as they broke into a glide a few hundred yards away. "They're from China originally. But they've really done well here. They seem so natural now."

I thought about this for a while as we walked back to the camp for dinner. Despite the predators, hunters, and weather, these birds somehow thrived; they adapted and managed to find their niche in the ecosystem. There was something to be admired about that. Before we got back to camp, we flushed another rooster. It exploded from the ground in a spectacle of color, and even James was surprised, since it was in a spot with little cover.

Back at camp, James took a portable grill and set it over the coals. He took the elk steaks and rubbed coffee grounds into them and placed them on the grill, along with a frying pan of thinly sliced potatoes and onions. We sat

The Eddy

around the fire and watched the meat sizzle, sipping cold drinks and anticipating the meal. The smell made me realize how hungry I was. The steaks were ready before the potatoes and onions, so we each placed a seasoned elk steak on our plates as an appetizer and gnawed on the meat, occasionally groaning our approval. We finished the meal slowly and watched the sun set over the fields. There were a few clouds, and the sun lit them up in spectacular orange hues. Normally, I'd appreciate something like this only for a moment or two, but tonight, time didn't matter. There was no schedule to keep. I could've sat there all night, taking in the fire and watching the night emerge.

Unfortunately, the wind died down and, just as it was getting dark, the mosquitoes set in. We put up with them for a while but finally called it a night and went into the tent. James put his headlamp on and settled back to do a little reading. It wasn't long before I was asleep.

I awoke sometime in the middle of the night to James' soft snoring. I had to pee, so I climbed out of the tent. The night was cool, and the stars were brilliant in the clear sky. I could hear coyotes somewhere in the inky darkness, howling back and forth. I'd never heard them before, so I sat around the dying embers of the fire and listened. It was solemn, slightly lonesome, but I was relaxed and content. As I got ready to turn back in, I heard an owl behind me add to the chorus of the evening. *Who indeed,* I thought.

Joe Paatalo

Chapter 13

James was up before me in the morning. When I got out of the tent, the coffee had been made and the camp cleaned up. He was ready to go.

"Thought we'd make the Black Hills today." He handed me a cup of coffee. "We'll cross the Missouri and head for the Badlands. I think you'll enjoy this stretch. How'd you sleep?"

"You snore," I said, "but I managed."

"Well, you fart in your sleep, but I'm not complaining." He pulled everything out from the tent. "You pack this up and I'll take care of the tent. We should be out of here in ten minutes."

I sipped on the coffee as I gathered the sleeping bags and mattresses and packed them away. It was pleasantly warm at seven in the morning, promising to be a hot day. Before we left, James made sure to douse the fire and spruce up the site. Other than a fire pit and a few tracks, there was little to suggest we'd been there.

We spent the next few hours on the road, sipping coffee and listening to The Band. James didn't say much, content to watch the road slide on by, singing quietly with the music while keeping beat by tapping on the steering wheel. The songs seemed to trigger some pleasant memories, because every now and then, he would break into a half-smile or give a quiet chuckle. I chose not to intrude on his memories.

When we reached the Missouri River, he pulled off the highway to get gas and pee. "Hey, you hungry?" he asked. "I'm sorry, I'm not a big breakfast guy. You gotta say something if you're hungry."

We went inside the station and he bought some jerky and a croissant. I got a bagel and an apple. We were standing in line to pay, behind this tall blond woman, when she suddenly turned around and looked at James. "Excuse me," she said, "but I'm having an issue with my car. I was wondering if you could help me for a minute? I'd be so grateful."

She was rather striking, maybe in her late twenties, with a bit too much make-up.

"Not sure if I can make a difference," James said, "but my friend here is a decent mechanic. We can take a look."

I looked at James, rolled my eyes, and bit loudly into my apple. We followed the woman to the gas pumps. James was grinning and told me to shut up.

"I think it's my radiator. The gauge says I'm running hot. I'm heading west, but I don't want to break down," she said.

"I can understand that," James said. "Let's have a look."

She was driving a red Pontiac, the kind of car lots of women drive because it looks cute. I opened the hood and took a look. The radiator cap came off easily and, while it may have been running hot, it was fine as far as coolant was concerned.

"Start her up," I said, "and let's see what the gauge reads."

She did as I requested and the gauge seemed slightly on the hot side, but nothing to be overly concerned about. "I think you're fine, but I'd watch it. Your coolant is okay, but if the gauge keeps reading hot, you might want to have it checked out. Could just be a thermostat, but you never know. I see you've been running the air conditioning and putting some pressure on the system. If you're going seventy-five and running everything, these four cylinders can get pretty hot." I replaced the radiator cap and tightened an air hose. "You should be fine."

She nodded and thanked me. "Where you boys heading?" she asked James.

The Eddy

"To the Hills," he said. "You?"

"Rapid City." She smiled and put her hands in her pockets. "Heading there to see a girlfriend." She turned away from James and shut the hood on her car. In the process, she dropped her handbag and bent over to pick it up. Her jeans were tight and both of us got a view of a sword tattoo below her jean line. She turned around to face us. "I appreciate the help, boys. I'd love to buy you a drink in Wall if you aren't in too much of a hurry. Place called Wolf Creek on Main. I always stop there. Name's Suzy." She held her hand out and James shook it.

"Mitch," he said, and looked her in the eyes. Her face seemed to flush a bit. I thought I might puke.

"Toby," I said, and offered her my hand. She shook it and looked back at James. "Hope to see you boys down the road. Don't be shy." She got into her car, waved, and was off.

"Wow," I said, "that wasn't exactly subtle."

James shrugged his shoulders and grinned. "Do you see why I like road trips so much? You never know what's coming next. Liked the tattoo, I must admit."

We got back in the truck and James unwrapped his jerky and took a big bite. "We're about to enter the west as soon as we cross the river. I always feel exhilarated when I reach the other side. It's like the trip has really begun. Watch how the topography changes too."

"Are we going to stop at that bar she told us about?"

James picked at his teeth and shook his head. "Probably not."

"Why? She was rather good-looking. Not your type?"

James rummaged around in his CD case and grabbed some Dylan. "No, she was pretty." He popped in the disc, eased the truck up to the speed limit, and hit the cruise. "Nice ass... Don't get me wrong. I like women. I like them a lot. But stuff like that is never as easy and casual as it looks. She's single, maybe thirty, probably coming off a few bad relationships and feeling the ol' biological clock ticking. She knows she's attractive but has her doubts at times, needs to feel like she's still got it. Likes the attention. She's one-part fun and two-parts misery."

I laughed. "How the hell do you know that?"

He took another bite of jerky. "That's not the first time I've looked under the hood. Trust me, I'm right."

"So, if I weren't with you, tell the truth, would you stop?"

"No," he said. "Seriously, I'm flattered, but no, women are too complicated. I don't need everything that comes with them."

"So you're just going to remain celibate?"

He stopped chewing and looked at me. "Listen to the music, Toby, or count the pheasants. I'm not going to talk about my sex life, okay?"

I laughed and looked out the window. The topography had changed. It was all rolling hills and cattle. "What's the next stop?" I asked.

"The Badlands and Wounded Knee." He reached in the back seat and rummaged around in the book bin he always traveled with. "Here, read some of this. It'll pass the time, give you some context." The book was *Bury My Heart at Wounded Knee*. "I've marked some passages."

I spent the next hour going through parts of the book. It was depressing. Some of it brought tears to my eyes. "You know, I knew some of this, but it really blows you away when you read it. Seems so sad. So unnecessary." I was reading about the 1890 massacre. "I've seen the film *Dances with Wolves*; it kind of reminds me of that."

James grunted. "That film was pretty to look at, but it's problematic."

I didn't know what he meant. "How so?"

"Well, Native Americans don't appreciate the old story of the white guy coming in and somehow enlightening them and doing things better than they can. It's an old Hollywood myth."

"Yeah, but the guy in the film, Dunbar, learns from the Indians, doesn't he?"

"Yeah, but he's still the hero, the noble white man who's the crack shot. Sure, he's the apologist for the white man and our sympathy lies with the Indians, but it romanticizes the past. It freezes Indians in time. The end of the film puts a gravestone on the Lakota, but the Lakota didn't die, Toby. They persevered despite all the shit."

"Huh. That's true," I said. "You know, Takeita asked me once why we still have names like the Redskins, or that grinning little Indian dude on the caps of the Cleveland Indians. I didn't know what to say."

"Well, it's a long story, and Indians have been fighting the battle for a long time. And occasionally, not very often, but occasionally, they win. At least a small skirmish here and there. But part of the problem is history, centuries of not being heard." James yawned and arched his back. "After a while, you lose your voice or get to thinking you don't have one. You get lied to enough, bilked and deceived enough, you stop trying. Not that different from all the gay-bashing you've endured, I suspect. After a while, you just get tired of barking, I guess."

James looked out his window and yawned again. "Never let anyone say history is in the past because it's not... And I need a cup of coffee."

I thought about what he said for a long time as we drove. I *wanted* history to be in the past. I survived by putting things in the past. It's not that I believed history didn't matter, but I didn't want to be consumed by it, and I sure as hell didn't want to be defined by it. I thought it best not to debate this point with James, however. I didn't like where it might go.

When we reached the Badlands, James pulled off the interstate and followed a back highway to a scenic overlook. We got out to pee and survey the landscape. It was hot and windy and, as we stood on the scenic overlook, I felt like I was looking at a lunar landscape, with its mountains of gray, stratified sediment and volcanic ash. It was desolate yet beautiful. I took a few pictures. "If I were a desperado, I'd come here to hide. Man, nobody would ever find me," I said.

"True, and you'd probably join the thousands of dinosaur fossils out here," James said. "If it didn't rain, you'd be lucky to last a week."

"Yeah, I guess. So what is all this land good for? What can you do with it?" I asked.

James turned his back to the wind and wiped at the dust in his eyes. "I'm not sure what you mean, but why does it have to have a purpose, other than being what it is?"

I shrugged and made my way back to the truck. I'd never thought of it that way before.

We drove for another hour until we reached Pine Ridge, where James stopped for gas. He said he always liked to throw some bucks into the community when he got a chance. We picked up some ice and a few groceries for the cooler and drove through town. The poverty was depressing, like looking at a third-world nation. James stopped at an arts and crafts store, bought some feathers, and drove out of town. For the next ten minutes, I didn't say anything.

"Just wanted you to see all this," James finally said. "Most people never bother, but it's part of *our* country. Part of *our* history." He continued to talk as we drove, weaving names and dates together, as if putting together a narrative quilt. He talked about the American Indian Movement, Leonard Peltier, and a dozen other stories that seemed to bleed into one another. As we approached the small town of Wounded Knee, James pulled off the road and drove up a little hill. "This is it," he said.

I looked around. There was almost nothing there, just a small cemetery with a brick arch that was falling apart. "This is it?" I couldn't believe it. I got out of the truck. "This is what I've been reading about?" There were no monuments, no testaments to the significance of the place, to the nearly four hundred men, women, and children who were slaughtered here. The wind had blown trash in from the town and it was scattered around a chain link fence surrounding the cemetery. "This is... this is sad."

I walked into the cemetery with James following behind me. There were two elderly Native women pinning something against the fence. When they left, I walked over

The Eddy

to see what it was. Two small bundles, one leather and one cloth, were tied into the chain links. I asked James about it. There were bundles and plastic flowers all over the grounds.

"Medicine bundles. They're offerings."

I nodded. "I pictured the place differently." I walked around and looked at some of the headstones.

"Have a seat," James said, and we plopped down against the fence. The wind was still blowing hot and hard. There was little protection from it out here. Two black crows were going at it in a scrub tree just outside the fence, arguing over something.

"First time here, I was surprised too. Thought maybe there would be more," James said.

"Why isn't there more?" I asked.

He shrugged his shoulders. "I don't know... Maybe monuments and tributes are more of a white necessity. Words put down on marble shrink history, as if to say *that's it*... And maybe that's not *it*. I don't know." He looked at me and smiled. "Anyway, I like this place. Thought you should see it."

I leaned back into the fence and surveyed the landscape. "It sure is different." At my feet, a potato chip bag spun in a little wind twister. I grabbed it and stuffed it in my pocket. "Lots of trash here."

James closed his eyes. "It's just trash. It blows hard out here."

"Do you ever wonder if people will forget what happened here? Or stop by and not know a thing?" I asked.

"Hadn't really thought about it." James's eyes were still closed. "Figure most people like their blissful ignorance. Guess if they want to know, they need to pick up a book or ask someone."

"I suppose," I said, "but most people don't do that."

"Nope, they don't," James said. He took a deep breath and seemed to drift off. Or maybe he was meditating; it was hard to tell with James.

When we finally got up, I asked him if we should

leave anything behind. "I mean, I think I'm part Indian, but I never think about it much. I wouldn't want to do something inappropriate or anything."

"Do what feels right," he said. "You don't need to feel funny about it. You won't offend anyone. Hell, they're just people."

I didn't have anything on me except some Tic-Tacs and a pen, but I placed them next to the bundles. I hoped no one would see it as trash.

Chapter 14

"Welcome to the Paha Sapa," James said as we approached the Black Hills. "Sacred land for the Lakota and Cheyenne, and a little piece of paradise for the fly fisherman. This is where you're going to learn how to fish."

"How long we plan on staying?" I asked, marveling at the change in scenery.

"Depends on water conditions. But we're in no hurry. I'd like to make a base camp, something comfortable in the mountains. I know a great place off the beaten path. Nice little campground next to a little stream with brook trout. Think you'll like it."

As we drove up the mountains, James turned off the air conditioning and we rolled down the windows. The smell of ponderosa pine hung heavy and sweet in the air. We were following a river as we moved higher. Sheer cliffs lined the banks of the river in places, and it was easy to see why this land was considered sacred. Occasionally, we'd reach a high open prairie, and in the distance, I could see the mountain peaks stretching high and green into the sky.

"Are we going to have time to see Rushmore?" I asked. "I'd like to get a few pictures."

James shot me a disgusted look. "Let's have a look at the water. If you want to see Rushmore, you can take the truck up there by yourself." He took a left off the highway, drove to where a bridge crossed the river, and parked alongside a gravel road. We got out and stood on the bridge to look at the water.

"This is Rapid Creek, one of the best trout streams in the Hills," he said. "There are fish all through here, from Rapid City up to Pactola Dam." He pointed down into the water. "Look, right behind that boulder, you see 'em?"

I squinted but couldn't see anything. I'd left my glasses in the truck. James took his off and handed them to me.

"Look behind that boulder, next to the foam line. Three fish. One must be more than twelve inches."

It took me a while, but I finally saw them. They were facing upstream. I noticed them when I saw a flash of white. "Wow, they really blend in." They seemed to dart almost sideways now and then, into the faster current and then back behind the rock.

"Lesson number one is to know where the fish hold," James said. "Think like a fish. You want cover for safety, a place where there's food coming to you, and a spot where you don't have to waste too much energy fighting the current. That's where it starts. If you give up safety and you move into the faster water, it better be worth it. In other words, there better be a lot of food to make up for the energy you spend retrieving it. Make sense?"

"Sure." I said. "What are they eating?"

"We'll cover that later. The thing is, you have to know where to fish. Otherwise, nothing matters. Good fly fishermen always spend time reading the water. They don't just jump right in and start fishing."

"So when do we start fishing?" I asked.

He looked at me and frowned. "Not until you get lesson number two: how to cast. If you can't cast, you're screwed. This water is great for a neophyte because it's forgiving to a new caster, but when we get to the bigger water where it's windy, and you can't cast, well, good luck."

We walked to the other side of the bridge and James had me point out all the likely holding spots. We didn't see any fish on that side, but James assured me they were there. "The water is running a little high from run-off, but it's gin clear. That's good. The fish will be spread out a bit, but I like that. Let's get you a license and then make camp."

We drove up to Hill City, where James made me buy a seasonal license, which was almost seventy bucks. I was

The Eddy

shocked by the price, but it was the first thing he insisted I pay for. "These streams are exceptionally managed," he said. "The money pays for that. Never begrudge the fees."

We drove out of town for forty minutes and finally pulled off the two-lane highway onto a forest road that had a small sign saying Ditch Creek. We drove the road slowly through the mountains for several miles until we came to a small campsite. It had ten sites, but we were the only ones there.

"I love this place," he said. "It's really quiet. I've camped here in the spring with a buddy when it snowed about a foot. Prettiest damn thing I've ever seen. In the morning, we found some mountain lion tracks about a hundred yards from the tent. We spent two hours following them to see what it was up to."

"What was he doing?" I asked. "The lion."

"I'm not sure," James said. "But it was an odd feeling seeing his tracks so close to the tent. Like I said, we followed them until they disappeared." He pointed to a ridge in the south. "His tracks just stopped up there. It became a ghost." He stood in silence for a while, staring up at the spot.

I found the story disconcerting, since I'd recently read about a few attacks in California, but I didn't say anything. Part of me wanted to see a mountain lion; part of me was content to see a picture of one in a book. "Have you ever actually seen one in the wild?" I asked, breaking the silence.

"Nope, but I've heard them plenty of times. I hope to get lucky one of these days."

I laughed. "Sure... But promise me. If we go out looking, you'll be the one wearing the sirloin aftershave."

We unpacked all the gear and set up camp. I collected firewood while James put up the tent. This time, instead of the two-man nylon tent, he put up an old canvas classic big enough for six people. He put a card table inside, as well as two cots to sleep on. I got the feeling we were going to be here for a while.

Once everything was settled, we sat down at the

picnic table with some thin rope, and James gave me lessons on how to tie knots. He taught me three knots—the improved clinch, the surgeon, and the nail knot. He made me tie them twenty times before he broke out the delicate tippet. He made me tie the knots another twenty times with this material until he was satisfied that he wouldn't have to babysit me.

Next, he broke out his old fly vest and had me put it on. He explained all the gadgets on the vest and how they worked – forceps, nippers, retractors, net release. I wanted to go through the fly boxes, but he said I wasn't ready for that.

"So," I said after I familiarized myself with the gear hanging off the vest, "are we ready to fish?'

He sighed. "No. Remember lesson two? Casting?" He broke out a four-piece Sage rod and put it together. He didn't string it up. Instead, he had me pretend like I was casting so I could feel the rod "load."

"You ever see the movie *A River Runs Through It*?" he asked.

"Yeah, with Brad Pitt. He's beautiful in it."

James rolled his eyes. "Yeah, well, besides that, forget everything you saw in that film, all that stuff about casting. It'll just confuse you." He strung up my rod and put a little ball of yarn on the end of the tippet and then placed twenty feet of line on the ground in a straight line in front of him. He then showed me how to hold the rod.

"Now bring your rod back fairly fast to twelve o'clock, with your wrist locked, and pause to let the rod load. Bring your arm forward and let the rod do the work. Do not throw the line. Four hundred bucks for a rod means you're paying for it to do the work. And no false casting. You're not ready for it, and it's overrated."

He demonstrated several times. It looked easy. "Now I'm going to make lunch while you practice casting. When you're ready, you can add a little more line, but just remember, the more line you add, the longer you have to let the rod load."

The Eddy

Casting was harder than it looked. My line kept collapsing behind me and I kept wanting to throw it. James watched as he made sandwiches, occasionally giving me tips, reminding me to watch my back cast. After twenty minutes, I started to get the hang of it.

When lunch was ready, I took a break. We ate turkey sandwiches with pepper jack cheese and alfalfa sprouts, and James opened a bag of sourdough pretzels. It felt like a king's meal. James washed down his food with a beer and I had a Coke. Whatever the reason, it felt like my taste buds had come alive. Afterward, we walked down to the little creek and looked for brook trout. We saw a few small ones. They looked like darting jewels in the water. I was ready to fish.

"Let's hit it," I said. I was already moving toward the truck.

"Not yet," James said. "I want to see you cast some more." He opened another beer and sat down at the picnic table. I sighed and went back to my practice.

"This is like fuckin' school," I muttered. It took me five minutes to get the hang of it again, but after I made a dozen decent casts, James got up and loaded the truck. "Okay, now we can hit it," he said. "I've got the camera; we're ready for your first trout."

We drove back through Hill City and then wound around to Pactola Dam and Rapid Creek. We stopped at the dam, checked out the scenic view of the tailwater, and then made our way to upper Rapid Creek. Above the lake, the river disappeared into a deeply cut gorge, and it was as pretty a place as you could imagine fishing. The river sliced like a ribbon into the base of the mountains, with granite cliffs surrounding the stream, reaching hundreds of feet into the sky. Ponderosa and lodge pole pine climbed up the mountainside, spectacular in their resilience, clinging to the sides of cliffs in the most unlikely places. Along the stream, birch, hackberry, and green ash thrived, providing shadows and cover for the fish. James pointed all this out to me as we walked upstream, and I began to think catching fish in this place was a secondary consideration.

"Here's our spot," James said after we'd hiked for forty-five minutes. We were near a bend pool where the water gathered in a deep spot and dumped into some fast-moving water in a narrow channel. It looked fishy. "I want you to sit here for a moment and watch how I fish this spot. I'll work it for ten minutes or so, and then you can have a shot at it."

I watched as he rigged up a two-fly system with a little split shot. He put a strike indicator—a little fuzzy bobber—near the top of his leader so he could detect when a fish took his fly. "I don't see anything hatching yet, so I'm going to fish subsurface. I'll work this run systematically, beginning at the bottom. You and I know there are fish in that pool, but we want to cover the water so we don't miss any fish or spook them. I'll start at the bottom of this run and work upward. Watch my indicator. If it hesitates or moves, I'm going to lift my rod firmly, but gently enough so I don't pull the fly out of the fish's mouth."

James walked down to the bottom of the run, made sure his shadow didn't cover the water, stripped his line out, and made a perfect cast into the riffles. On his fourth cast, his indicator seemed to hesitate in the water. He lifted his rod and it bent back sharply.

"You got one!" I yelled.

James let out a whoop and looked back at me. "Nice one. A 'bow.'" The fish made a run up into the pool, and I could hear the line sing out from the reel. It ran for about ten yards and then James began to bring him back, keeping his rod high. Within a couple of minutes, the fish was near his feet.

James removed his net from the back of his vest and landed the trout. It hung heavy in the net. He wet his hands, gently removed the trout, and turned it upside down so it was disoriented. He removed the small fly and then lifted the fish for me to see. "Sixteen, maybe seventeen inches. Fat, healthy, and gorgeous."

The fish was beautiful, olive green with a swath of

The Eddy

pink down its side. I took a quick picture and James put the fish back in the water and watched it dart away downstream.

James stepped out of the water and walked back toward me. "God, I just love that. Nothing better in the world." He was grinning like a little kid. "Now it's your turn. I'm just gonna sit back and watch you. I won't say a thing unless you ask me. It's a little tougher than it looks, so don't get frustrated. If you get a fish today, on your first time out, consider that a great success, okay?"

I put my one fly on, adjusted my leader with the strike indicator, and stepped into the water where James had been. It took me a while to get my line under control as I pulled it off the reel, but, when I did, I pulled the line back for a twenty-foot cast and immediately put the fly into the hackberry on the bank. It took me a while to get it untangled, but James never said a thing. He just sat there with that half-smile on his face, leaning against a rock, admiring the scenery. He continued to watch as I botched a few more casts. I finally moved up toward the deeper hole where the casting was easier, and I managed to put the fly where it needed to be. I looked back at James and he gave me the thumbs up.

I must have fished the hole for twenty minutes with nothing happening. I was beginning to wonder if I was doing something wrong when my indicator suddenly darted sideways in the current. I lifted the rod and felt the heavy, pulsating resistance. "I got one!" I screamed.

James ran down to me. "Get your line on the reel! Keep your rod tip up! Let him run!"

I was trying to do as he instructed when the fish ran and snapped the line. "Shit!" I screamed. "God, he was a pig! Shit!" I turned to look at James and he was laughing. "God damnit, you said you wouldn't say anything. You confused me!"

"Sorry, I got excited. That was a big fish."

I plopped down on the bank to retie my leader. "I'm gonna get him," I said.

"Well, good luck. He won't be eating for a while." He threw me a box of flies. "I'm going upstream a ways, so I won't bother you. You have fun. If you want me, just give a holler; I won't be far. We've got about two hours before it starts getting dark in the canyon. If a hatch starts, keep fishing those nymphs; just take off the weight and fish 'em shallow."

He walked away and I was grateful to be by myself. I worked the pool for some time without any luck and then moved upstream. The two hours passed quickly. I never got another bite, but I did see fish starting to rise. It looked like raindrops hitting the water, except occasionally there was a swirl left behind.

Just as it was getting difficult to see, James came up from behind and startled me. "Had enough?"

I jumped. "Geez, don't do that." I reeled up my line. "I didn't get any, but I think I had a few hits. How 'bout you?"

"A few," he said. He didn't elaborate.

"Tomorrow," I said. "Tomorrow, I want to come back here. I don't care if you have to drop me off all day, I'm gonna get some fish tomorrow."

"All right, then," James said. "Let's go get something to eat."

We stopped at a burger joint in Hill City, and James slowly ate his burger while I rattled on and on about fishing—the things I'd observed, the flies I tried, when the fish started to rise.

Finally, when I took a break to work on my malt, James said, "You know, I had a hunch you'd be a natural. You're inquisitive, analytical, observant. You like a challenge. You've got all the qualities to be really good at this."

"Thanks," I said. "You know, I can't remember when I had so much fun. I mean, it was frustrating, but in a good way."

James nodded and smiled. "When I started fly fishing years ago, nobody I knew did it. I spent hours reading about it, looking at catalogs, buying magazines. For years, I really

The Eddy

sucked. I was enthusiastic, but I wasn't any good. Those were some of the best times of my life. I learned through failure, by myself, on my own. I haven't found anything yet that brings me so much joy on such a consistent basis. I thought of that today as I watched you fish. You reminded me of that... It was good I left you alone."

"Yeah," I said, sipping on my malt, "maybe fucking up is a good thing."

James lifted his diet Coke. "Well then, here's to fucking up."

On the way back to camp, James put McMurtry back on and we drove in silence, listening to the music. It was better the second time through. When we got back to camp, we made a fire and James and I opened some beers. We didn't say much; there was no need. When we finally retired to the canvas tent and settled down into our sleeping bags, I felt as if I could sleep for twelve hours. James was snoring before I got settled, so I cut a loud fart to see if he was really out. He didn't say anything, so I figured that was it. Just before I dozed off, he said, "Do that again and I'll shit in your waders." We laughed for five minutes like a couple of junior high kids before conking out.

Joe Paatalo

The Eddy

Chapter 15

The next morning, we went back to upper Rapid Creek. It was overcast and looked like rain. We put on our rain jackets and walked back into the gorge. James said he'd stick with me until I caught my first fish so he could capture the moment on film. It didn't take long. There was a blue wing olive hatch, and James gave me a small emerger to fish in the film with a strike indicator. Fifteen minutes later, I hooked a six-inch brown. James took about six shots of me wrestling with it, trying to get it off the hook, and then releasing it.

"You gotta start somewhere, kid," he said. He gave me a few more flies and went further upstream. We agreed to meet in a few hours for lunch, so I was left on my own to experiment. I ended up catching six more before I reeled in and went to look for James. The biggest was only twelve inches, but I was proud of myself.

I found James fishing some riffles in a narrow part of the stream. He was directing his casts near the banks where there was a foam line and some overhanging grass. It was a tight area to fish. He was concentrating and leaning forward with each cast, unaware I was behind him. I sat quietly and watched. Each cast seemed perfect; there was little wasted motion. He had a dry fly on with another fly below it, and each time he cast the rig, it turned perfectly over. I saw him lift, miss a fish, swear out loud, and then put another cast right next to the overhanging grass.

I saw the fish take the dry casually, but as soon as James lifted the rod, I could tell it was big. It made a run upstream and then came partially out of the water. It was a pig of a rainbow, wider than a two-by-four. It pulled out line and tried to get behind a log upstream. I watched as James lowered the rod and tried to move the fish's head in another direction. The 'bow would pull out line, stop, and then James would reel in a bit and move upstream. He kept the line taut so there was never any slack. Finally, the fish seemed to tire and started back downstream toward James. It got close to his feet, saw him, and started running again, this time downstream. James took off after it.

"You almost had him!" I yelled.

James looked up, surprised to see me. "Been trying to get this fish for the past hour," he yelled. "Tough son of bitch!" He stumbled as he tried to keep up with the fish. "As soon as he stops running, I'll get him. Get your camera ready!"

Sure enough, the fish stopped running. It went to the far shore near the deepest water it could find. James kept the rod held high and slowly made his way to the fish. He made a point to get behind it and then pulled his net from the back of his vest. He placed it in his teeth. The fish came to the surface on its side, and the fight was over. He netted it and let out a yelp. He held the fish in the net for me to see. It was so big, the net could barely contain it. He walked back to shore and placed the net in the water to get the hook out.

"Oh, man," he said, catching his breath. He held the fish up for me to see and I took a picture. "Twenty-four inches. Brood stock, I'd guess. Biggest fish in a long time."

He placed the rainbow in the water and gently moved it back and forth into the current to help it recover. It took a few minutes, but then it darted away downstream. James got out of the river smiling and sat down next to me. "That just made my day."

He took off his vest, grabbed a couple of Cokes out of the back pouch, and handed me one. "How'd you do?"

"Seven," I said. "Nothing like that, though. How many did you get?"

"Four, including that one. You out fished me."

"By numbers, maybe," I said. "But that one weighed more than all of mine combined."

The Eddy

"Yeah, it was a beauty. I saw it sipping near the bank about an hour ago. I kept working that fish. I put him down a few times, but after a few minutes, he'd start sipping again. I had to switch flies a few times and lengthen my leader, but I finally stuck him. Not bad for a 6x tippet."

"I'm impressed," I said. "I want one like that."

"Well, what makes a fish like that so memorable is the challenge. I could have given up and moved on, but sometimes getting the hard fish is more worthwhile."

I nodded and looked around. "It's hard to imagine a more beautiful place," I said. "Do you ever think you could live here?"

James leaned back on his elbows and sighed. "Yeah, I could. It crosses my mind all the time. It's always depressing to leave."

"Why leave? You're not attached. You could work out here. Teach or guide or something. You'd be happier."

"It's not that easy," he said.

"I know, you keep saying that, but I don't see why."

"Trust me. It's a long story. Doesn't matter."

"Are you going to tell me the story? I've got the time." I looked at him, but he didn't say anything. He just rubbed his right knee and winced.

"Bothering you?" I asked.

"Yeah, when I tripped back there, I twisted it. It acts up now and then. No big deal."

"Well, I want a big fish. Do you mind if I fish the rest of this run?"

"Have at it," he said. "There's another nice one up ahead too. I'll just sit here a while and then move further up. If it starts raining hard, I'll come back and find you."

I stepped into the stream and started working the run. After a few minutes, I had a nice hit but lost it. I turned back to see if James had seen it, but he was gone. I fished for another two hours, catching a few, but they were mostly small, the biggest maybe thirteen inches. When it started to rain, I put my hood up, but I was getting wet and cold. James came back and said we should head back. By the time we got to the truck, it was pouring hard.

"Don't think we'll be able to wait this one out," he said.

We loaded up the truck, took our waders off and climbed into the cab. James put the heat on, and before I knew it, I fell asleep to the rhythm of the wipers. I awoke as we turned onto the dirt road to our camp. It was still raining hard.

"Looks like we'll be playing some cribbage," James said.

A quarter mile down the road, James got out of the old truck and switched the hubs into four-wheel drive. The road was a mess. Water was streaming off the mountainside, forming gullies across the road. Pools of water in the low spots made driving treacherous, and we crossed them cautiously, careful not to bottom out. It was a relief to get back to camp, but I was concerned we'd be stuck there if it kept raining.

"What's the worst that can happen?" James said. "We get stuck here for a day or two, no big deal. We've got plenty of food. I might have to ration my beer, but *I'll survive*."

In the canvas tent, James lit two lanterns and we sat around the table, nice and dry, chewing on venison sticks and playing cribbage. There was something soothing about the sound of the rain on the old tent. The canvas gave off a musty smell, but it was nice. I imagined it was like camping back in the '50s. I kept glancing at my watch and James finally said, "What do you need that for? Time doesn't matter out here. We get up when we get up. We eat when we're hungry. We leave when we're ready. Stick it in your vest; you only need it so you don't lose track of time and forget to meet me. If you're wondering how much daylight you have left, put your hand out like this, just below the sun." James put his thumb flush to his index finger and held his hand up. "Count the hand lengths down to where the highest land point meets the sky. Each hand length is about an hour."

"Cool," I said. "Very mountain mannish." I put the

The Eddy

watch away. It took a while to understand what he was talking about, but he was right. There was something liberating about not having to track time.

When the rain finally stopped, James went out and started a fire. It was pitch black and chilly, so it was nice to have the light and warmth. We sharpened a few sticks and sat around the flames roasting bratwurst. They went straight from the fire onto the bun with a squirt of mustard. I had three and James had two. I think I could've eaten six.

After our dinner, James broke out a bottle of single malt scotch, poured it into a tin cup, and washed down about four ibuprofens. I opened a beer, made sure he didn't mind if I had a few, and we watched the fire, mostly in silence. After James' second cup of scotch, I asked him, "So, are you going to tell me that story or not?"

James cleared his throat and leaned closer to the fire, considering it. I opened a new beer and leaned back in my chair, not sure what to expect.

"When I was your age," he began, "I'd made a name for myself playing hockey. I was really fast, knew how to score. I was offered a few scholarships, but I chose Duluth, since it was close to canoe country and I liked being next to the big lake. There's something about Superior, its size and all its possibility. Anyway, I got drafted my junior year but turned it down. Figured I could play one more year of college and then give it a shot. I was in no hurry." He smiled and slowly shook his head. "Guess that was a mistake.

"Late in May, after I finished my finals, I decided to go into Canada, into the Quetico, north of the Boundary Waters. For three weeks. On my own. I didn't tell anyone. I sold my Chevelle, bought a Toyota truck, threw all my gear in the back, and tied my dad's old canoe on the top. I drove up to Canada and entered the park from the north side. Because I was stupid, and poor, I went in illegally, not wanting to pay the fees. It was a dumb move because no one, and I mean no one, knew where I was... Trust me, Toby, never go somewhere remote without telling someone.

"Anyway, the trip was great at first. It was late May,

no one was up there, and the fishing was better than anything I'd ever experienced. I spent my time exploring, marking all the lakes on my maps—where the fish were, the best campsites, that kind of thing. Each day, I set out with a new challenge. It was hard, but I loved it. I never felt lonely. It felt natural for me to be out there.

"So, sometime toward the end of the second week, I was on this big lake, Sturgeon. The fishing was great, but the wind was tough to manage on the big water. I checked out the maps and decided to go down the Maligne River, which was just south of the lake. I had a fly rod with me and wanted to see if I could catch some smallmouth, so one morning, I broke camp and paddled over to the river.

"It had been raining a lot and the river was running high and fast. I was smart enough at first to portage the tough spots. I had been in whitewater a few times and handled it without a problem, but this was different. This river had some tough Class IIIs—you know, standing waves, ledges, that kind of thing.

"After about three days on the river, putting up with the rain, I got this gorgeous eighty-degree day, a north woods postcard. Naturally, I figured it was a good day for a swim, so I took the canoe out and ran a few rapids. No problem. I was able to maneuver into the eddies when I needed to; I was able to backpaddle and ferry, perform all the right moves. I knew what I was doing. But I got a little cocky.

"The next day, the weather turned cold and rainy again. It was late in the afternoon, but I figured I could put some distance in on the river. I was fairly fresh, so I portaged the first rough spot, but when I got to the next one, I decided to run it. I got lazy and overconfident. I didn't want to get out of the canoe, so I used bungee cords and secured everything into the canoe in case I tipped. I mean, the stuff was in there tight. I thought I knew what I was doing. When the rapids came up, I got down on my knees to paddle, keeping my center of balance low. I hit the first chute just fine, but then…"

The Eddy

James stopped talking and took a long drink of scotch. The night had turned colder. "Life is funny," he finally said. "I've thought about this moment a thousand times. I've woken in the middle of the night dreaming my way out. Sometimes I see it play out differently. But usually, it ends the same way."

"What exactly happened?" I asked.

"Exactly? Who knows? Here's how I remember it now. The loaded canoe did not respond as well as the empty one. I hit a rock, turned sideways, and dumped. I fell downstream of the canoe, and that was the problem. I barely had time to come up for air when I got pinned between the canoe and a boulder in the river. I was pinned right below my knees and the canoe was submerged. I couldn't get the canoe off me and I remember screaming in pain, flailing in the water. I could literally hear the canoe breaking. It felt like my legs would be severed. With adrenaline flowing, I was able to lift on the far gunwale to loosen my left foot. When I freed it, I stepped down on the canoe to try to get my other leg out, but I slipped back and fell alongside the canoe. The problem was my right leg never moved. I could feel the tendons and cartilage rip. My body went one way and my knee never moved." James rubbed his right knee and smiled. "Sounds pretty bad, right?"

"How did you get out?"

"You know, I'm not exactly sure." He rubbed his chin and spat into the fire. "I was close to drowning because I couldn't stand. Like a fool, I didn't have my life jacket on. But I think the river shifted the canoe because my leg suddenly popped free. I was in so much pain, I can't be sure of what happened exactly, but when my leg came loose, I broke away from the boulder and began bouncing downstream. I was on my back and could barely stay afloat. I must have swallowed gallons of water. When I finally got free of the current, I crawled to shore and started heaving. Afterwards, I managed to crawl up on shore, but I couldn't stand. I crawled into the woods and passed out.

"I'm guessing I was out for hours, but I have no way of knowing. When I came to, I tried to stand, but my right knee was literally on the side of my leg. My other leg was bad too, but at least it was stable. I found a stick and managed to stand, but it was tough. I started to look for the canoe and the gear, but it was either washed away or pinned under that boulder. I remember praying it had come undone because, without the gear, I was dead. Unfortunately, the canoe *was* pinned. And all my gear with it."

James shook his head and took another drink. "It's hard to describe what goes through your mind at a time like that. I was cold, in agony, and it was starting to get dark. I had no shelter and no food. I could try swimming out to the canoe, but I wasn't sure I could make it... I remember thinking about my dad, how appalled he would've been at my predicament. That and the fact I smashed his fuckin' canoe. The man hated waste. He also had little tolerance for stupidity. Anyway, what would you have done?"

I shook my head. "Jesus, I have no idea."

"Well, neither did I. The thing was, I knew I needed matches to survive. I knew hypothermia would kill me. I had nothing on me to survive, so somehow, I had to get to the canoe to see if I could get into the daypack where I kept my lighters in waterproof baggies. If I got those, I had a chance. I was pretty sure I wouldn't last the night without them. So I limped way upstream of where the canoe was pinned and dove back into the water. It was a calculated risk. I managed to make it past the boulder where the canoe was submerged, and I sort of flopped over behind the rock in the eddy where the water was calm...

"That eddy saved my life. I was spent, had nothing left. It gave me the respite I needed. It gave me a chance to form a plan... When I was ready, I crawled up on the boulder and looked down. Dad's canoe, his favorite possession, was in two pieces. I could see my gear strapped tight in one end of the submerged canoe, and in the other half my daypack. It was wrapped around one of the thwarts that was sticking upward. I had to go for it, so I stuck my head and shoulders

The Eddy

into the water in a kind of half-dive, trying to get at the pack or loosen it. It was a miracle I didn't drown. The current kept banging my head against the rock and I'd have to come up for air and try again. Finally, it popped free.

"After I rested, I tried for another twenty minutes to free the other packs so they could at least float downriver, but I couldn't do it. They were wedged too tightly, and I was too exhausted. I finally just gave up and slipped off behind the boulder to rest in the eddy."

James stopped talking and took another long, slow swallow of scotch and cleared his throat. "You know, I was seriously tempted to just stay there in the comfort of the calm water, to let everything slide on past me. Resting there, behind that rock, I saw the whole world rushing past me, a raging torrent of water—loud, constant, wild. I had underestimated it... I had underestimated everything. I wanted no part of it again." He looked up at me and smiled. "But, of course, I couldn't do that, could I?

"I waited until I regained my courage, said goodbye to Dad's canoe, took a deep breath and let myself slip back into the rushing water. I held on to that daypack for all I was worth and tried for shore. The river battered me pretty good again, and I swallowed more water, but I made it."

"When I got to shore, I didn't have time to feel good. It was getting dark, and I was getting cold, so I rifled through the pack for the lighters, hoping I'd remembered to put them back. I found them in Ziploc bags. They were the only thing dry in the pack. I didn't have much else in there, just a pocketknife, a little rope, a few waterlogged granola bars and a wet novel. I took the knife and shaved some sticks and got enough dry shavings to start a fire. I have no doubt without that fire, I would've died. Sometimes it's the little things, you know. Anyway, it's funny, but I remember thinking about that old Jack London story I read in high school, *To Build a Fire*, and how that guy was out in the Yukon at minus 60 degrees and couldn't get a fire going. That story kept going through my head. Later, as I was lying next to that fire, I swore I would not move until someone found me. I remember drifting off that night thinking I would sleep by that fire for a week if I had to.

"But when I woke the next morning, I knew the ordeal was just beginning. My knee was swollen like a huge sausage. It made me sick to look at it. My other leg was a mess too. I was bruised everywhere, and I was sure I had cracked ribs. I tried to stand, but it was difficult. I half crawled to the river and drank about a gallon of water. I couldn't believe how thirsty I was after all that. I crawled into the woods for more wood and heaped it on the fire, figuring I'd just stay there a while, but it wasn't rational. I knew I was dry and safe for the moment, but nobody was going to find me. It could be weeks, or even a month, before someone might come along. On top of that, I was in so much agony I could barely stand it."

"So you *had* to move," I said. "How far were you from help?"

"Well, I wasn't sure. I didn't have my maps anymore, but as I recalled, I was at least twenty miles from Lac La Croix, which is a fairly busy lake. Somehow, I had to make it there. I figured if I followed the shoreline, I might get lucky enough to see someone, or at the very least, I could keep moving until I hit the big water and could signal someone. As awful as it was, I had to try it. I didn't see any other option. I considered taking some of the rope and trying to get my gear out of the canoe, but I didn't think I'd be able to get enough leverage to budge it, especially since I could barely stand. Most people have no idea the power of moving water. And I sure as hell didn't want to go for another swim. So, as soon as my fire burned down, I found a few stout sticks and fashioned one as a splint and the other as a walking stick. And then I began to move."

"Shit, that must've hurt," I said.

James took a deep breath and looked into the fire. "Yeah, it did. Walking the shoreline up there is no picnic. It's busting brush, essentially. I kept falling. It wasn't so bad going down but getting back up was brutal. If I made three miles the first day, I was lucky. At night, I had to stop, make

The Eddy

a fire, and cover myself with pine boughs for warmth and sleep as best I could next to the flames, praying it wouldn't rain. Sometimes it would, and it just increased the misery.

"By the third day, the hunger really kicked in. For a while, it had been held in check by the pain, but my stomach started turning to knots. The only thing I'd eaten was a few soggy granola bars, and they didn't last long. To make things even worse, I was getting pretty weak. I spent a lot of time trying not to panic. But it gets hard. I started thinking I was lost, that somehow, I was on the wrong river. My mind started playing tricks with me. And here's where the story gets weird."

James paused and looked at me. "This is one of the reasons I've never talked about this. I don't think most people can understand the panic and pain, but they sure as hell wouldn't understand this. The thing is... I started hearing voices. It was late at night and I was propped up against a boulder near my fire when I heard it, as clearly as I'm talking to you right now. How do you explain something like that? I had moments of delirium; I know that. But I *felt* lucid at the time.

"What did you hear?"

James stared into the fire. "It's not you."

"*It's not you?*"

"Yeah, as plain as that. I spun around, scared as hell, and started yelling. Someone had to be there. But no. My heart was racing, I just sat against that rock and stared out into the darkness for a long time, straining to hear anything. Just when I had convinced myself I'd been hearing things, I heard it again. '*It's not you.*'"

"Coming from where?"

"I'm not sure. Above me, somewhere in the darkness. Just a disembodied voice. Very calm, very clear."

James stopped talking and kicked at the fire. When he spoke again, it was almost in a whisper. "I heard it twice more before I got out. Once in the daytime."

I sat there looking at James. He was rubbing his chin, feeling the scar line. "It's understandable. You were at the breaking point. What were you thinking before you heard it?" I asked. "Do you remember?"

He thought about it for a moment. "The same things, I guess. How I was going to get out. Whether or not I should try to move. Survival stuff."

"Were you talking to God?" I asked.

"Talking to God?" He looked at me curiously. "No, not really. I'd said a few prayers, I guess, but no, I wasn't asking for a sign, if that's what you mean. It was a fear response… You know, for the past eighteen years, I've tried to convince myself that what I heard was a manifestation of my mind under duress. It makes complete sense. But part of me has wondered over the years why *those* words. If I created them, which I guess I did, why *those* words? What exactly did they mean?"

"What do you think they meant?"

He shook his head and looked up into the darkness. "I don't know. Not really." He laughed. "But I guess I took it to mean my life was more than just about me." He looked at me and shrugged his shoulders.

"Anyway, the last time I heard the voice, I was sitting down on a log overlooking this wide part of the river. It was this humid, buggy day. I was having a hard time breathing and my right knee was throbbing so bad, I felt dizzy. Part of me wanted to crawl into the woods and die. I just wanted it to be over. And then I heard it again, clear as can be… It was then I had to decide how much I really wanted to live.

"In the end, I made this deal with myself. I made the first promise of my life that I truly swore I would never break. I promised, if I got out of there, I would do something that would give my life meaning, something that would make a difference. Up until then, I never really thought about having a purpose beyond me. I wasn't exactly self-serving, but I was playing hockey, totally independent, working at school. I just figured I'd find something down the road that gave me satisfaction and made me some decent money. As long as I didn't end up like my dad… But I made that promise, then and there. It sounds clichéd now, but I meant to keep it."

James kicked at a log that had fallen out of the pit. Sparks shot into the night air and disappeared into the dark.

I sat there for a while, sipping my beer, not knowing what to say. It was a cool mountain night and I could see my breath. I watched James as the flames occasionally illuminated his face. He was rolling the scotch in his tin cup, staring into the fire.

"You know," he began again, "I'm well aware of how trite this all sounds. It's why I've never talked about it. It's my deal, no one else's."

"*This* is why you chose to teach? Because that's how you would keep that promise?"

James sat straight up and looked at me. "Listen, Toby, it's more complicated than that, but yeah, that's part of it. In case you haven't noticed, I'm not exactly The Natural when it comes to teaching, but it's what I chose. I can be pretty good at it, but it gets tougher and tougher. It takes more energy to do it right, and I'm not that resilient anymore."

"But you've given enough years. Quit if you want. Do something else. You've fulfilled that promise."

He got up to get another log. I could see his knees were aching when he stood. "Yeah, I've thought about that. A lot actually. But I'm only forty, and just because I've put some distance behind it doesn't mean the promise has worn thin. Listen, I'm no saint. I made a promise, just as solemn, when I married Maggie. But I broke that one… I broke that one. No one else. This isn't a sob story. I don't feel sorry for myself. It's context I'm providing for you, that's all. I'm just giving you some meat on the bone."

I drained the last of the beer and got up to pee. "So what if you're wrong about all of this, about the voice, about what it meant? Isn't that possible?" I had my back to him while I was urinating and, when I turned around, he was staring at me.

"Toby, you ask the same damn questions I've asked myself for years. And I keep asking them. The thing is it doesn't matter why it happened; it just did. And I made a promise I need to keep."

The word *need* really struck me, but I left it alone. "Well, I guess I admire that, but I would've found another way to keep it if I was unhappy."

"You mean you'd compromise," he said.

"No, not compromise, just—change, that's all."

He smiled. "It's not that easy, Toby. It's not a promise if you can manipulate it to suit your needs."

"No," I conceded, "I suppose not. Still…"

"Look," he said, "it's not that big of a deal. It's just that the world beats you up sometimes in ways you never see coming. Maybe it was just a shitty-ass promise under duress, but it's *my* shitty-ass promise. And I'm all right with it."

He looked at me and could see I was skeptical. "I don't expect you to understand any of this," he said, "but when a camping buddy reveals something like this, you're supposed to just listen, nod, and say 'That's deep, dude. Good luck with that.'" He laughed and knocked back the rest of his drink.

"So how did you get out?" I asked.

James leaned back in his chair and finished the story. "By the sixth day, I was pretty much on fumes. Didn't think I could go any further. But sometimes, when you think you can't possibly take another step, you take another step. Then another, then another. Anyway, I caught a glimpse of Lac La Croix from the top of a hill and pushed myself until I found a portage. I followed it until it came out on a bay. And I figured that was it. I was done. I'd make a fire and stay there. Either someone would find me in the next couple of days or that was it.

"On the seventh day, I awoke to a teenage girl standing over me. She was with her father on a trip and they were heading up the Maligne. I think I scared her pretty good because she screamed and woke me up. I must've looked pretty rough. When her dad got to me, he was calm and clearheaded, but he could tell I was in bad shape. He told me his name was Ray and he promised to get me out.

The Eddy

He forced some juice into me and gave me a little to eat, but not too much. The two of them helped me up and packed me into the canoe. The thing is, they couldn't get me into it without removing the thwart, so Ray just cut it out so I could lie down. Beautiful canoe too. They left all their gear at the portage and just started paddling for all they were worth. They were amazing. Nothing short of amazing. After about four hours of nonstop digging, they spotted a float plane and waved it down. The pilot got me aboard and flew me to a hospital in Duluth. There they stabilized me and then I was flown to the Twin Cities. I was in the hospital for two weeks."

"Did you ever hear from those two again?" I asked.

"Yeah, they looked me up and came to the hospital in the Twin Cities to see me when they got back. They were from the suburbs. Ray and Caitlin. For years, we exchanged Christmas cards. We got together a few times after. Great people. Haven't heard from them in a while. Guess I dropped the ball on that one."

"And you had surgery?"

"Six of them. My right knee had to be reconstructed and my left knee had a torn ACL and MCL. I had cracked ribs pretty bad too. It took me a long time to recover. I was out of hockey and school for a year, trying to rehab. When I came back and tried to play, I wasn't much good. I couldn't cut, and every time I checked or got checked, it seemed like I would double over in pain. The school was good to me and kept me on the roster, but I was taking up a scholarship, and that wasn't fair. So I quit. Hockey career over, no professional puck for me."

"That's too bad," I said.

"Not really. I was lucky to be alive. I never, ever felt sorry for myself."

"So, then you went into teaching," I said.

"Yup. Figured I'd make a good coach. That didn't work out so well. But the teaching, for the most part, has been okay. And that's the end of the story." He stood up and stretched.

I didn't think it was the end of the story. But, if he had anything left to say, I could see it wasn't going to come that night.

"Geez," he said. "I think I drank too much. If I feel like shit tomorrow, I'm gonna blame you." He walked over to the woods to take a leak and then relit the lantern and took it in the tent. I banked the fire and followed behind him. Once I got settled in, he blew out the lantern. I tried to sleep, but my head was swimming with scenes of his misadventure.

"Are you asleep?" I asked.

I heard him roll over. "No. Kind of hard to shut down after that."

"Yeah, I hear you... James, I tried to kill myself about a year ago."

He was silent for a long time. I wasn't sure if he'd heard me.

"I was just thinking about what happened to you and how hard you fought, and then I started thinking how I tried to off myself. I can't imagine two more different stories."

I gave him a brief synopsis and he listened quietly. Finally, he said, "Seems to me it's the same story. Two stories of survival."

"Yeah, but I was trying to kill myself," I said. "In an insanely stupid way."

"You survived," he said. "You made it through the storm."

"That's true," I said. "But I'm so ashamed of it, I just want to forget. I just want to put it behind me forever."

I heard him chuckle softly and roll over. "Well, good luck with that."

Chapter 16

The next morning, we slept in late and then had a hearty breakfast of eggs, bagels, and venison sausage. James was quiet, perhaps a little hung over. Either that or talked out. We decided to try the road and, while it was slow going, we managed to get out. It didn't take long to see the streams had been blown out, though, and were unfishable. I tried to talk James into seeing Rushmore, but he wasn't interested. I finally dropped him off at a lake where he could take his float tube out and fish for cruising trout. I took the truck to see Rushmore, but I had to promise to visit Crazy Horse Mountain as well.

I came back for James in the early evening. He was lakeside, cleaning a few fish, when I pulled up. As I got out of the truck, he held up four medium-sized rainbows, eviscerated and ready for the fry pan. "Hope you're hungry," he said.

As we made our way back to camp, after James filled me in on still-water fishing, he asked about my trip. "What did you think of Rushmore and Crazy Horse?"

"They're really different. Crazy Horse is so much bigger."

"Which did you like more?"

I had to think about it. "Rushmore is more refined. More polished. But I think I liked Crazy Horse more, even though it's far from being done."

He smiled. "Why's that?"

"I don't know. I guess because it seems more fitting for this place. I liked the idea it was being built without any federal money."

He kept smiling and drove in silence for a while.

Finally, he said, "Do you know anything about the Fort Laramie treaty of 1868?"

"Nope," I said. "Important?"

"Yeah, it was. It was an agreement between the government and the Lakota and Arapaho, designed to end the hostilities, in particular Red Cloud's war with the government. In essence, it promised the Black Hills to the Indians forever. It recognized this land as sacred to Native people."

I looked out the window at the landscape. We were passing a manufacturing plant. "Well, I take it that didn't last too long," I said.

"Nope. Word spread about gold after the Custer Expedition a few years later. Prospectors started flooding the Hills. Hostilities broke out, and in 1877, the government seized the Hills back. This was around the time of Custer's Last Stand, so you can imagine the anti-Indian sentiment. Anyway, the government essentially turned a blind eye to another one of its treaties. Economics and racism."

"Too bad," I said. "Bad part of history, I guess."

"Well, it doesn't end there. Never does. Sometime around 1980, the U.S. Supreme Court ruled in favor of the Indians, claiming the government owed them money for the Hills. I don't remember the exact dollar amount, but it was never paid, in part because the Indians refused to accept it. So now the money supposedly sits in the Treasury collecting interest. You have to respect the Lakota for not taking it."

"Why won't they take it?" I asked.

"Because it's blood money. Would you take it?"

"I'm not sure," I said, "but they'll never get the land back. May as well take it and do something smart with the money."

"Well, that's one argument. There are plenty of Indians who believe they should take the money, but it hasn't happened yet. The thing is, when you look at Rushmore what do *you* see? A tribute to America and its presidents? A tribute to the craftsmanship of Borglum?"

The Eddy

James paused. "What? How do you figure Native people see it?"

"I don't know," I said. "How *should* they see it?"

"I'm not sure, but if the government steals my sacred land and carves the heads of four dead white men into the side of my cathedral, I think I have a right to be pissed."

I thought about it. It was history rearing its ugly head again. "Well, they do have Crazy Horse. I'm not sure if that makes it any better, but at least it's something," I said.

"Well, even that's more complicated than it looks. From what I understand about Crazy Horse, I'm not so sure he would approve of his likeness being carved into the side of a mountain on holy land. There are plenty who believe he would not like it. But there you have it."

"So is that why you didn't want to go to Rushmore?" I asked.

"Yeah, partly. But I can't be too sanctimonious about it. After all, I come here to use the land and its resources. I hunt and fish here. I treat it as my own and as my right as an American to use it. I'm conflicted about it, but it doesn't stop me from being here."

I thought about that for a while. "So what do you suggest we do? We can't change the past. You didn't screw them, and I didn't screw them."

"Nope, you're right, we didn't. But I'm not sure that takes us off the hook completely."

"What do you mean?"

James looked at me. "I don't know, but as I get older, I'm starting to believe in ghosts."

I shrugged and waited for clarification. It never came. "You ever think about teaching history?" I finally asked. "Seems maybe you'd be good at it."

James shook his head. "Don't really see a difference between history and English. History is just stories packaged differently. I've long surrendered the distinction between the two. Truth is truth." James looked at me and laughed. "It's all just stories, Toby… Look, forget it. Hand me the CD case." He took out a Bonnie Raitt disc and slipped it in. "We need a change of pace."

"I was beginning to think you were sexist, didn't like women musicians."

"Sexist? No. Ignorant maybe. That's why I need Bonnie. I've got some Mahalia Jackson, Etta James too. It's all in there if you look." He pointed at the CD case.

"Man, you need some new stuff," I said.

"What do you mean? I've got Neil Young's latest."

I laughed. "Man, you *are* stuck in the past."

We joked about music for a while as we drove. It made the long trip back to camp go faster, but it was still a decent haul from where we fished. I asked him why we didn't camp closer to the water.

"Sometimes distance is a good thing. You gotta *earn* certain things. They shouldn't come so easy."

"Yeah, but why do we have to stay so far from the water?"

James laughed. "Reach into my book bin behind me and grab that Hemingway anthology. Crease the corner on *Big Two-Hearted River*. When you get a chance, read it."

I dug around in back, found the book and marked the spot. "And this is supposed to answer a simple question?"

"Just read it. It's about fishing. And a few other things."

"Well, at least it's short," I said.

"Yeah, well, it's a lot denser than it looks. We can talk about it on the road sometime. Or better yet, you talk about it, and I'll listen. This ain't school."

That night, James baked the fish in tin foil over an open fire, along with a huge pan of beans, rice, and elk sausage. Later, we sat around the fire in the dark and poked at the coals. James was quiet, but I didn't mind. It was nice to just sit still and listen to the evening.

In the morning, we decided to break camp and fish Spearfish Canyon on our way out of the Hills. It was sunny and warm, and we hoped the water would be clear. Unfortunately, it was still off-color. We tried fishing it with streamers but gave up after an hour and decided to try Sand

The Eddy

Creek just over the Wyoming border.

Sand Creek was in different geography, much flatter, with cedar and juniper lining the banks. The water was slower, fewer riffles, lots of bend pools. It seemed to be in no hurry. The trout were visible as soon as I looked closely into the clear water. They scurried when they caught my shadow, taking refuge under the undercut banks. "There must be a hundred fish right here," I said, peering into the water. "This is amazing."

James stripped down to his shorts and put on his wading boots. The afternoon was bright, clear, and hot. "Let's wade wet," he said. "And don't let this river fool you. You'll see a thousand fish before the day is done, but that doesn't mean you'll catch any. These fish are spooky, especially on a day like this. We'll be lucky to take a few."

We strung up our rods and James had me put a beetle on, while he fished with a cricket and an ant. I started above him since the river was narrow. Mostly he stood behind me, watching me cast hopelessly to trout. After a half-hour of nothing, James took a spot on the bank and had me join him. "We need longer leaders. Lengthen your leader another three or four feet with 6x tippet. You're spooking the fish."

I sat down on a rock near the bank and did as he suggested. James stepped back into the water to give it a shot. I was tying my leader when I heard the splash of an aggressive take. I looked up and James was grinning. He had a nice trout. I watched him land a fourteen-inch brown.

"Nice," I said. "The cricket or the ant?"

He slipped the fish back into the water. "The cricket. I'm slamming it near the banks wherever there's some shade or deeper water. We should've lengthened our leaders straight off. My fault."

It took me a while to get used to casting with the longer leader; I lost a lot of flies to tress and bank-brush, but it did get easier as the day wore on. We spent most of the day leapfrogging one another, each taking a few runs and then moving upriver. The fishing was challenging. I had to remember to move slowly to avoid scattering pods of fish.

When I landed a fish, which wasn't very often, it was usually on my first few casts. After that, the fish would scatter upstream or under the cut-outs beneath the banks where they couldn't be seen, leaving the pool or run appear barren.

Every now and then, I'd walk by James as I moved upriver, and I'd see him landing a fish. He'd be grinning or laughing to himself, oblivious to me or anything other than the fish and the water. He seemed at his happiest when he was standing in moving water, intently casting a fly rod.

I was discovering, however, that he was a moody bastard. At times in the truck or at camp, he'd shut down as if someone had thrown a switch. He'd just go quiet. It didn't happen too often, but I couldn't help but wonder what triggered it. Something I said? Some unpleasant memory jarred loose? A personality quirk? Whatever it was, I saw no discernible pattern to it.

For my part, I was beginning to love fly fishing. It drove me mad at times. I'd screw up my leader, get tangled in the brush, make a series of horrific casts, but every now and then, I'd get it right and hook a fish. It was like the satisfaction you get after solving a puzzle. And it was a puzzle—reading the water, making a proper cast, recognizing how fish were behaving. Most of it was still a mystery to me, but I liked that about fly fishing. It was complicated, and each time I figured something out, there was something new to learn.

What I enjoyed most, I think, was watching a take, fooling the fish. I lost more than I landed, but I always got a thrill when the indicator stopped in the water or when a fish came up and sipped my fly. It meant I was getting better. I hadn't caught anything big yet, but at some point, I knew I would.

We took a break early in the evening to have sandwiches and a cold beer. We sat on the tailgate of the pickup and talked about the fishing, trying to decide if we should stay there or push on to some new water. We were leaning toward moving when James started to notice the first signs of a hatch. Swallows were diving over the riffles,

The Eddy

plucking mayflies out of the air. James took it as a sure sign, so we grabbed a few cold drinks and sat on the bank to survey the action. "Watch this closely," James said. "This should be good."

At first, the rises were mostly from small fish, little sips, or tail swirls. James described the hatch as baetis flies, and he detailed the process of how they emerged from the rocks in the shallow riffles, broke through their nymphal shucks, and ended up as little sailboats on the surface of the water, drying their wet wings before flying off to mate.

"The little fish often feed first on the surface, but watch the rise forms for bigger fish." He pointed one out to me. "You see that swirl? That's a fish taking the insect as it's coming up in the water column, before it has a chance to break free and dry its wings. You can tell because you don't see a bubble on the surface of the water. A bubble means they're taking the dry. A swirl means they're taking an emerger."

I noticed the difference right away.

"The little fish are so theatrical," he said. "They're like little kids playing in the pool, all splashy. The bigger ones are usually less showy. They stay down more, feeding on the emergers where most of the action is. They'll come up as the hatch continues, but only when they realize the party has moved upstairs."

"Don't you want to fish?" I asked.

"No," he said. "You can if you want. Sometimes I just like to sit and watch the show."

I was tempted to grab my rod, but I stayed on the bank and watched. Just as James predicted, the hatch started moving up and the bigger fish started to surface. The shadows on the water were longer now, the fish less exposed.

"Check this out." James swiped at the air and caught a bug. "You see this?" He opened his palm. "This is a caddis fly. We have two events taking place. Unlike the mayfly, these flies tend to bounce on the water instead of sitting there casually waiting for take-off. The females, after they've mated, dive down into the water to drop their eggs. It's called ovipositing. It really triggers aggressive strikes. You fish these flies differently than mayflies. You can skate or dance your fly across the surface and trout will hit them. Can't do that with most mayflies."

"Which do the fish prefer?" I asked.

"You never know. You can't predict it. It's what makes it so challenging. Sometimes there'll be millions of caddis, and they won't take anything but a few mayflies. Sometimes it goes the other way. Sometimes fly fishers call it a masking hatch, because you're sure you have the right fly, but the fish are taking something else. If they're on one, they hardly ever take the other. They can be pretty discriminating at times."

"So you have to keep switching to see what they're taking," I said.

"Yeah, but you also have to remember to use the right size and color, because that might put them off too. I usually figure out what they're taking and fish two flies, a dry with an emerger fished in the film as a dropper."

"Is that harder than fishing below the surface?" I asked.

"No, not really. It's just different. The thing is, you have at least one advantage. When the fish are high in the water column, they are less able to see you. You can get closer. Just make sure you have a longer leader, because you can line them easier when they're up."

I watched for a while and then couldn't stand it any longer. "I need to try it."

"Go ahead," James said. "They're still on the blue wings. Make sure to use a little floatant on your fly so it doesn't sink."

He watched as I lengthened my leader, prepared my fly, and stepped into the water. I tried casting upstream to the rising fish without any luck.

"You're dragging your fly. It has to look natural on the water. Try across and down the river. Mend your line."

I gave it a shot, but I didn't know how to mend my

The Eddy

line.

"Can I show you?" he asked.

I shrugged and came to the bank. "Give it a shot," I said.

James took my rod and stepped into the water, pulled out some line, and looked for a rise he liked. "See that big rise across and down a bit? I'm going to lay this fly out ahead of him so I don't scare him, and I'm going to mend my line so it doesn't form a downstream bow." He laid out a perfect cast and, with his wrist, flipped the fly line upstream so the fly drifted naturally. After the fly passed where the fish was holding, he picked up the line and made another cast, this time a little closer to shore.

The fish took the fly and James pulled the rod high. He chuckled and fought the fish for a few minutes and then landed him without his net. It was a fifteen-inch brown with the beginnings of a hook jaw. He placed him gently back in the water.

"That was the biggest fish of the day. See its jaw? That was a male." He handed the rod back to me. "I'm done now. I'm going to head back to the truck for a beer. You stay as long as you want."

I watched him walk off, glad he was out of sight. He made it look disgustingly easy, like that athlete who, with a flick of his wrist, can knock down twenty straight jump-shots without sweat. The minute you try it, however, it's a different story.

I put a dropper on below my dry fly, stepped back into the water, and tried again. For the next two hours, I fished intensely but only landed one small fish, and that one took the emerger as I was lifting my line. I must have missed at least a dozen. They'd hit my fly, but I just couldn't hook one. It was frustrating because I was so close to success. I finally gave up in disgust and returned to the truck. James was sitting on the truck's tailgate writing a letter. I changed into some dry clothes and tried not to break his concentration.

"How you'd do?" he asked finally.

"Not so good." I told him how many I missed.

"Yeah, I forgot to tell you," he said. "When fish take a dry, especially downstream, hooking them is a little harder because you tend to pull the fly out of their mouth. You need to count *one-one thousand* before you lift."

"Thanks," I said. "It would have been nice to know that two hours ago."

"You're welcome." He handed me a Coke. "You want to drive or stay here?" he asked.

"I don't care. I don't see a campground around here."

"Who needs one?" He grabbed his Therm-a-Rest from the back of the truck and threw it on the ground. "I doubt it'll rain. Let's sleep under the stars. Mosquitoes shouldn't be too bad. Pretty arid out here."

We made a small fire in an old pit and moved our sleeping bags next to the fire. James pulled the portable chairs from the back of the truck, and we sat around the flames and had salami, cheese, and crackers for dinner. James put the hard salami on a stick and heated it over the flames. It was a simple dinner, but it went down well with a cold beer.

Later, with a full moon, we lay on our backs and looked at the stars and listened to the coyotes howl in the distance. Occasionally, we'd hear a slap of a beaver tail on the river, warning someone or something to keep its distance. It was nice not hearing cars or other people, just the crackle of a fire and the sound of water moving over rocks. Every now and then, James would roll over and poke at the fire, reminding me of his presence. But, for the most part, I felt as if I were alone at night. The feeling was not unpleasant.

The Eddy

Chapter 17

The next morning, I awoke to the sounds of James packing the truck. "I take it we're hitting the road," I said. I yawned and crawled out of my bag. James had been out fishing with the first light and was breaking down his gear. "Get anything?" I asked.

"A few. Pale morning duns were coming off, so I had to give it a shot. Here's breakfast." He tossed me an apple. "Thought we'd make for the Big Horn today. I think you're ready."

I got up and jammed my sleeping bag into its stuff sack and deflated my pad. We broke camp in five minutes and were on our way.

"How long to the Big Horn?" I asked as we got back on the highway.

"A few hours, not too bad. It'll be a different kind of fishing. We'll see a lot of people. Early June isn't so bad because the water's up a bit, but you'll learn something about fishing etiquette."

"What makes this river so special?" I was rifling through his CD case, looking for something new to play.

"Big fish. *Really* big fish. It's a tailwater, nutrient rich. Perfect conditions for fish year-round. The wind can be a challenge, but the water will hold your interest, especially after you lose your first big one."

For a change of pace, I popped some jazz in. "Maybe I'll land that first big one."

James laughed. "You might. This river is an education on how to fight big fish in fast water. It humbles the best. Once you learn, though, the lesson really sticks."

James set the cruise on the truck and we sat back and

listened to the music. When the tunes were playing, he didn't care to talk, which was fine with me. I was content to look out the window with Miles Davis as the scenery changed from arid low plains to the rolling foothills of the Big Horn Basin.

In Hardin, we picked up some groceries and then followed the lower Big Horn River through the agricultural landscape and into the Crow Indian Reservation. Rock croppings and tree-dotted ramparts punctuated the landscape, until finally, as we neared the upper river, we could see the dramatic sandstone and limestone cliffs along the river, rising steeply for hundreds of feet.

I was eager to see the water, so James pulled over at the three-mile access point above the dam so we could make a close inspection. It was almost noon. Big cumulus, popcorn clouds dotted the June sky and, as I got out of the truck, I was immediately aware of the wind.

"Wow, this might make for some tough casting," I said. "Will I be able to handle it?" We walked down to the landing.

"The wind tends to pick up in the late morning and early afternoon. If it's sunny like this, we'll be on the bank somewhere taking a nap or drinking a cold one," James said. "When we fish this river, we fish it from sunup to sundown."

I looked at the water off the boat ramp. It was a side channel, maybe thirty yards across to a narrow island. The water was clear and swift. Two men were standing off one of the island's points. One was casting and the other held a large net.

"That guy's being guided," James said. "The guide looks a bit bored. May be a tough client. The water is up. That can be good. It means the back channels will be holding fish."

We walked up the bank to look at more water. "You ever guide?" I asked.

"Yeah, I did. Generally, out here, but some in the Midwest. Haven't done it in a while, though."

"Did you like it?"

The Eddy

"Mostly. It's like teaching, though. It can get on your nerves. If you have a streak of bad clients, it can be a tough way to make money. If you have a steady clientele, it can be fun.

"I used to guide these two guys out here every summer, a couple of Jewish brothers from Chicago. They were great. Very funny. Very generous. The brothers had this ritual of toasting their dead father before every drift and at the end of a long day. They insisted I partake with them. They made me an honorary Jew. They called me Shecky for laughs. Anyway, I liked them. They took their heritage and fishing seriously, but not so much they couldn't have fun with it. They had something I admired: *balance*. Stuff like that you don't forget."

"What is it about religion and fly fishing?" I asked. "Seems like they get associated a lot."

James shrugged. "They're both mysteries. Anyone who says they have either figured out is a fool."

I nodded. "Guess I'll remember that... You think I'd make a good guide?"

"Sure," he said. "If you put enough time in. But don't do it for the money. It's never as much as it seems."

"Why did you do it?"

"I don't know." He pointed to a rise on the edge of a riffle. "They're starting to come up... I guess I just liked an excuse to be on the water. I also liked it when I could get people into fish, especially those who hadn't had much success... Anyway, it's an interesting life. Maggie came out here one summer before we got married. She was in law school at the time and needed a break. She wanted to see why I spent so much time out here."

"Did you teach her to fish?"

He laughed. "Sort of."

"Was she any good?"

He shook his head. "No, she was terrible. I could teach a poodle to fish, but I couldn't teach her. She was enthusiastic, though. Fishing at night always made her... Well, we had some good times."

"Hmm... She's a really nice woman, Maggie. I'm sorry you guys didn't make it."

James didn't say anything. We walked back to the truck and got in. "You know, I'm not sure what *making it* means," he said. He leaned back in his seat. "But just because something ends doesn't mean it wasn't worthwhile."

"You mean your marriage?" I asked.

He took off his glasses and rubbed his eyes. "Everything ends, Toby, sooner or later. Marrying her was one of the best things I ever did. No regrets." He started the truck. "Guess I'd make a lousy marriage counselor, eh?"

I laughed. "You and my mom both. You should try hooking up with her. She gives everyone a shot."

James looked at me and frowned.

"That didn't come out right," I said. "It's just that she's really giving and sees the best in people, guys especially, even when everyone else doesn't see it. I don't know, maybe it's a virtue. Maybe it's a flaw."

"Hmm... A flawed virtue, more like it. Means you give a lot more than you ever get. I like your mom. Wish there were more like her out there."

"Are you looking?" I asked.

He backed out of the lot and laughed. "No way. I told you before. I like women. I enjoy their company. But I'm solo from here on out. End of story."

James wanted to stay at the Cottonwood Campground, not far from the three-mile access. When we pulled in, he said, "Put up the canvas tent. I'll walk up to the fly shop, check in, and reserve a drift boat. Make sure you stake it down really well. Tents around here have been known to blow away in the afternoon."

While he was gone, I unloaded most of the gear, figuring we'd be here a while. We were in a long, narrow field lined by ancient cottonwoods on one side and open prairie on the other. There were RVs, tents, campers, and new trucks with trailers. I found a picnic table and tried putting the tent up next to it. It was a struggle, and I looked around to see if someone knew how to do it, but apparently,

The Eddy

everyone was off fishing. Every time I got close to getting it up, the wind would catch the canvas and I'd have to scramble to keep it from flying away.

It took me some time to set the tent up. As I was nailing in the last stake, I looked up and noticed James behind me, sitting against one of the old cottonwoods. "Geez, you could've helped me." I was a little irritated.

He shrugged and I could hear him chuckle under his breath. "You did fine. Next time, pay attention to the wind. You had the opening set like a sail, right smack into the wind."

"Thanks," I snapped. "Couldn't you just tell me this stuff in the first place?"

"I could," he said, "but then you might not remember it." He got up and stretched. "Everything is set for tomorrow. Tonight, we can fish from shore. I'm going to take a nap." He grabbed his sleeping bag, pad, and a cold beer and climbed in the tent. Within minutes, I could hear him breathing heavily. I wasn't tired, so I took Hemingway and went for a walk down by the river to figure out what the hell James saw in him.

Joe Paatalo

Chapter 18

The next morning, we were up by seven. It was cool and cloudless with no wind, a perfect western June morning, so much cooler and drier than I grew up with in the Midwest. James loaded the cooler with beverages and bagel sandwiches and then prepped the camp stove for dinner later that night. He took two large vacuum-sealed bags of dehydrated vegetables and venison meat and placed them in a pot with water to reconstitute while we were fishing. "When we get back tonight, all we have to do is heat it up and add spices. We'll be tired, so this will save us time."

We grabbed some fruit for breakfast, jumped in the truck, and were off. "We're going to float thirteen miles today, starting at the dam," James said. He handed me a tube of sunblock. "Be sure to put this on. You'll regret it if you don't." He reached down for his CD case and found the Allman Brothers. "Time for 'Blue Sky,' don't you think?"

"Do we need to pull over so you can dance?" I asked.

He cranked it up. "I'm dancing in my head."

I rolled down my window and let the cool air wake me up. James sang along with the song. *Don't fly, Mister Bluebird, I'm just walking down the road, early morning sunshine tell me all I need to know.* As it broke into its jam, we both began bobbing in the cab of the truck, exchanging high fives and grooving to the guitar. Had anyone seen us, it would've looked pathetic—a forty-year-old guy moving like, well, a forty-year-old guy, and a teenager swinging his ponytail like some Woodstock throwback. By the time the song was winding down, we were pulling into the boat launch.

"See that green and white drift boat down there?

That's ours," James said, catching his breath. There was a man standing next to the boat looking up at us. "We need to take all our gear down there. You're in for a treat."

The man by the boat was grinning when we got down to the water. "It's good to see ya, Mitch, ya old river rat." The man thrust out his hand to James and the two exchanged a quick guy hug. "You look a little thin," he said. "We need to get you on the oars."

"Nick, this is Toby, my fishing partner. Toby, Nick is going to guide you today." We shook hands. His grip was firm and friendly. He was tall, strongly built, and looked like what I imagined a guide should look like. Short blond hair, deeply tanned, with forearms that seemed disproportionately large for his body. He wore a faded Sage fishing cap, expensive but well-worn waders, and a canvas vest that looked as old as he was. When he took off his sunglasses, I could see the raccoon mask that indicated he was the actual "river rat." He was a handsome guy, maybe not in the mail catalog sense, but his features were pleasant, his eyes blue and clear, his smile genuine.

"All right, Toby," he said, "let's get you set up." Nick took my fly rod, pieced it together, reset the drag on my reel, and then put a new leader on for me. "We'll start off nymphing this morning, so I'm going to put a big indicator on with two flies. No wind, so you can handle it. Mitch, why don't you start on the oars, and I'll work with Toby. Let's see if you can still handle a boat."

James just smiled and pieced his rod together and then pushed the boat into the water. Nick and I jumped in. James got behind the oars, swung the boat so that its bow pointed downstream, and said, "I love this Goddamn river. Let's tear it up."

"Go ahead and start fishing, Toby," Nick said from the stern. "Cast out to the left and mend your line so the drift is timed with the speed of the boat. Try to avoid any drag."

Five minutes into the drift, I stopped and looked down into the water. "Oh my God! Look at the fish! They're huge." The fish were darting four feet below me. They

The Eddy

looked like something in a zoo aquarium. James laughed and kept rowing.

It took me a few attempts to get my cast away from the boat, but when I did, I turned back to look at Nick. He was putting a big wad of Beechnut tobacco in his cheek. He spat a brown stream into the water and winked at me. "Six thousand fish per river mile," he said, "and it's up to us to rip some lips." He grabbed James' rod. "Watch how I do this."

He let out some line and put the tandem flies thirty feet from the boat, mending the drift the way James had taught me. Then, dissatisfied with the cast on one side, he lifted his rod and effortlessly flipped the thirty feet out to the other side. "Get me by the seam over there, you piece of shit guide." He pointed to a section of the river where it picked up speed and parted around a boulder.

James corrected his drift and put Nick on the spot. "Backrow a bit, Mitch." James bit his oars into the water and slowed the boat. Nick picked up his line and cast it back upstream. All three of us saw the indicator sink. Nick lifted the rod and it bowed with the heavy weight of a fish. "They're always stacked in that spot. Here, Mitch, give this to Toby to land."

James handed me the rod to finish the fight. It was by far the biggest fish I've ever had on the end of a line. Nick coached me as I fought it, making sure I never lost tension on the fish. When I got it to the boat, he landed it with a long-handled net. It was a twenty-inch rainbow.

"Now, like any worthwhile fisherman, Toby, I know you ain't satisfied with this fish because you didn't hook it. But you played it well." Nick unhooked the fish and lifted it so James could see it. "Thing is, you learned how they fight." He spat another stream of juice in the water and grinned. "And tell me, ain't that fight the sweetest thing? Trust me, it's addicting."

James spun the drift boat to avoid a rock and then back rowed to put me in a good spot. "You got about four drifts here," he said. "That's as long as I can hold it."

I flipped my flies onto a seam. On the third cast, I had

a hit but lost the fish. James lifted the oars out of the water and the boat lurched forward.

"Hey, it's time you earned your money," James said to Nick. "I'm gonna stop at my G spot ahead, and you put Toby on some fish. I'll wager a bottle of Dalmore I get the biggest fish today."

Nick looked at me. "Hear that, bud, I think the gauntlet's been thrown. Let's kick his sorry ass."

And so, the day truly began. Nick was able to correct my casting flaws in short order. I had a few kinks to work out, but within the first few hours, I caught a dozen fish, the biggest eighteen inches. James, on the other hand, was landing fish consistently, including a brown that measured twenty-two inches. I tried not to watch him as he fished, but it was hard to avoid.

"Keep your eyes on your business," Nick said. "We got all day and I know some secrets." He was switching flies for me while we fished a back channel. "Biggest fish will probably come in the evening anyway."

"How long have you known James?" I asked.

Nick clipped off the tag end of my tippet. "I was nineteen when I came out here the first time. Your age. I was green and enthusiastic, just like you. I could fish all day, from sunup to sundown." He spat his wad of chew on the shoreline. "I wasn't that good, but I got to know Mitch on his days off. I'm from New Jersey originally, and I headed west out of high school, looking for adventure." He handed my rod back to me. "I was out here with two hundred bucks, looking to find a job. I had a beat-up Ford Taurus and not much else. I was living on ramen, camping at Cottonwood, cleaning up after campers for a free stay. Man, I'd walk the shorelines for miles every day."

Nick reached into his vest and pulled out some fresh Beechnut. He put a big, brown wad in his cheek and took a slug of water from a container. I cringed. "Cast to that seam," he said, pointing to some fresh water.

"Was James guiding out here then?" I put out a nice cast and mended my line like I'd been taught.

The Eddy

"Yeah. He wasn't exactly living high off the hog, but we got to know one another. He'd make these great meals at night and invite me back to his trailer. In fact, I lived with him for a while until Maggie came out. We'd go out in the boat when a client canceled; usually, it was in nasty weather. That's when I learned to fish. Man, that guy could fish. He never got tired of it. I learned more in those three months than I've ever learned since."

I recast my line, this time a little further out. "Is this your favorite river?"

"The Big Horn? Nah. It's where I make my money, but I prefer free-stone water, fewer people... Hey, you missed one."

I put the fly back in the same spot. "Yeah, it caught me off guard. So, you don't like crowds?"

"Crowds are good for guiding but lousy for fishing. Some people can be real pricks. Act like they own the water and you don't exist. I've seen a few fights out here."

I thought about that and put another cast out. "Well, I guess fly fishing is like religion then. They both cause conflict."

Nick laughed. "I take it you saw that movie too. Never thought about it that way, but, yeah, I suppose you're right. Let's go see how Mitch is doing."

As he said that, I started to lift my line out of the water and a fish hit one of my flies. It shocked me and, as I tried to get control of my line, the fish ran and snapped me off.

"Son of a bitch! I yelled. "That was a big one!"

Nick slapped his knee. "Biggest of the day so far. I saw it. A real fatty." He was laughing. "You know why he took your fly? He thought it was an emerger on your lift. Remember that. Happens a lot."

I reeled my line in. "I'll remember that. It won't happen again."

Nick patted me on the back. "Yeah, it will. Trust me. And you'll be just as pissed."

We found James near the drift boat, munching on a

bagel and sipping a beer. As we approached, he threw Nick a beer. "Get what you want, Toby," he said. I grabbed a bagel and a Coke.

"How's it going?" Nick asked.

"Got enough to satisfy the lust," James said, "including one slightly over twenty-five, but I'll round down to keep it fair." He pointed to the spot on his rod where he marked the fish's length. "Had spots the size of nickels."

"Wow," I said, trying to envision the fish. "That big? That'll be tough to beat."

Nick popped open his beer and laughed. "I've never seen him lie about size before, at least with fish, so we've got our work cut out, Toby. The day is young, though."

James munched his bagel and looked out over the water. "She's in nice shape, Nick. Nice to see some high water again. Scours things clean. Hatches been down?"

"A bit," Nick said. "Bothers some of the purists, you know." He smiled.

James took out a handkerchief and cleaned his sunglasses. "Everything changes, especially rivers. If you're too much of a purist to respect that and adapt accordingly, you don't deserve to be here... You still seeing Pam?"

Nick took a drink of beer and wiped his mouth. "No, she's in Helena now. Guess she got tired of living without health insurance."

"Too bad. She was a doll." James looked at me. "She was gorgeous. Way out of Nick's league. Centerfold material. Smart and independent."

Nick let out a loud belch. "She was all those things, for sure. Except independent. I don't know any truly independent women. When we broke up, which was only supposed to be a cooling-off period, she had another guy within a week. I found out when I went to Helena to see her one weekend... *Helena* long ride there. *Helena* longer one coming back." He laughed and raised his beer to me. "Trust me, Toby, no woman is ever independent. If she's good looking, she needs to have it known all the time, in one way or another. Pick the cute ones; stay away from the lookers."

The Eddy

I looked at him. "I'm gay, Nick, so I'm not sure if that applies to me."

Nick cocked his head, opened his mouth to say something, and then burst out laughing. Beer ran out of his nose and he had to wipe it off on his sleeve. "Man, you got good timing... Well, fuck the love lesson then. I was just trying to be a good guide."

James had his head in his hand. From behind him, I could see his shoulders quaking in laughter. He looked back at us and started singing "Love Stinks" by the J. Geils Band. Nick joined in and, although I didn't know the song at the time, it was pretty funny.

I fished hard the rest of the afternoon, while James mostly watched and put away beers. He and Nick spent a lot of time sitting in the boat talking about the past, which was fine with me. I wanted to surprise them both with the biggest fish. After one run where I lost a few big ones, I slogged back to the boat. I was beat from casting and standing in the fast current.

"You look shot," Nick said as I collapsed in the boat.

It felt like my right arm was jelly. "How much longer to the put-out?" I asked.

"Another three hours," James said. "That's why we've been pacing ourselves. There should be a hatch tonight."

I closed my eyes and leaned back in the seat. "You could've told me," I said.

And in unison, both men said, "Yeah, but you might not remember it then."

"Assholes," I said. I wanted to punch them both.

Sure enough, there was a hatch that night. Blue-winged olives. James had an extra rod and insisted that Nick fish. The two men seemed to have renewed energy and, when the hatch got thick, the fishing got furious. All of us, including me, landed dozens of fish, although nothing that came close to twenty-five inches.

Just after the Soap Creek tributary, it started to get dark. James jumped behind the oars and let the two of us fish from the boat while he took us to the thirteen-mile access point. He kept singing Elvis Presley's "It's Now or Never" as he rowed. I think both Nick and I wanted to dump him in the drink.

When we pulled up to the launch, it was almost ten. There was a pickup truck with a trailer waiting for the boat. James' pickup was in the lot. We unloaded all the gear and James gave the trailer man forty bucks, thanking him for waiting so long. We were the last ones off the river.

"You boys ready for some hot stew?" James asked. I didn't know if I was more tired or hungry.

"Elk or venison?" Nick asked.

"Squirrel," James said. "New recipe."

Nick leaned back in the truck and smiled. "I could eat your grandma, I'm so hungry."

Back at camp, James lit the stove and put the stew on. We made a little fire and James broke out his scotch. "Guess I can get rid of this crap now I've got a new bottle coming." He took out three tin cups, poured two fingers in each, and added a splash of water. "Here's to the Horn and good company," he said.

We toasted and clinked tin. The scotch felt like a hot coal going down. I felt its warm burn all the way to my stomach.

We leaned back on the picnic table and, in the fellowship of fisherman, talked about the day, teasing one another while the stew warmed. James broke out a loaf of good French bread, and we munched on it as an appetizer. Every now and then, James would get up to stir the stew and sample it, adding a few unknown spices. When he finally pronounced it ready, he handed each of us a bowl and a spoon and then put a large jug of water on the table. "Enjoy it, men. I think it's right fine."

Each of us loaded our bowls to the top with stew and ripped off pieces of bread to dip in the juices. Like hungry men, we didn't say anything for a while.

"Chrise," I finally said. "Jeezus Chrise."

Both men looked at me and started laughing.

"Made him read *Big Two-Hearted River*, did ya?" Nick

The Eddy

said to James. "I should've guessed. Once a teacher, always a teacher. And yeah, I couldn't have said it any better."

They continued talking long into the night, both of them sipping on scotch. I was content to listen and tend the fire. Eventually, the conversation turned to relationships. Whether it was the whiskey or the fatigue, Nick spoke tenderly of Pam, of his regrets. James listened sympathetically. It was clearly an open wound for Nick.

"And here's the thing." Nick got up to relieve himself. "It's not like I'm some slug. I've got a degree in geography from Montana State. I make decent money building decks and additions when I'm not guiding. I do okay. But, for Pam, it was too much of a vagabond life. I guess she figured I'd grow out of it." He zipped his fly and spat into the fire.

"Could you get her back?" I asked. "I mean, hypothetically. If you were willing to make some changes."

Nick turned and looked at me with scotch-glazed eyes. "Now why would I want her back? I just said I missed her. I didn't say I wanted her back. I'm not changing." He swayed a bit on unsteady legs. "To thine own self be true!" He lifted his cup and laughed loudly. "A little blue balls is better than having no balls!"

We drank to his toast, although I only had water. I liked the macho reverie, the ritual of late-night guy-talk. I'm not sure any of us really believed what we were saying, but we sure weren't going to shed any tears. We'd be damned if we'd break that code. At least in front of one another.

By 1:30 a.m., I was so tired, I couldn't keep my eyes open anymore. I was glad Nick was staying up the road at a friend's cabin and didn't have to drive. When James finally called it a night, he turned to Nick and said, "Here, this is for you." He peeled off three hundred-dollar bills and tried to hand them to Nick. "Thanks for being a great guide."

"No way," Nick said, shaking his head. "This one's on me."

They argued about this for a while until James finally stuffed the cash down the front of Nick's pants. "There, it's over. I won't touch it now that it's rubbed against your package. I'm hitting the hay now, so I'll see you on the river." He slapped Nick on the shoulder. "We'll be here for a while, so join us for dinner when you can."

Nick grabbed me by the arm. "C'm'ere, bud. Let me give you some final fishing advice." He steered me toward the darkness. He took the money out from his pants and stuffed it in my shirt pocket. "I won't take this. Give it back to James when you leave or keep it yourself. Mitch is an ass sometimes, but he's given me a lot without ever asking for a thing."

"Yeah, I know," I said.

"I worry about him. He goes AWOL sometimes, if you know what I mean." He handed me his card. "Call me if he ever needs anything. I'll drop whatever I'm doing. That goes for you too. Any friend of his…" He put his hand out and gave me a firm handshake. "See you on the river."

I walked back to the tent and crawled inside. James had his flashlight on and was taking off his clothes. "Thanks, James," I said. "That was one of the best days I've ever had." I collapsed on my cot.

"Well, you're welcome… He gave back the money, didn't he?"

"Yup."

"Guess that means you're buying groceries for a while." He rolled over. "See you in five hours."

The Eddy

Chapter 19

The next morning, I awoke with James McMurtry coming from the truck. *You kept all that meanness inside you so long, you'd fight with a fence post if it looked at you wrong.* I groaned and rolled over. I hadn't moved all night and I was stiff and sore. Had I been on my own, I would've rolled over and slept until noon. Instead, I got dressed and went outside to pee.

James was preparing the cooler and cleaning up the site. Apparently, he'd slept well. "Coffee's on. Pour yourself a cup. We're out of here in fifteen minutes." He was looking at me with that half-smile. "Looks like the hair fairy assaulted you last night."

I rubbed my eyes and felt the back of my scalp. It was sore from wearing a cap all day. "I feel like I just woke up from a nap." I took a leak and sat down at the picnic table and poured a cup of coffee. "What time is it?"

"Six thirty. We'll launch at seven and be into fish in an hour. Here, try one of these." He handed me a hot bagel with melted cheese and cold salmon. It was weird but tasted great.

"Were there ever any gay Indians?" I asked.

James bit into one of his bagels and gave me a look. "What?"

"Gay Indians. I dreamt of this gay Indian... Weird."

"You dreamt of a gay Indian." It was a statement, not a question.

"Yeah. Just a dream." I yawned. "No big deal."

"What do you think? Of course there were gay Indians. Just like there are gay Iranians, gay Amish, gay dolphins, and gay circus clowns. Why?"

"I don't know. I just had a weird dream, that's all."

"So that you know, Toby, many Native cultures viewed homosexuality as a kind of gift, an ability to see and understand both genders. Homosexuals were not ostracized; they were embraced."

I yawned again. "Yeah, well, I was sure embraced last night."

"Jesus Christ." James rolled his eyes. "Get your shit together. We're out of here in ten minutes."

We launched again from After Bay and, for the first time, I got on the oars. It took a while getting used to rowing while facing downstream, so I made sure to stay away from shore or any obstructions that might make me react quickly. James fished from the bow, and I enjoyed watching his smooth casts as I rowed. He was fishing a streamer combination—two big flies tied twelve inches apart and stripped to make it appear as if they were chasing one another.

We were about fifteen minutes into the float when James hooked a big fish. I heard him shout as he lifted his rod and, in the next instant, I saw the fly combination shoot out of the water right at James' head. He had just enough time to turn so he didn't get it square in the face. But he still got it.

The biggest of the two flies, something called a Grey Ghost, was buried in his skin just below his ear. James tugged at it, cut his line, and turned to me. "There's a nice run up ahead on the left. Beach the boat and we'll fish it. I'm going to need your help getting this fly out of my mug."

The Ghost was buried deep. I tried to back it out gently, but its large barb had hold of some cartilage and wasn't about to let go. James finally got tired of my tugging at it.

"Here. Back off. I'm going to push the hook out like I'm putting in an earring. When the barb pops out, you take those pliers and pinch down the barb so I can back it out." He grabbed the fly, twisted it, and I saw the tip pop out from a new hole in his face. Blood was streaming steadily from

The Eddy

both places. I pinched down the barb as directed.

"I don't have any antiseptic, so do me a favor and reach into the back of my vest. I think I have a flask in there."

I got it out and handed him the thin metal container. He unscrewed the top, took a big swig, and then backed the fly out from both holes. On the pinched-down bard was a piece of flesh. He looked at the bloody fly curiously and then put it on his drying patch. "Let that be a lesson, Toby. Always wear sunglasses, and always pinch down the barbs." The right side of his face was still streaming blood.

"You better put some antiseptic on it," I said.

James took another drink and then poured a palmful and splashed it on his face. "Just like putting on aftershave," he said. "Let's fish."

It had to hurt like hell. He wiped the blood off and tied on a new rig. For the rest of the day, I looked at the dried, caked blood on the side of his face.

We fished with less urgency that second day, more methodically. That happens when you know you have fourteen hours of fishing ahead of you. Sometime in the late morning, some stoneflies started coming off. James had me switch to a fly called a Yellow Sally, and we took fish on dries for several hours. I landed one rainbow over twenty inches, and James caught several even bigger than that. Both of us lost fish we thought might have challenged the twenty-five-inch mark, but in the fast water, it was tough to get control of them. In the afternoon, the wind started kicking up and storm clouds moved in. It made for great fishing while the weather held. Finally, we stopped at a place called the Drive In for lunch and to look for some cover. A rain squall began pelting us as we ate our sandwiches, so we put on our rain jackets and took cover under some old cottonwoods. Before long, the rain came down in sheets and we were forced to put our hoods up and hunker down. It felt as if the temperature dropped twenty degrees.

"Man," I said, "this is hard core. You could get hypothermic out here." The rain had gone down the top of my jacket and I was shivering.

"Just because it's June doesn't mean it's a picnic. People get caught unprepared all the time out here in nasty weather. Once you float past the three-mile exit, there's no getting off for ten miles. You just have to tough it out. As a guide, I used to hate it when I had some milquetoast who insisted I get him off the river. I learned to carry extra clothing with me all the time." James looked at me. He had rain dripping off his nose. "I'll tell you something. You learn a lot about a person when things go south."

I leaned in closer to the tree and put my legs up to my chest. "Did it rain like this when you were in the Quetico, after you dumped?"

"No. If it had, I would've died," he said matter-of-factly. "It would've sapped what little energy I had left just trying to keep warm. I got lucky that way." I could see his breath as he spoke. "As bad as it was, it could have been worse. At least I didn't have to eat anyone." He reached into his vest and pulled out a beer.

"Man, how can you drink that now?"

He shrugged. "It was taking up weight in my vest."

"Yeah, well now it's gonna take up weight in your bladder."

We sat under that tree for nearly two hours. I got chilled and had to get up and walk around occasionally to stay warm. When the worst of the rain passed, we got back into the boat. The wind was still blowing. James rowed and I tried to fish, but I was shivering uncontrollably. Finally, I turned to James and said, "I'm a wimp, but I have to warm up. Can we pull over?"

"That's not being a wimp," James said. "That's being smart. You gotta say something when you get that cold. That macho shit means nothing out here." He beached the boat and threw me his daypack. "I've got long underwear in there. Strip down and put those on."

I put the long johns on and felt the difference immediately. "Wow, that's a relief," I said.

"You were shivering because your body was losing more heat than it could generate. It's the beginning of

The Eddy

hypothermia." He threw me a stocking cap. "Keep your head covered. It's where you lose most of your heat. You'll be fine now."

And I was. It seemed like a small lesson, but I didn't take it lightly. I fished comfortably for the rest of the day. The wind never did let up, but there was a nice blue-wing hatch and we both caught fish.

By seven that evening, we were both so tired, we called it a day and rowed hard to the take-out. By the time we got back to camp, it started to rain again. We decided not to mess with a fire, instead opting for the tent and a dinner of sandwiches and chips. James lit the lantern and read a book while I wrote a few postcards to Takeita and Mom. Afterward, I was too tired to read, so I drifted off listening to the hiss of the lantern and rain beating down on the canvas.

The next day broke clear and fairly cool. James was up before me as usual. He had the coffee on and breakfast ready when I crawled out of the tent.

"Ready to hit it?" he asked.

"I'm game."

"The third day is often the best," he said. "Don't ask me why. I have a hunch fishing will be great."

In many ways, James was right. It was the best day. I was getting into fishing shape. I was able to wade easier; my knots weren't as many or so hard to untangle; I was able to select and change flies without advice. For his part, James could fish for an hour or two without checking on me. Occasionally, he'd slip off on some side channel and I wouldn't even know he was gone until it was time to get back in the boat. Best of all, the temperature was in the 70s and there was very little wind. The only problem was there were more fishermen.

On one of our favorite spots, we had to wait for an hour until someone was done fishing it. James didn't want to crowd them, so we pulled over, gave them plenty of space, and had a nice long lunch until the spot opened up.

When it finally cleared, we decided to beach the boat and fish the run for at least an hour. Unfortunately, ten minutes into it, a boat with two guys pulled up next to ours and started fishing the same run. James was livid. He reeled up his line and, without hesitation, marched right over to them.

"Hey, guys! Give me a break here. It's a big river. Have some etiquette."

One guy completely ignored him and kept fishing, but the other guy reeled up his line. James was talking to him. "I don't mean to be rude, but you should respect a guy's space."

The guy was middle-aged, slightly overweight. He had expensive gear. "I'm sorry," he said. "I've never fished here before. I'm from back east."

"No problem," James said. "Sometimes people just don't know. At the very least, when in doubt, just ask the other fishermen if you're too close."

The guy smiled. "Thanks, I will. Al here," he pointed at his buddy, "he's been fishing here for years."

"Then he should know better," James said.

Al kept fishing. "C'mon, Al, we better move," the heavy-set guy said.

Al ignored him. James waited.

"Hey, Al," James said. "You need to move, or you need to talk to me."

The guy kept fishing. James turned to the overweight guy. "Is he hard of hearing?"

The guy shook his head.

"Fine," James said. He set down his rod and marched over to the guy. "Hey, asshole, I'm talking to you. What's your problem?"

Al reeled in his line and looked at James. "Nothing says I can't fish here. So back off. I'm not going anywhere."

James put his hands on his hips. "Really? And nothing says I can't take your fucking rod and break it over your thick head."

"Do that, and I'll sue your ass." The man was calm, self-assured. He reminded me of an older version of

The Eddy

Wheatley's Hedstrom.

"Be my guest," James said. "But you've got thirty seconds to start moving before I break your rod and a few more things."

"You wouldn't dare," the man said.

"I'm already counting."

The man hesitated, seemed to calculate his odds, and then backed down. "I'm going to report your ass. There'll be cops waiting for you when you get off this river."

He stormed away. The other man was already in the boat. "This isn't over, you prick!"

He got into his boat and shoved off. As a final gesture, he gave James the finger.

James turned to me and chuckled. "Happens every now and then. Like I said before, some guys think they own the river." He picked up his rod to resume fishing.

"You really wouldn't have broken his rod, would you?" I asked.

"Oh, absolutely. Without question." He shrugged. "I never bluff."

"Great," I said. "Now we have to worry about the cops."

James flipped his line out into the current. "No, we don't. Guys like that never do anything. He's just a self-important asshole who likes to assert himself. Hates the world, his brothers used to beat him up, never made the varsity team, has a little prick. The world is full of guys like him." James cleared some gunk from his fly and looked at me. "And you know what? He'll never get in a fight because he can't stand the pain. He's afraid of it."

"Sounds like you think you've got him pegged," I said.

"Maybe. But don't you ever let those pricks back you down. It makes it worse for the next guy."

"Okay," I said, "but you ever been wrong about these guys?"

He smiled. "Not that I recall."

We fished the rest of the day without incident, catching fish consistently, except for a stretch in the late afternoon when everything seemed to shut down. We were content to wait it out, napping along the bank with the grasshoppers, listening to the boats drift by. Occasionally, I'd hear someone yell and I'd look up to watch a fly fisherman battling a fish. It was the Big Horn cheer, a shout of pure adolescent joy. I couldn't help but smile, especially after it was followed by a few choice cuss words when the fish came off.

In the evening, as the shadows lengthened across the water, the fishing picked up again. A prolific caddis hatch came off so thick, it was hard not to breathe them in. We rigged up multiple dry patterns and had a blast skating the flies on a downstream cast. The takes were wild, and my right arm got tired fighting fish in the swifter currents. We had planned on staying out until dark, but there was nothing left to prove. We decided to head out early.

On the way back to the landing, James started to talk about moving on soon, but I lobbied for a few more days. I felt like I was starting to get competent, and I wanted to break that twenty-five-inch mark. James laughed and agreed to stay on for a few more days. We did decide, however, not to rent a boat for the next day but to walk the shoreline instead.

When we got back to camp that night, James made a tuna and rice hot dish and served it with a glass of Happy Camper Chardonnay. Nick came by later in the evening as we sat around the fire. He and James told stories of strange and horrific clients, and we laughed deep into the night. It was probably midnight when I finally climbed into the tent. The days of five hours of sleep and fourteen hours of fishing were starting to catch up to me. I fell asleep as soon as my head hit the pillow. All night in my sleep, I dreamt of moving water.

Chapter 20

James and I were both a little slow getting out of the tent the next morning. Without a boat waiting for us, there seemed to be less urgency. We had breakfast, sipped coffee, and watched the other fishermen in camp as they prepped for their day. It was another cloudless morning, already warm at 8:00 a.m.

"We'll need to pack light today," James said. "Take everything out of your vest you don't need. I've got water bottles with filters, so we can just drink out of the river. Forecast doesn't call for rain, but put your jacket in the back of your vest anyway."

We went through our gear and eliminated anything redundant, then made a few bagel sandwiches for lunch. Mine had thick pieces of summer sausage with pepper-jack cheese and a slice of onion. I wrapped them tightly in tinfoil and stuffed them in my vest. Their weight would be a comfort as the day wore on and my belly started grumbling.

"We'll fish Three Mile, walk the shore, and then make our way back," James said. "I'd like to get a few pictures today."

"I'd like to get that hog today," I added.

"Then fish streamers with a stout leader. I'll give you a sinking line so you can get deeper. You won't catch as many, but you'll have your best shot at a beast."

We went back to where we were the first day when we checked on the river and then walked upstream for half a mile. James fished a combination rig, a bead head pink sow bug with a pheasant tail soft hackle behind it. I opted for the heavy artillery, a sinking line, and two gaudy streamers, one predominantly yellow, the other mostly white. We began by casting upstream and across, but I made a point to let my streamers drift further downstream before stripping them back.

It wasn't long before James began catching fish and, while it wasn't as wild as the night before, he caught them consistently enough to stay focused. I, on the other hand, was getting shut out. After an hour and a half, I was ready to switch back to what I knew would work.

"If you wanna switch rods," James said, "I'll fish the streamers. Just let me know."

I declined, mostly out of stubbornness. Finally, after nearly four hours, I landed a twelve-inch brown. It wasn't much to show for the effort, but at least it gave me some confidence. I released the fish gently and sat down on the bank for a break. James joined me. He had his water bottle filled, and he handed it to me. "Take a cool drink of the Horn. It'll bring you luck."

I opened the filtered bottle and let the water trickle down my throat. James took off his sunglasses and wiped them on his shirt. His face was beginning to resemble a raccoon's. "I call this place *The Jake,*" he said. "Friend of mine buried his pup right over there." He pointed to a couple of cottonwoods on an island across from where we were fishing. "Said it was the toughest thing he ever had to do, tougher than divorce, tougher than burying his father."

"Wow... I never had a dog," I said. "Always wanted one, though."

James put his sunglasses back on and sighed. "I had a yellow lab a few years back, Bonzer. Helluva hunting dog." He stared out at the river. "Always liked the smell of dogs."

I waited for him to say more, but he was quiet. "I heard dogs' feet smell like buttered popcorn," I said.

He looked at me, shook his head in disgust, and began rubbing his knee.

"Bothering you?" I nodded at his knee.

"Barking like a hound dog," he said. "Think we need a break. You interested in a ride into Billings? I know a good bar where we can catch the Twins. Think they got the Yanks today."

"Sure." I was ready for a break. My right shoulder was aching.

"Grab some clean clothes, if you've got any," James said when we got back. "We can shower and then head in."

Cottonwood had clean public showers, and it was nice to wash away the grime of the past few days. I finished showering before James and went out to listen to some music in the truck while he shaved. When he came out, he was wearing a pair of faded blue jeans, cowboy boots, and a gray t-shirt with a picture of six Apaches on it. Below the picture it said *Fighting illegal immigration since 1492*. He wore it untucked. He looked handsome, tan, and fit. But, when he climbed in the truck, I just about gagged.

"Jesus, James, what the hell is that smell?"

"What? My aftershave? It's called Grey Roan." He sniffed his t-shirt.

"Well, I think your pony just died," I said. "Where did you get it?"

He shrugged. "Got a jug of it on sale a long time ago. I kinda like it."

I rolled down the window. "I gotta tell you, man, that's the worst five-dollar investment you ever made."

He frowned. "You know, come to think of it, I don't think Maggie cared all that much for it either."

I laughed. "You think? If I were you, I'd wash that stuff off and use the rest of your jug for starting a fire." I reached in the back of the truck for my day pack. "Seriously, put some of this on instead." I handed him some of my cologne. "Trust me."

Surprisingly, he didn't argue. He just chuckled, got out of the truck, and went to wash it off. When he came back, he was smiling. "Guess you were right. A couple guys in there were bitching about the smell when I walked in. Guess it had some hang time. Said they'd rather smell a donkey's ass." James put the truck in reverse and backed out of the lot. "You like baseball?"

"Baseball? Yeah, I like it enough. I'm a big Royals fan,

but that's a constant source of pain."

"The Royals have some rich history. George Brett, Frank White, the '85 World Series."

"Since I've been around, they suck," I said. "They never have enough pitching, their hitting is suspect, and they never hold on to a decent player. It's hard to be a Royals fan, but once you're blue, you're always true."

James looked at me and nodded. "I like your attitude, kid. You're not a front-runner. Anyway, I'm a big Twins fan. I like the way they're managed; I like the way they play ball. They get a lot of mileage from their players."

"I thought you were a hockey guy," I said.

James shook his head. "I'm too close to that game. I love the sport, but it gives me indigestion watching it. Brings back too many memories. I like baseball; it's more like life."

"In what way?' I asked.

"Well, baseball doesn't have a clock. Baseball is played out on its own terms. Baseball is about failure. I mean, if you're a .333 hitter, you're one of the best hitters in the league, but that means you fail two out of every three times. A baseball player has to know how to deal with failure. The season is long and drawn out. It's epic. Baseball is about the narrative of summer, the long, slow progression of a 162-game season."

"Yeah, it's long," I said. "But with the Royals, you know you're out of it by the end of May."

"Maybe," James conceded, "but there's always the game within the game to enjoy. The Royals might suck, but on any given night they might rise up and beat the Yankees. On any given night, they might be capable of great and noble things. That's the beauty of baseball. One or two players playing beyond their gifts for one night, and it's magic. Some kid, fresh out of the minors, throws the game of his life and everyone around him rises to the occasion. It happens."

"I suppose," I said. "But when your team loses a lot, it gets tough holding your interest."

"Yeah, well, think of the Cubs fans. They show up because they love the game and its rituals. They relish their

The Eddy

role as the pathetic loser. But most importantly, they love the game for what it is—an epic, tragic story. And they get to participate. It's Shakespearean."

I looked at James and frowned. "You're making this shit up, "I said.

"Of course I am." He started laughing. "It makes the ride go faster and allows me to perfect the art of bullshit. But that doesn't mean the Cubs aren't a Shakespearean tragedy. That I truly believe."

The Wooden Nickel was a high-ceilinged western tavern, complete with the long oak bar and a mirror behind it. Elk and whitetail mounts covered what wall space wasn't taken up with brewery advertisements. From the tines of the animal heads, people hung everything from hats and beads to bras and panties. One mount, near the pool tables, had a pair of boxer shorts, size 10XL. Someone had painted a huge brown streak down the middle seam.

The bar was dimly lit, with most of the light emanating from neon beer signs and wide screen TVs. The lack of light made the patrons look mysterious or sinister, depending on your temperament.

The place was crowded, so we waited for two seats near the end of the bar to open up. They were near a TV mounted behind the bar, so we could easily see the ballgame. The Twins and Yankees were in the fourth inning with no score. We sat down and ordered burgers. James ordered a microbrew while I settled for a Coke.

Next to us, two guys in their twenties were drinking bottles of Budweiser. They'd had more than a few because the peeled labels from the bottles were scattered on the bar top. The one sitting next to James wore a cowboy hat and a blue striped button-down. He looked lean and rangy, like an athlete. He smelled of drugstore aftershave. His friend was stout and broad-shouldered. His hair was closely cropped, his t-shirt tight. He looked like an ex-marine. Both of them were making suggestive comments to two women at a table behind them. One woman, a pretty Hispanic gal, was trying hard to ignore them. Her friend, who was blond, gave them the finger. It didn't stop the men, though. James ignored all of this and sipped his beer. He seemed fixated on the game.

"Hey, let's order some wings." The cowboy was talking to the marine. "I like white meat, Gusser, but I know you prefer the dark." They laughed and looked into the mirror to gauge the women's reaction.

"Maybe we should move," I whispered to James.

He never looked at me. Instead, he elbowed the cowboy and said, "You see that?" He was pointing to the baseball game. "That's called striking out... Take a fucking hint."

The cowboy looked at James and then checked me out. He began to grin. "Aw, hell, they love it. You got no sense of humor."

James kept staring at the screen. "No, I don't. And I would appreciate it if you'd stop annoying all of us." He said this with a flat, monotone voice that scared me. He then turned to me. "I'm going to the head. If these pricks bother you, take a walk." He got up. The two guys watched him walk away and then looked at me. I shrugged my shoulders and went back to watching the game.

I was grateful when the women at the table got up to leave. The cowboy and the marine watched them go. Their fun was over. Bored, they grabbed their beer and went to play pool.

"I scared them off," I said to James when he got back. "I think they saw my pipes and knew it was in their best interest."

James leaned back in his chair. He glanced over at the pool table and shook his head in disgust. "Assholes," he said. "Let's enjoy our burgers and watch this game, okay?"

"Sure," I said. And we did. Unfortunately, the Yankees scored five runs in the eighth and the game was all but over. The Twins, James said, played a brand of baseball called "small ball," which was a euphemism for not being able to hit. A rally was highly unlikely.

James finished his beer and said, "You ready to

leave? I can't stand the Yankees."

I nodded. "Yeah, I guess."

James glanced over to the pool table. "Okay, here's what's going to happen. When you and I get up, those two shitheels are going to follow us. They didn't get laid, so they're looking for the next best thing—a fight. When we hit the door, I want you to sprint to the truck." He handed me his keys. "Pull up next to me as soon as you can. Get ready for a quick exit, okay?"

"What are you gonna do? Don't do something stupid, James. It isn't worth it."

He smiled. "Trust me, okay. Just do as I say."

Sure enough, when we got up to leave, the men put down their pool cues and started for the door behind us. James walked casually as if he had no worries. I was sick to my stomach. As soon as I stepped outside, I broke into a sprint. I looked behind me and James was walking slowly.

It took me a few minutes to get to the truck, which was parked behind the bar. I hopped in, spun it around, and headed for the front of the bar, expecting to see a brawl in progress. Instead, I saw the two men on the ground in fetal positions. James was standing over them. I saw him glance at me and then he turned back to the men. With his boot, he delivered a savage kick to the cowboy's ribs and then turned to the jarhead, who was trying to crawl away. The man was cowering, and it made me sick to watch him. James buried his boot in the guy's back. I could hear the blow. He then turned away and walked calmly back to the truck and got in the passenger's side.

"Let's go," he said.

I was stunned. "What the hell did you do?"

"Maced 'em." He took a small can of pepper spray from his pocket and threw it on the dashboard. "Fuck 'em. They started it; I finished it."

"Jesus. Did you have to kick them?"

He just looked at me and didn't say anything. I drove away with an eye on the rearview mirror.

"When you went to the can, you went out the back

and got the mace from the truck, didn't you? You planned that."

James was now glaring at me. The scar on his chin stood out from his freshly trimmed goatee. "So?" He paused. "What the hell did you expect? That I'd fight fair? They don't deserve fair. Besides, I'm wearing boots. Can't fight in boots."

"But you kicked them. That was—"

"What? What was that?" He thrust a finger in my face. "You don't like it? Because I don't give a shit what you think about it. I should've kicked 'em harder. They'll live. I don't want to talk about it." He turned and looked out the window. I kept my eyes on the road and didn't say anything.

About halfway back, I got tired of the silence and popped in Merle Haggard. I wasn't mad at James; I wasn't even disappointed in him. And I sure as hell didn't feel bad for those two guys. I was just shocked at the level of James' viciousness, at how easily and calmly he could do that. It was hard for me to understand that kind of savagery, much less its source.

Back at the camp, James made a fire and we sat around the flames, not saying much. It was a great summer evening with a cuticle crescent moon hanging in the southern sky. The stars were clear and sharp and, in the cool Montana evening, sitting in the foothills of the Big Horn Mountains, I felt alive in a way I'd never felt before. I was becoming a part of the landscape. I could feel the wind burn on my face; the satisfying ache of days spent moving against water. Most of my clothes smelled of smoke and sweat and fish, and it was not altogether unpleasant.

And despite James' occasional surliness and temporary retreats into darkness, I was happy to be here. There was nothing I wanted for, and I could not recall a time in my life I'd felt that way.

The Eddy

Chapter 21

We left the Big Horn the next morning with Neil Young cranking from the truck. James was in a good mood, but I, for one, was sorry to be leaving and told him so. James said that was a good sign. Like a great song coming to an end, a good river should leave you wanting more. I wasn't sure about that but didn't care to debate it. Instead, I listened to Young wail and looked out the window. *The same things that make you live can kill you in the end.* The guy sounded like someone trying to sing with his nuts in a vise, but I liked his lyrics.

James had decided it was time for some pocket water and fewer fishermen, so we made our way to the Stillwater River, a thirty-six-mile, blue ribbon stream descending out of the Beartooth Mountains, slicing its way through the high plains of the Absarokee Range and finally dumping into the Yellowstone at the town of Columbus. It was a river known for its summer caddis hatches. In the spring, large rainbows from the Yellowstone came upriver to spawn and often stayed into the early summer season. In the fall, the browns, which tended to hold more in the river, moved into the smaller tributaries. Unlike the Big Horn, where fish could be located anywhere in its first twenty miles, the Stillwater's fish tended to move, depending on temperature and water conditions. It was the difference between a tailwater and freestone river.

James had fished it a number of times, loved its beauty, the boulder-strewn water, the accessible campsites. He also appreciated that there were stretches of water that required miles of walking to reach. People, he said, would not be an issue.

In Columbus, we went grocery shopping and then James hit the local fly shop for some information. I took advantage of the time and went across the street to make a few phone calls. In short, I found out that Mom missed me, that Takeita had a new boyfriend with a motorcycle who wasn't nearly as hot as me, and that Maggie didn't know the first thing about fly fishing. She kept calling flies *lures* and everything else *tackle*.

"Geez, Maggie, you sound like you've never been fishing, and I know that's not true."

"So, you've been talking. That's good. Has he shut down on you yet?"

The question caught me off guard. "Uh, he goes quiet sometimes, if that's what you mean." There was a long pause on the line.

"If he goes cold, Toby, don't take it personally. When he's fishing, it usually doesn't last too long—most of the time."

I considered telling her about the bar incident but thought better of it. "No, it's all cool," I said.

"Well, keep checking in with me, okay?"

And then it suddenly occurred to me. "Maggie, did you want me to go on this trip to keep an eye on him?"

I heard her laugh. "No, not really. But it works as a *twofer*. You get the ride of a lifetime and I get to keep track of him. It's an old habit I'm trying to quit." She ended the conversation by saying, "Tell Mitch I love him. He already knows it, but sometimes he needs to hear it."

When I hung up, I got the feeling she said this often, although I'm not sure how much weight it carried. As I walked back across the street, I wondered if anyone else ever said that to him.

When I entered the Otter's Den, he was chatting about fly rods with the proprietor. "Maggie says she loves you," I said. He looked up at me and didn't say anything. He handed the owner fifty bucks and put a small container of flies in his pocket. I shrugged and followed him out to the truck.

The Eddy

We left Columbus, following the river, and searched for a campsite that would suit our fishing needs. James wanted a site without people, so we looked for something halfway up the river. We found a spot outside of Nye, a little hamlet consisting of a gas station and a convenience store with a post office. We stopped in to see what the locals had to say, which was mostly a lot of rambling about the need for rain. When we got back in the truck, I noticed one of those road signs on wheels next to the post office. In bold letters, it said Worthless Checks: Gary Sisler, Andy Bigwater. It made me cringe.

Instead of making camp right away, we decided to cruise the river, checking on its flow and looking for holding water. After driving gravel for a while, we stopped at a place called the Moraine, got out of the truck, and walked down to the river. In the tall switchgrass and clover of the high plains, we kicked up a few grasshoppers. They fluttered and buzzed on take-off.

"Make a note of that," James said. "On breezy afternoons, they tend to get blown into the water. Fishing hoppers can be some of the most exciting fishing of the season. Slam 'em against the banks and twitch 'em. Watch what happens."

When we got to the water, James let out a long, slow whistle. "Wow, this looks great."

The river was wide, maybe a hundred and twenty feet across, and it was littered with boulders the size of pick-up trucks. Behind each of them, the water was dark and deep, perfect holding water for fish. The only problem was the conflicting currents that would make presentations challenging.

"This, I assume, is what you mean by pocket water," I said. I found myself calculating casts, imagining how I would mend my line.

"This is perfect," James said. "Most pocket water is smaller, more high mountain, but this fits the definition."

The bottom of the river was rocky with little vegetation. James lifted a rock from the water and held it up for me to see. Dozens of tiny, sand-cased caddis clung to the underside. He pinched one lightly and its green head emerged from its protective casing. "Amazing, isn't it?" he said. "If you dissect a fish, he'll be loaded with these things."

He placed the rock back into the stream. "This river may look sterile up here, like it's been scoured clean from the mountain run-off, but there's a whole other world alive in the water. You just need to look closely to see it." He took off his ball cap and scratched his head. "Remember how I told you to turn a fish upside down when you handled him?"

"Yeah," I said. "It works; they stop squirming."

"I learned that from an osprey. I was fishing the Snake years ago, and this osprey dove into the water ahead of me and took a big cutthroat. The first thing he did was to flip the fish upside down in his talons so he wouldn't drop him." James smiled at the memory. "He knew more about fishing than I did. The fish must have been sixteen inches. Anyway, you learn a lot when you really look. It's more than just having your eyes open."

"Well, my eyes are open, and I don't see any fish here," I said. I was leaning over a boulder trying to look into a pool next to the shore. "You think they're up this high on the river?"

James put his sunglasses on and peered into the water. "I don't know, but I would guess so. The thing is, they're hard to see. In the spring, rainbows from Boulder Creek, some seventy river miles away, slip down into the Yellowstone and then make their way up the Stillwater to spawn. Apparently, they like the cobbled bottom. But unless you see them move or feed, you might miss them. Their colors adapt to the changing environment; you'll notice that when you catch them. They look different. It's survival, you know, keeps them from getting picked off by herons and other birds."

I sat down on the boulder and looked downstream to where the water narrowed into a canyon. "I know all about blending in," I said. "And it is about survival."

James cocked his head and looked at me. "Yeah, I

suppose you do. But you don't exactly try to blend in, do you."

I reached behind and undid my ponytail. "No, not really. I used to, though. Guess I'm not so much like a trout."

"Well, in some ways, maybe you are," he said. "Remember, trout adapt and survive. They live in a pretty tough environment."

I looked down in the water and considered this. "Yeah, they are tough. I mean, at first you might not think so, but they put up with a lot." I stopped to think again. "So, you wanna break out the gear?"

He bent down and splashed some cold water on his face and then looked up at the sky. "Pretty bright, but what the hell else are we going to do? You don't have to twist my arm."

Once again, it took me a while to get used to the new water. Because it was so clear, I had a hard time judging its depth. Several times, in attempt to reach a pocket, I waded past my waist and had to wrestle with the current to keep my footing. I spent more time trying to figure out wading strategies than actually fishing.

James, on the other hand, was more adept at wading and was able to send out long, precise casts, reaching water I could only dream about. I finally gave up trying to reach the deep water and switched over to a grasshopper to work the banks. It made for easier fishing, but I wasn't able to catch anything. I was beginning to think the water was sterile when I looked up and saw James landing a fish. A few minutes later, he landed another one, so I walked downstream to see what flies he was using.

"Griffith's gnat," he shouted over the wind. "They're rising to midges!" He reeled up and walked over to the bank. "Those are my first two fish. I spent the last hour and a half throwing everything I've got with no luck. I finally saw a rise and played a hunch. They weren't that big, maybe twelve inches."

"I never saw a rise," I said.

"Me neither, until a few minutes ago. It's hard to see

rises in swifter water. Wanna call it for now and come back in the evening? We might get a good hatch then."

I was fine with that. I'd gotten pushed around by the water and was ready for a break.

We drove back to camp and lounged around. James got into the cooler, grabbed a few beers, and then walked down to the water to do some reading. I decided to take the truck and told James I was going to do some more scouting, but that was just an excuse. I felt like driving. I wanted some private time.

It was late afternoon, sunny and warm, so I changed into shorts and sandals, cranked the window down, and drove the gravel backroads. I found a CD by John Fogerty and turned the music up. I drove in the general direction of the Beartooth Mountains, taking in the landscape. It was breathtaking country, with its mountain plateaus covered in purple owl's clover and buttercups. Packs of mule deer were everywhere, casually grazing. They hardly looked at me as I drove by. Near the river, to the south, steep granite cliffs rose dramatically. In the sunlight, they had a reddish hue. It occurred to me, as I drove that gravel road, that I could live the rest of my life in this place and still not see it all.

I had lived most of my life in flat country, in places where possibility ended at the vanishing point of a two-lane highway. But out here, the world seemed infinite, the possibilities endless. Somewhere in those mountains, thick with lodge pole pine and spruce, lay grizzly, elk, and bighorn sheep. Out here, I could get lost. Out here, I was surrounded by mystery and majesty. I found myself wanting to live here, to make a stand in a place like this and call it home.

I knew, deep down, some of what I was feeling was romantic and not practical. I guess some of that comes with being young—the desire to have and hold everything. But, for the second time since the trip started, I experienced the elation of being truly alive. Although I could not have articulated it then, it was as much about hope and possibility as anything. These things were new to me at eighteen, and all I knew for sure at that time, as I drove

The Eddy

down the endless gravel road, was that I never wanted to be without them again.

I drove for hours that afternoon, listening to music, watching the scenery, breathing in the dust from the road. Nothing happened of note—just a kid in an old truck, listening to music on a mountain road. But when I returned to camp, I felt different, as if the world had somehow shifted.

I found James at the picnic table reading a biography of James Madison. He had another pot of stew hydrating in the sun. "Hey," I said, "I'm not sure how long you plan on being here, but I'd like to spend a night alone along the stream. Would you mind?"

He put down his book and looked at me. I think I surprised him. "Really?"

"No offense, I like your company, but I want to do this—if you don't mind."

"Mind? Hell no." He looked at up me and squinted. "I'd be happy to help with the details. Are you sure?"

"Yeah, I was thinking maybe a full day, twenty-four hours."

He got up and gave me a jab to the gut. "Damn, Toby, you keep surprising me. When do you want to do it?"

I looked at the sky and shrugged. "How about tomorrow?"

We fished next to each other that night, near the confluence of the Stillwater and Yellowstone. The scenery wasn't as pretty in the foothills, but the fishing was better. I used a bead head hare's ear and an emerging caddis and caught fish consistently. The biggest was seventeen inches. The fish were chunky and beautiful and fought with spirit. The bigger rainbows made a point of leaping out of the water during the fight and, when this happened, James would laugh out loud and yell, "Did you see that? Did you see that?" He was like a kid on the water. He never tired of it.

We stayed out until it was almost too dark to see, returning most of the way back to the truck with the aid of our headlamps. Both of us tripped several times in the darkness, and I managed to put a pretty good gash in my waders. Back at the truck, I showed him the damage. "Waders can always be repaired," he said, "but perfect nights of fishing are few and far between."

The Eddy

Chapter 22

We didn't get to camp until after 11:00 that evening, and we decided against a fire. In the morning, we'd each pack our gear and head out alone. I was excited for the challenge. I'd never spent a night alone outdoors.

That night, I dreamed of standing in the current, unable to move, while a bear slowly approached me from the shoreline. I jerked awake just as I was about to get clawed. I was in a sweat, not sure of where I was, and it took me a moment to get oriented. James was snoring softly. When my heart settled down, I took my headlamp and went outside to take a leak. I went to the far end of the camp near a cluster of trees and, just as I undid my pants, my light cut out. Sometime in the night, the clouds had moved in and it was so dark, I couldn't see my hand in front of my face. I banged my headlamp again and again against my thigh, but the light was dead. I was only fifty yards from the tent, so I didn't panic, but the thought of being out alone the next evening and having this happen was sobering. I made a mental note to check all my gear in the morning.

When I finished peeing, I walked in the direction of the tent, feeling my way in a crouched position with my hands out. Just as I thought I was getting close, I heard James crack a loud fart. It was twenty feet behind me and to my left. I was that far off. By the time I made it back to the tent, I did all I could do to not laugh out loud and wake James. I couldn't wait to wake up in the morning and tell him how his ass saved me.

As I suspected it would, the morning broke gray, with low clouds moving in from the northwest, shrouding the mountains in a hazy mist. I had some reservations about potentially bad weather, but James didn't seem fazed by it.

"Do you want the tent or the bivy?" he asked. "The bivy's lighter, but obviously isn't much for room."

I chose the bivy. "What if it starts raining hard?" I asked.

He shrugged. "Be prepared. Line your backpack, make sure you have your good knife, and take a back-up lighter. You'll be fine."

He went through my clothes, made sure I had only what I needed, and showed me how to set up the Whisper Light stove. He then packed my dinner, which consisted of three packs of ramen and some dehydrated stew meat and hot chocolate. I packed elk jerky and dried fruit for my lunch. All the food was stuffed into a large Ziploc baggie.

We drove to the river's halfway point above the town of Absarokee. It was eight in the morning and already drizzling.

"You might want to put your rain jacket on. You know what happens when you get wet. And take this." He threw me a small can of pepper spray. "You won't need it down this low, but we're talking grizzlies. You'll feel better having it."

I stuffed the canister in my front vest pocket. "If you don't mind, I'll go upstream. I'll probably go up about five to seven miles, depending on the fishing."

"You can't get lost if you stay near the river." He hoisted his pack on his back. "We'll meet back here about ten tomorrow morning. Try not to be late." He turned and walked away.

"Good luck," I yelled, but I don't think he heard me. I threw on my pack and started upstream. It would be two hours before I sat down and geared up for fishing.

The Stillwater above Absarokee had a different personality; broader, with the water braiding around small islands. Punctuated by long runs and slicks, it was difficult for me to figure out where to start. It all looked good. I decided to find the deepest water and any obstructions that would give fish a place to hide.

The Eddy

I chose a spot to camp along the river under an old aspen tree, figuring I would work upstream the rest of the day and make my way back in the evening so it would be a shorter walk out. I was eager to fish. I took my lunch out of the Ziploc bag and tossed it in my vest along with my water bottle, leaving everything else behind. Following the riverbank, I walked until I found a narrow spot in the river. On the outside bank, there were two large boulders with deep eddies behind them, perfect spots for big fish. Since nothing appeared to be rising, I tied on a caddis nymph with some heavy weight and started working the water.

For twenty minutes, I tried casting ahead of each boulder and mending my line so I could get a natural drift, but to no avail. The conflicting currents kept dragging my fly and I couldn't get it deep enough. I tried adding weight, but that made casting almost impossible. I should have conceded right there, but I just knew if I could get a good drift, I would land a few fish. The only reasonable solution to this puzzle was to cross the stream and fish from the other side, or wade further out so I could shorten my cast and control my line. I opted for the latter since it would mean less work. Or so I thought.

With my second step, the water was up past my waist. As I tried to widen my stance for support, the rocks below my left foot gave way and I did a half-split. For a brief moment, I held on, rod high in the air, feet spread, like a silhouette of a surrendering soldier.

And then the river exacted its punishment. Both feet lost what purchase they had, and I went completely under water. I held tight to the rod in one hand as I was swept downstream. With my free arm, I tried to keep myself afloat by staying on my back, but my waders filled so quickly with water, it was almost impossible. I began to sink. Thankfully, the run got shallower. After a horrifying twenty yards, I was able to roll over and touch bottom. Once I gained traction, I crawled out of the river and flopped down on shore. Gallons of water gushed from the top of my waders. Had the river not thinned out, I would've drowned.

I picked myself up, walked up the bank, stripped off my waders, and emptied the rest of the water. Somewhere in the event, I'd lost my sunglasses. I was stunned at how fast everything had happened. I kept staring at the river, which looked so benign from shore. I had underestimated the power of the current and made the mistake of not wearing a wading belt. And it almost cost me my life. For the third time in the past year and a half, I'd almost killed myself. It was becoming an unpleasant trend.

It didn't take long for the adrenaline rush to wear off and for the chill to set in. I needed warm clothes, so I began the soggy trek back to my pack. Once again, the shivers overtook me. I wasn't in peril, but I was disgusted with myself for being over-confident.

By the time I got back, I needed warmth. The dry clothes helped, but I was still shivering. Because I had not taken the time to gather firewood before I left, I was forced to scramble for wood. Had I returned in the night, this would've been more than a mild inconvenience.

After I warmed up with a fire, I set up my bivy and placed the dehydrated meat in water so it would reconstitute for my ramen stew. The whole episode took more than two hours, and it was another sobering lesson. I did not resume fishing until two that afternoon, and it was four p.m. before I caught my first fish, a whitefish on a deeply sunk nymph. It wasn't exactly what I envisioned when I set out in the morning with grandiose hopes.

The day was not a total loss, all lessons aside. By the evening, there was a caddis hatch, and I managed to catch a few respectable rainbows, and browns on dry flies skated across the surface. The rainbows were caught in remarkably thin water, while the browns seemed to hold in the deeper, classic spots. I made a mental note to ask James about it and continued to fish until it was too dark to see my fly on the water.

The long walk back to camp was made easier with the headlamp. I was grateful it was waterproof. James was right. Gear was important. But it didn't matter unless you

The Eddy

used it wisely.

That evening, I sat by the fire, exhausted but comfortable. I had hoped for a clear night, but the incessant misty rain made everything damp. I finally put on a stocking cap and crawled into the bivy next to the fire. There wasn't much room to move inside the sack, but it had a hoop at the top with netting so I could see outside, not that it mattered in the darkness.

For a long time, I listened to the pleasant sound of the river moving in the darkness. As lovely as rivers were, they could be frightening. Never again would I think of them in the same way. Never again would I allow them to lull me into a false sense of security. The Stillwater could babble innocently all night if it wanted to. I knew what it was really saying.

Just before I dozed off, it occurred to me that I was a sitting duck wrapped tightly in my bivy—or more like a large piece of *meat candy* in a wrapper. James said there wouldn't be grizzlies at this elevation, but I was tempted to put the pepper spray next to me. I was warm and cozy but, if I'd learned anything that day, it was better to be prepared. I crawled out of the sack, took my headlamp, and searched my vest for the spray. Sadly, it too was a victim of the river, lost somewhere in the water along with my sunglasses. If I was going to meet my demise that night at the claws of a bear, I would go out knowing the river could take you in more ways than one.

I woke with the sun, glad to see the weather had turned favorably sometime in the night. It was cool when I crawled out of the bivy. The coals from my fire were still smoldering, so I gathered some wood and in no time had a nice fire to warm me up.

I cleaned out my stew pot, added some water, and put a small baggie of wet coffee grounds in the water to steep. When the coffee had been boiling for five minutes, I pulled it from the fire and poured a cup of cold water in it to let the grounds settle. James had taught me the trick and I felt deeply satisfied with myself as I sat on a stump near the water, sipping my river coffee, letting the day come to me slowly.

A few fish rose as I was sitting there, but I could see nothing on or above the water to indicate a hatch. Although I was tempted to grab my rod and try a few casts from shore, the days were getting longer as we were nearing the solstice, and I felt no need to get greedy with time. I had all day.

I broke camp, making sure to douse my fire and clean the area so that it looked unused. It was another thing James always made a point to do, and it seemed like a good habit to develop. He was a conscientious camper and tried to live by the *leave no trace* ethic as much as he could. He went out of the way to clean up after other people, whether at a campsite or on the river. He never asked me to do the same; he just assumed I would.

On my way back to the truck, I saw my first bear. From the distance, it looked like a large, black root wad near the river. And then I saw it move. It was a black bear and, when it saw me, it bolted into the tree line and disappeared, apparently more afraid of me than I was of it. I was impressed by its speed. Although black bears seldom attack humans, I made a note to purchase some pepper spray as soon as I could. One thing was obvious; there was no way I could outrun a bear if I needed to.

James was waiting for me at the truck, standing in his underwear and applying a large bandage below his knee. He looked up at me as I approached and smiled. "Took a tumble this morning," he said. "Goddamn turkey came out of its roost and startled me. Did a header and ripped up my knee on a downed tree. How'd you do?"

I told him about my day and then filled him in on my swim. He was quiet for a while.

"You know," he said, "I can't be expected to think of everything. You should've worn a wading belt. When you're on your own, you can't afford screw-ups. Try not to die on my watch, okay."

The Eddy

I was taken aback by his lack of empathy, but I shouldn't have been. He was nothing if not emotionally unpredictable. "I'll do my best," I said. "I'm piling on the lessons."

James slid into his pants and then loaded the truck with our gear. "You know, Hemingway was right," he said. "He was right about a lot of things, especially about doing things the right way as opposed to the easy way. And he was right about the cost of being a participant." James patted the gauze on his knee. "You remember that. There's a price to be paid, eh."

"I guess so," I said. The reference was still a bit vague to me. I crawled into the cab of the truck and leaned back. "I forgot to ask. Did you catch fish?"

James rustled around in the back of the truck and came back with a wet heavy bag. "Check it out." He held up a half-dozen whitefish.

"What the... Why?"

"Gonna smoke 'em today. They're supposed to be good. You'll see. Natives eat them all the time."

"Oh, boy," I said. "I hope you know what you're doing."

"Haven't a fucking clue. Just always wanted to try it."

I laughed. "Mind if I'm not a *participant* in this one?"

"Of course," he said, straight-faced. The ambiguity was not lost on me.

For the first time since we'd left St. Paul, we did not fish that day. Instead, we went back to camp and cleaned the whitefish, cutting them into thin strips and placing them above a small fire, which we fed with live pine boughs to add smoke and flavor. We read books, cleaned our fly lines, and patched our waders. Late in the afternoon, James took out his tying gear and gave me a beginning lesson on fly tying. Mostly we worked on nymph patterns and soft hackle flies, since we tended to lose more of them. It was a laid-back day, with lots of talk of fishing and planning for the rest of the week. Throughout the day, we tended to the fire and played with spice combinations. On some fish we put lemon pepper, on others a hot Cajun spice, and on a few we added just salt and pepper. Toward evening, as the fish shriveled, James basted them with olive oil.

By sunset, we deemed the fish ready to eat, so we made a pot of rice and beans and opened another bottle of Happy Camper Chardonnay to toast our experiment. Neither of us had tested the fish throughout the day, so there was a great deal of anticipation.

"Here's to living in the moment," James said, and he lifted his glass.

"Here's to the underappreciated whitefish," I added. James grabbed a piece with lemon pepper and I took one with Cajun. We both chewed deliberately, not wanting to make a judgment until we were ready.

When I finished, I cleansed my palate with a sip of wine and grinned broadly. "Now, that," I said, "is outstanding. I had my doubts, but I'm impressed. Not too fishy or oily, slightly chewy, absolutely delicious."

James nodded in agreement and sampled a Cajun piece. "You know, I also had my doubts. If you can believe it, not everything I try works out. I've just gained a new respect for the mountain whitefish. Perhaps we should try carp next."

I scooped a big helping of rice and beans and piled them on my plate. "You're on your own there. At least whitefish are pretty, other than their mousy lips. Carp are downright homely."

"So are halibut. But no one complains about their taste."

I looked up at him as I took a mouthful of food. "Are you comparing halibut to carp? Because if you are, this conversation just took a radical turn toward stupid."

James laughed. "Yeah, that is pretty dumb. I guess carp are out, at least for now."

I raised my glass again. "Here's to hoping we're never that desperate."

We stayed at the Stillwater for another seven days, covering much of its thirty-six miles. In general, the fishing was good in the mornings and evenings, but slow in the afternoons. As the summer progressed, the weather warmed, and we took to taking long breaks during the middle of day. At one point, we took a trip into Billings to resupply our reading material, and I bought a half-dozen fly fishing magazines and a collection of essays on fishing that James had recommended. Since we were in town, I took the opportunity to give Mom a call. She sounded good.

"You seeing anyone these days?" I asked her. There was a pause on the line.

"Sort of. A nurse at work. He's a little younger than me, a real health nut." She laughed. "Can you believe he's got me into running? I've lost five pounds."

"You look great, Mom. You don't need to lose weight." It was rhetorical, but I meant it. "What have you got *him* into?"

She thought about it for a moment. "Old movies, I guess. Maybe red wine."

"Mom, don't forget about you, okay? How much younger?"

She laughed again. "Ten years. That's not so much, is it?"

"Of course not. As long as you're happy."

I could hear her take a deep breath. "You know, Toby, even if things go south, it's still worth it, you know."

I couldn't help but smile. "Yeah, Mom, I've heard that before... And thanks for being a good mom."

Her voice cracked. "You're going to make me cry. Everything okay with you?"

"Couldn't be better. I'm figuring a few things out." I imagined her smiling on the other end.

"Well, be safe out there, Toby. Don't take any chances."

I thought of my swim the other day. "Of course, Mom. I'm not into taking chances."

She laughed. I think she knew more than she let on. She wrapped up by telling me she loved me and all that other stuff that moms are obligated to say. She ended with,

"I'm glad you're learning something."

Driving back to camp, I started to think about what exactly I was learning. It was hard to put into words, but it had a lot to do with *doing*. It made me think of Winiski, who understood that education needed to be tactile and relevant. I asked James about it later that day.

"How come more teachers don't make their stuff relevant?"

He was sitting at the picnic table tying a complicated wrap on a parachute fly. He didn't say anything for a while. Finally, he took off his cap, rubbed his eyes and gave me a quizzical look. "What brought that question on?"

"I don't know," I said. "I was just thinking about Winiski, her style of teaching. That and how much time I've wasted in classrooms."

"I'd rather not talk about teaching," he said. He went back to tying.

"Okay," I said. "But in case you're wondering, I think of you as an excellent teacher. And I'm not the only one."

"Look," he said, irritated by the subject. "I'm not wondering. And I don't consider myself an excellent teacher. At best, I'm above average. Sometimes a bit better, on my good days." He finished his last wrap on the fly and looked at me. "The thing is, I'm like that major league hitter who's a lifetime .280 guy and every now and then goes on a tear for a few weeks and carries the team. I just can't keep it up for long. The game is too tough for me. I can't hit the junk-ballers. Administrators are the junk-ballers. They throw that sloppy knuckleball shit at you and screw you up for weeks. The great ones can ignore that stuff. Me? I just get pissed off and flail at it and end up on my ass."

I opened a warm cream soda and shook my head. "Guess I'll stay clear of that topic." I waited for another response, but James put another hook in the vise and began a new fly. I finally gave up and went for a walk.

The Eddy

Chapter 23

We left the Stillwater on the first of July, deciding it was time to cross over into Wyoming and visit Cody and the Shoshone River. We'd been on the road over a month and were beginning to get that leathery look from living outside in the sun and wind. James was deeply tanned on his arms, neck and face, and it looked to me like he'd lost a few pounds.

I was eating like a horse, but I noticed some weight loss as well. On any given day, we'd likely hike ten miles and stand in rough currents up to our thighs for hours on end. I'd yet to grow tired of it, and I liked the fact that every day had some physical and mental challenge. My life to this point hadn't been exactly sedentary, but it was nothing compared to this. Each day was interesting out here. Each day, I could measure success or failure. I didn't want the summer to end. I didn't want to go back to where the days were something to endure.

In Cody, we stopped at the North Fork Fly Shop for supplies and information. Fishing was excellent on the lower Shoshone right in town, and word was the north fork of the river, which led into the east entrance of Yellowstone, was producing nicely. We were cautioned about grizzlies up there, so I made a point to buy another canister of pepper spray, along with a new pair of sunglasses.

As James gathered his usual information, I wandered over to a huge 3-dimensional map of the region, stretched across a table next to a rack of expensive wading boots. All the rivers on the map were highlighted, crisscrossing wildly through mountain ranges and high plains. The map showed the lower Shoshone as a tailwater, spilling out of Buffalo Bill dam, a few miles above town. From the dam, the river carved its way through a deep canyon on the north side of Cody and then continued its flow eastward through the town of Powell, some forty miles away. Eventually, the river hooked up with the Big Horn, and from there, as I ran my finger along its length, it took me back to After Bay in Montana.

Looking at the map, I started to think about how since the trip began I'd had the feeling of drifting, as if somehow I was moving westward against the prevailing winds, without a point of reference and any feel for the vast geography. To be honest, I liked the sensation, the feeling that the world stretched out before me endlessly. But it was clear to see that everything *did* eventually connect, in some way or another, that even the vastness of this country had its limitations. Sure, I could stand alone in some isolated river, feeling happily removed from the rest of the world, but I was always a part of something bigger, whether I wanted to acknowledge it or not. And I wasn't entirely sure how that made me feel.

I was standing there, thinking about all of this, when James slipped out back to test an expensive Winston rod. When he returned, I saw the owner ring up the sale. I was shocked. It was almost seven hundred bucks, and a six-weight to boot, which he already had. When we got back into the truck, James handed me the rod. "Give it a shot today. Let me know what you think."

"This thing is worth almost as much as your truck," I said. "How can you afford this?" I took it out of its case and admired it. It was a four-piece beauty with a German silver uplock and burl maple spacer. "I'd be afraid to use it."

"Look," he said, "just use it. It's only money. I have no mortgage or rent, and I drive a crappy truck. I spend money on that albatross of a car back home or on trips like this, so it's no big deal, okay? It's windy today and you need to work on your casting, so enjoy. It's light enough to keep you from blowing out your shoulder. Enough said."

With the new rod in hand, I could hardly wait to see

The Eddy

what I could do, but before going down to the river, James pulled into a motel and reserved a room. He figured we'd earned a good shower and a bed, and it would give us an opportunity to go out in the evening for a burger after a long day on the water. The shower, in particular, sounded good. I'd noticed lately my waders were starting to give off some funny smells. They were labeled as "breathable," but I think that term was loosely used.

From the motel, we drove a few blocks to the edge of town and parked in a lot overlooking the Shoshone. It was windy, and as I got out of the truck, my hat blew off. I chased it down and walked over to the edge of the parking lot, looking down into the canyon below. From high above, it was easy to see all the good holding water, the runs and riffles, the deeper-colored pocket water. I made a mental map of the good spots, knowing once I made my way down to the water, everything would look different. James came over and stood beside me with a cold beer in his hand. He didn't say anything. He just stood there, smiling, taking in the view.

The first twenty miles of the lower Shoshone is considered blue ribbon fishing, with large Bonneville cutthroat, rainbows, and browns. James had fished it many times and assured me it was worth our effort, although I thought it strange fishing in the heart of the town. The saving grace was that we were in a gorge. Once we were down at the water, other than the muffled sound of a truck now and then, it felt like we were miles from people, which was always a good thing. It wasn't the prettiest spot we'd worked, with its steep, soft banks and scrub flora. But the water itself was lovely, with a slightly aqua color.

The rocky shoreline and steep banks made wading difficult, but, as soon as I landed the first fish, it was just a minor distraction. With the Winston rod, I was able to reach water I couldn't before. A light, fast action rod can do that. I felt like a pro, if only for a short time. I caught the first fish, an eighteen-inch cutthroat. James came over to take a picture.

"Geez, it's beautiful," he said, admiring its buttery color. He had me hold the fish away from me toward the camera. "You might want to blow this picture up. It's an important first."

"Hooked him on one of those soft hackles you tied." I placed the fish into the water and moved him back and forth in the current until he recovered. "Geez, this rod is something. It throws some serious line." I pointed to a rock in the middle of the river. "I got it all the way out there. Guess the rod really matters."

"A little bit," he said. "But you're just getting better. Your casting doesn't waste as much energy. Notice it's a ten-footer. I bought it longer for rivers like this. Helps you to roll cast against these banks and high-stick through the pockets."

I couldn't help but grin. Not only did I know what he was talking about, but I could actually do those things. I understood those arcane words and phrases and, for the first time in my life, I felt like part of a fraternity. Sure, it was only a loosely affiliated group of people who liked to stand in moving water waving a stick, but I was part of it.

Later, as I was getting into the rhythm of casting, I got to wondering why it was that I'd never been part of any group. I'd spent my life always on the outside looking in. Lately, I'd managed to put my past away, assuming most of the pain and anger—the suicide debacle, all of it, was simply the result of coming to terms with who I was. But maybe that was too simple an answer.

As I continued upriver, enjoying the power of that fine rod and the challenges of new water, it occurred to me that I had never allowed myself to fail. Not really. I couldn't have articulated it then, but what I was coming to understand was a large part of my life had been about avoiding the tough water. But it was the people I admired most who plied those waters. Mom did it with relationships and a big heart, thinking she could make a man better; Winiski did it by going against convention and investing in the discarded; James did it by defying the system and

The Eddy

defining his own set of standards. And Takeita? Hell, she practically swam in it. And yet all of them failed consistently. They all got hurt.

I can't recall exactly how my epiphany took form that day, but I remember sitting on the bank of the Shoshone on a sunny July mid-afternoon thinking about that new rod and what it meant. I remember knowing with certainty it wasn't the rod that made me better. What made me better was where I was willing to go. From that point on, I knew I would be a different kind of fisherman. What that meant in terms of my life, I had only a vague notion. But whatever it meant, there was no going back.

The day on the middle fork of the Shoshone was the best day of fishing I'd had so far. Not only had I out fished James in numbers, but I caught bigger fish. He actually stopped fishing at one point and sat on the bank to see what I was doing. I wasn't in his league, but, when we were walking out that evening, I stopped and looked at him. "Remember when you said that in baseball even the Royals can beat the Yankees?"

He shook his head in disgust and then laughed. "Indeed, I do."

"Well, today I was George Brett, hitting that homer against the Yanks. I'm going to enjoy it for as long as I can."

"You deserve it," he said. "I was impressed. But tomorrow, if you have another day like this, I'm checking for illegal pine tar."

That evening, we went to the South Fork Tavern for dinner. It was a western-themed bar in the heart of Cody, and it was renowned for its burgers. It felt nice not to have to prepare a dinner or worry about a campsite being set up correctly. James ordered a Red Lodge microbrew and I sipped on a Coke, watching the people come through the doors on a Friday night, all gussied up. It didn't take long to figure out who was a local and who was a tourist on his way to Yellowstone.

James looked around the bar and said, "Start with the cowboy boots and work your way up. That'll tell you all you need to know."

As he said this, an '80s song by Journey started blasting from the jukebox, and I could see James cringe. "Jesus Christ," he said. "You can bet a local didn't play that shit." He got up and went to the jukebox with a stack of dollar bills. He was on a mission.

While he was shoving bills into the jukebox, a woman with long dark hair and cowboy boots came up behind him and put her hands on his ass. He turned, there was a short exchange, and the woman hugged him. I hadn't seen that coming.

James came back to the table with the woman and introduced her. "Toby, this is Amanda, a good friend of mine." He pointed to me. "Amanda, Toby."

We shook hands and they sat down. She was a pretty woman, perhaps thirty years old, with dark skin and high cheekbones. She looked half Indian. She wore an untucked denim shirt with faded, tight-fitting jeans. She was on the taller side, and I suppose she had the sort of body and look that would make men of all ages turn their head.

Amanda was a nurse at the local hospital and that was where she had met James. He limped through the doors late one night with an excessively swollen left knee and needed to find out if he'd damaged it again. He had fallen earlier that day while fishing, but instead of stopping, he fished the rest of the day. By the time he got back to his truck in the dark, he could barely walk.

"He was hurtin'," Amanda said. "His knee was only badly sprained, but I made him sit in one of the waiting rooms with his knee packed in ice until the swelling went down. When I finished my shift, I went to check on him. He was lying on the floor with his knee elevated, snoring. It was kinda cute. Anyway, before I left, he asked me out for a beer. I figured he was harmless. If he got too fresh, I knew I could always outrun him." She looked over at him and winked. "We've kinda had this long-distance thing going on ever since. I keep telling him he's going to have to move out here or one day he's going to show up and I'll be introducing him

The Eddy

to my husband."

James listened to all of this and I could tell it made him a little uneasy.

"How long you guys known each other?" I asked.

Amanda answered before James could speak. "We met six years ago. I remember because it was the day before I turned twenty-five."

James looked over at Amanda and said, "Toby is one of my former students. He knows Maggie pretty well."

Amanda looked at me for a moment with a blank expression, and then it dawned on her. "Well, I've never met her, but I understand she's a fine woman."

"I'm going to find a cash machine," James said, and stood up. He was looking at the floor as he walked away.

"Well," Amanda said, turning her attention back to me. "I feel a bit awkward."

I looked at her and said, "Not me. I don't give a shit if you guys were hooking up before he was divorced. That's none of my business. I guess I'm just curious if you knew he was married."

Amanda cocked her head and looked away. "You're pretty forward, but, yes, I knew. He never lied to me. I knew when he got divorced too. Guess I figured he'd be coming my way after that, but he never did, at least for a long time. How well do you know Maggie?" she asked.

I was trying to read her, but she was tough to gauge. She seemed comfortable in her skin. "I know her fairly well. I like her a lot. I respect her," I said.

She put her elbow on the table, rested her chin in her hand, and looked at me for a while. She was smiling slightly. I had the sense she was trying to see if she could make me look away, break me with some quiet feminine display of power. I just stared back at her, waiting. Finally, she let out a low, soft chuckle and said, "I get it."

I didn't say a word. I just kept looking at her.

"You Indian, Toby?"

"Nope."

She kept looking at me as if she didn't believe me.

"Toby, are you like this a lot? Pissed, I mean."

"I didn't know I was pissed."

She took a swig of beer and pointed her bottle at me. "I admire your loyalty. It's noble. Not enough of that in this world." She smiled. "Toby, do you think it's possible to love more than one person at a time, romantically speaking?"

I shrugged. "I don't know. Why do you ask?" I kept looking at her. She had this oddly serene look. "I guess so, why?"

"Because I think Mitch did. I'm not saying whether it was right. That's not my call. I'm just saying it was real. And love makes you vulnerable. It makes you do things you never thought you were capable of."

"What about lust? That makes you vulnerable too," I said.

She leaned back in her chair and let out a hearty laugh. "Honey, you are *too* much. Lust makes you careless; love makes you vulnerable. There's a difference. I need to buy you a drink."

"I'm not of age," I said flatly.

She kept laughing. "Oh, yes, you are. You're older than that." She bought me a Budweiser, which I really hate. I sat there and peeled the label.

"So, you didn't answer me. Are you like this a lot? Angry, I mean." Her eyes continued to read me. "It's just life, you know."

I looked at her a long time, again trying to get a read on her. She never once turned from my gaze. What I wanted to say, what I wished I'd have said was, *Well, it's like this, Amanda—My mom loved a lot of men. I mean that in a good way. But men never loved her back in the way she deserved. They cheated on her all the time. Sometimes it was other women, sometimes it was with things like motorcycles. But they never gave her what she deserved, which was their full attention. So I'm awfully sorry, but you remind me of something that makes me feel ill. And don't tell me it's just life. That's too damn easy and lets everyone off the hook.*

But I didn't have the words at the time, or if I did, I

The Eddy

certainly couldn't form them. Instead, I said, "I'm really not angry. I don't get angry much anymore. I guess I'm just surprised."

James returned with two beers and a large Coke. He settled next to Amanda, and I could tell she liked his proximity.

"We were just talking about Maggie," she said.

James looked at her and didn't say anything. I had to admire her. Bold, brash, confident, pretty. She put the elephant right on the table so there was no looking past it. "So, tell me all about the fishing," she said.

I stuck around long enough to be polite and down a burger, but eventually, the conversation left me in the distance. As I got up to leave, I said, "I'm assuming you can catch a lift back, James. If I don't see you until the morning, well—I won't wait up." I grabbed the truck keys off the table and nodded toward Amanda. "I enjoyed meeting you. Thanks for the beer."

Amanda squeezed past James, stood up, and shook my hand again. With her back to James, she said quietly, "Watch out for him."

"Sure," I said.

As I was walking out, I had to laugh. There were two ways you could take that statement.

When I got back to the room, I called Mom. I wanted to talk. I wanted to tell her how much I loved her. But I got the answering machine instead. Her message was bright and cheerful, not exactly what I was looking for. I expressed my love to the machine and then considered calling Maggie. Bad idea. I hung up the phone before it could ring and instead called Takeita. It was great to hear her voice. We spoke for over an hour, laughing it up pretty good, all on James' dime.

Joe Paatalo

The Eddy

Chapter 24

James did not return until the early morning. I was still asleep, so he crawled in bed and I let him get a few hours of shut eye. By nine, I was packing and making a lot of noise. I watched him as he crawled out of bed and dragged himself into the shower. He hardly said a word. We didn't speak until we were a half-hour out of Cody. "Did you know she was going to be there?" I asked.

"Yeah, I was pretty sure. I hadn't given her a specific date, but I thought she might be there." He yawned. "We've known each other for a while."

"Yeah," I said. "Six years."

He looked at me, started to say something, then turned back to the road.

"Cause I got the feeling you'd been sleeping with her for a long time. I'm not that good at math, but—"

"I know where you're going," James said tersely. "And you can quit counting on your fingers."

We drove in silence for a while. Finally, I asked, "Why did you do it?" I could see I'd hit a nerve. The tendons on his neck were dancing. He kept staring straight ahead at the road.

"Shit happens," he said. "It just happens."

I wasn't satisfied. "That's a bumper sticker, not an answer. How could you do that to Maggie?"

He turned and glared at me. He was pissed. "It's none of your damn business... You know, you keep mining for answers, as if digging deeper, you'll find something. But sometimes the further you dig, all you find are more questions. There is no answer."

I turned away and looked out the window. I couldn't

help but think of Maggie. "I wouldn't have done it," I mumbled.

James slammed his hand on the steering wheel and I jumped. "Don't be so fucking self-righteous!" he shouted. "What the hell do you know anyway? Huh?"

"You don't need to be an asshole about it," I said.

James took a deep breath and pinched the bridge of his nose. "Yeah, well, I am an asshole." He turned toward me. He had the look of someone chewing on sand. "But before you get too self-assured, be careful of absolutes. They'll bite you in the ass."

I felt like saying more, but I knew better. He was wrong about one thing for sure, though. There was an answer. He just didn't want to face it.

Not long after that, James seemed to slink back into his dark place again, and I guess it was to be expected. He wasn't mean around camp or on the river; on the contrary, he was quite pleasant. But he was detached in a way that made me feel he was not all there. I'd seen shades of it before, and it didn't bother me. I figured I had opened an old wound, and it would take time before the scar tissue would form again.

What was odd, though, was that he stopped fishing. Most days, he would join me on the river, but he spent a lot of time reading on the bank, messing with his equipment, or just sitting silently. He would move up or down the river with me, occasionally fish a hatch, and then drive back to camp early while I fished the remainder of the day.

We camped along Highway 19, which followed the length of the river all the way to the east entrance of the park. The river was accessible at all times. Unlike the middle fork below the dam, the north fork was spectacular, with its high red cliffs, pines that clung to the mountainside, and its astonishing array of fishing opportunities. It held runs, riffles, pocket water, bend pools, glides, and slicks—almost every variety of water you could fish. Our first camp was near the town of Wapiti, and every day or so, we would move up the river to a new site, each one prettier than the

The Eddy

last.

The fishing was excellent, with lots of fish in the twelve-to-sixteen-inch range. I caught them easily, so, after I'd land a few in the morning, I found myself fishing the more challenging water. Some of it was beyond my skill level, but I would try it for a while, making mental notes of what I needed to do better, and then go back to less challenging water before I shot my confidence.

One day, as we were walking upstream, we came across a man and his son fishing a nice-looking pool. The man appeared to be in his forties. The boy was maybe ten. Normally, we'd walk around people as silently as possible and move well upriver, but for some reason, James approached them. "How's the fishing?" he called out.

The man turned and waved. "A little slow," he said. "But we're having fun."

The boy was sitting on a rock trying to untangle a knot in his line. He didn't look like he was having fun. "Want some help?" I asked the boy. He looked up at me and then looked at his dad. "Sure," he said.

He held a nine-foot, five-weight St. Croix rod, pretty decent equipment for a kid. He was fishing a stonefly nymph with a chunk of split shot. Somehow, they had become hopelessly entangled.

"We'll just cut this off and re-tie," I said. "Do you know the surgeon's knot?"

James and the man were chatting. "I'm not too good," the man said. "Charlie and I are sort of learning together. We're from Missouri. Mostly we spincast for bass and panfish, but since we were coming out here, we wanted to fly fish. We practiced a little on ponds before we left, but it's different out here."

"Having some problems with the wind?" James asked.

"God, yes. We pretty much quit fishing in the afternoon."

James looked at the man's gear. He had a Scott five-weight, a good rod. "You've got enough rod there, although a six-weight might be better if you're new to this. I can show you a few things that might help if you want."

The guy was all for it.

James proceeded to show him how to read the wind and use it to his advantage when loading the rod. He showed him how to lower his profile and haul the line. Within twenty minutes, James had corrected the guy's glaring problems. Afterward, he walked over to where I was standing with the kid, who was struggling with everything.

"Charlie," he said, "can I show you something?" He pointed to a barely submerged rock in the river. "I just know there's a fish behind it." James grabbed a pebble and flipped it about five feet in front of the spot. "If you put your fly right there, I know you'll catch one."

James took a small piece of split shot and put it above the one I'd put on. "Trust me," he said. "Charlie needs to go a little deeper."

Charlie struggled with the casting, but eventually, he got one where it needed to be. His dad was standing there with us, and I know the poor kid felt pressure. As the fly drifted past the spot, it hesitated slightly in the current. "Lift your rod," James said calmly.

Charlie did as told and the line tightened with a fish. I thought his dad was going to crap his pants, he was so excited. James said nothing, preferring to let father and son scramble around on the shore, Dad yelling encouragement and boy doing all he could to get the loose line on the reel. Finally, as the exhausted fish came toward shore, Dad plunged into the river with his enormous bass net and started flailing at the water. After an excruciating two minutes, he managed to net the fish. Downstream. How they managed to catch that poor thirteen-inch rainbow was nothing short of a miracle. I looked at James just as the dad was lifting the fish out of the water. He wore expression of extreme relief.

We stayed for another fifteen minutes, taking pictures of Charlie with his fish in various poses. Dad finally joined in and we took a few more pictures. It was clear the

The Eddy

poor fish was not going to be released, which was fine. James knew it before me, and I saw him dispatch the fish as soon as he could by breaking its neck. It was an act of mercy. The fish had been handled and dropped so much, I had the feeling its last piscatorial thought was something akin to *Thank God.*

As we walked away, I said to James, "That might be the most nerve-wracking five minutes of fishing I will ever experience in my life."

He chuckled. "I wouldn't doubt it. That poor fish died for a noble cause. That kid and his dad will remember that for the rest of their lives."

"Do you think they'll catch any more fish?"

James burst out laughing. "God, I hope not."

That night around the fire, James talked about the things we normally talked about after a day on the stream. He seemed to be coming out of the black hole, so I was careful not to say anything that might get him riled. Just before we crawled into the tent, he looked at me and said, "You know, I really liked that kid today. I sometimes wish I had a son." It was as close to regret as anything I'd ever heard from him.

By the fifth day on the North Fork, James was back to his old self and fishing as hard as ever. We were high up on the river, not far from the entrance to the park. James was having a blast throwing terrestrials near the banks. He had a beetle on top and a black ant below it as a dropper. He let the ant sink, and it seemed more often than not the fish took the submerged fly.

I was fishing nymphs, occasionally catching a fish here and there, but I got tired of watching James catch fish after fish. I finally switched over to a similar rig, and things picked up considerably. Neither of us caught anything of size—the biggest was maybe seventeen inches—but we caught fish on every fifth or sixth cast.

Late in the afternoon, we were sitting on the bank eating bagels, when James turned to me and said, "I think we've pounded these fish enough. Let's give this river a rest and go fish the Green."

"And skip the park?" I asked.

"No, we'll drive through it, around the big lake, and then drop south through Jackson Hole and then over to Pinedale. I'll show you on a map."

"Good fishing along the way?"

"Great fishing. Lots of famous water. Let's play it cool and see where the wind takes us. The park in July will be packed, though, so let's just head in the direction of the Green and see what happens."

I liked the idea of having a loose plan, something that was fluid and could change at any moment. I found that I did not miss my watch and did not care what day it was. In fact, all I knew for sure was that it was early July. I started to wonder how many people would ever experience such a thing, to be free from the constraints of time. The notion seemed almost un-American, suggesting laziness or lack of productivity. I remember in Kansas hearing the phrase *Indian Time* in reference to someone who was out of step and couldn't keep beat with the rest of the world. Well, good for them, I thought. Maybe what Indians understood better than anyone was that time could be measured in more ways than the turning of hands on a clock.

The park was every bit as beautiful and crowded as James said it would be. There are so few roads in the park that they easily get congested. As frustrating as this was, I decided it was a good thing, since I knew what the building of more roads would lead to. It was, in the larger scope of things, no more than a minor inconvenience. We didn't have a schedule to keep.

After driving several hours, we stopped at the famous Fishing Bridge and stared down at thousands of big trout finning in the slow current. It looked like a hatchery. A recent mayfly hatch had left lots of dead flies on the underside of the bridge's railings, so I scooped them up and dropped them in the water, one by one. From above, I could see how the trout moved to feed. They'd come up, sip the dead fly, and then drop back into the depths for protection.

The Eddy

The sky was bright, so it made sense to me. But the fish were so casual about the dining experience, I got to wondering whether I was seeing the real deal or the equivalent of circus-trained trout who were accustomed to being fed.

A young guy standing close to me remarked, "Damn, I wish it was legal to fish here. I hear it used to be."

I smiled to myself. No way in hell would I fish here, even if I could. It wouldn't be right.

After leaving the park that day, we crossed over the Continental Divide and camped near the little town of Moran. I suggested we keep on driving, but James didn't want to drive through the mountain passes at night. I was eager to get to the Green, and I attributed that to my experience on the bridge. There was something about looking at big fish that was titillating. I asked James that night whether he still got as excited about fishing as he did when he first took it up. He thought about it for a long time.

"Yes and no," he finally said. "When I was younger, I used to fish harder, cover more ground. It was like I was always having a contest with myself to see what I could accomplish that day. It was thrilling in the way that new things can be. I suppose it's like the start of a new relationship, where there's almost a physical ache to it, partly out of desire, partly out of curiosity."

We were at a small public campground, not far from the Grand Tetons, and even in July, the mountain air was crisp. I threw another piece of wood on the fire. James continued, "But you reach a point where you begin to see there's a lot you've been missing in your zeal. That it's about more than catching fish because more fish can't sustain you. So you either step back and rethink your approach, or you quit altogether and find something else, anything that will provide you with what you think you've lost."

James reached into his daypack and uncorked his bottle of scotch. He took a swallow from the bottle and shivered. "Nothing like scotch in the high mountains on a cool evening." He wiped his lips. "Anyway, to answer your question, I still love fly fishing, perhaps more than I should.

But I love it like a long-time lover, I guess. I still have the desire for her, but it's a different kind of desire. Often, it's enough just to know she's there, if that makes sense."

"I think so," I said. "I mean, I get the analogy and all."

"Well, it might be a tortured analogy, I'm not sure. It's been a long day. But I know a few old souls who have been fishing for a lot longer than I have, and they've said, in one way or another, that in the end it's not even about the fish."

I shook my head. "Hmm, sounds more like the loss of—" I couldn't remember the word.

"—Libido?" James asked.

"Uh, no. I was thinking along the lines of mental faculties, but I like 'libido.' That's like sex drive, right? It's kind of consistent with your tortured metaphor."

James took another pull of scotch and shook his head. He was amused. "You know, you have this habit of asking these real complicated questions. And, at first, I thought you were sincerely interested in what I had to say. But now I understand you do it to torture me."

"I was wondering when you'd figure that out," I said. I flipped a coal at him and got up for the tent. "See you in the morning." I was bushed.

James sat around the fire until it started burning down. Occasionally, I heard him laugh out loud, which was weird. Finally, he said, "Hey, wake up. I've got a new extended metaphor for you."

"I can't wait to hear it," I said. "In the morning."

Chapter 25

The next day, we drove down Highway 191 toward Jackson Hole, admiring the mountain scenery. James used words like *dramatic* and *humbling*, which was true, but it was more than that. I kept thinking about the mystery of mountains, how I never knew what was beyond the next ridge or what the next pass would reveal. I began to understand what those mountain men must have felt as they traversed this country for the first time, not knowing what lay ahead, the possibilities both titillating and frightening at the same time. Landscape is powerful in that way. I could understand why some of them never left the mountains, and it made me wish I didn't have to go to school. I, too, could wander the mountains, maybe find a job out here guiding or working in a fly shop. It sounded better than the routine of school.

But I knew I had money committed to me, and I couldn't turn that down. I was obligated. The more I thought about it, the more depressed I became. I guess part of it was my old fear of failure and exposure, that if I went to school in Oregon and couldn't hack it, I'd let people down. I could talk all I wanted about having the courage to try hard and fail, but it was easier said than done.

When we got to Jackson Hole, we visited another fly shop for the latest fishing recommendations. The place was called the Hoback Hut, and it had a beautiful electric cutthroat trout above its front door. The old guy behind the counter looked like he'd spent his share of time on the water. He seemed happy to be there. I assumed he was the owner.

He went into his routine right away. It must have felt like a recording to him. "The Snake is fishing well right now, good flow for drifting. She's down a bit, on account of lack of rain, but fishin' good. Caddis and Yellow Sallies or a 12-to-14 Adams for dries. Standard big stones for nymphing."

"And the Hoback?" James asked.

"Down a bit, but good for wading. Nice cutthroat river, as you know. Fish aren't as big, but they're pretty as can be. What are you guys interested in?"

"Mainly getting off the beaten track," James said. He was gathering some flies and putting them in a plastic cup. He didn't need them, but it was customary to buy flies if you were asking for information. "We're not so interested in the standard fare."

"How long you boys been out?"

I imagine we looked a little ripe. James shrugged. "I don't know, I guess it's been six weeks."

"No kidding," the old guy said. I could tell he was impressed. "And how long you got?"

James looked at me. "Another three weeks, maybe a bit more."

The guy stuck his hand out. "Name's Frank. Used to own this place but gave it to my son. Just like to fill in now and then."

We both shook his hand. "Tell you what," he said. "If you promise not to tell anyone, I'll show you a stretch of water that most people don't know of. It'll take a few hours of hiking, but I think you'll like it. You guys look like you can keep a secret and might appreciate a robust walk."

James grinned. "Frank, you know men of character when you see them. And I just remembered I needed some new fly lines."

The guy took out his personal map and showed us the spot. I wish like hell I could've photocopied the whole thing. It looked to be at least thirty years old. It was creased and stained and marked up in a code only he could decipher. It was worthy of framing. He took a pencil and pointed out a tributary to a tributary to the Snake. "Most people don't fish it because it looks a little thin. But if you're willing to walk a ways, it opens up into some gorgeous water.

The Eddy

Occasionally," he added with a wink, "some of the monsters of the Snake work their way up there, especially this time of the summer when things heat up a bit."

James made a few notes on the shop's generic map of the area. "And how is the Green fishing, around Pinedale?" he asked.

"Not sure," Frank said. "Haven't heard much." He carefully folded the map and put it away. "Lot of folks like to hit the big water around here where everyone else is, but I like your thinking. Last I heard, the flow was good, but that was over a month ago. The wind down there can be a real bear, so use something stout. This time of year, you might get some gray drakes, so be prepared. That's dry fly heaven when they come off. Anyway, just stop in at one of the Pinedale shops; tell 'em Frank sent you. They'll let you know what's happening. If you do fish it and come back this way, I'd appreciate a report."

"You can count on it, Frank," James said. "Much obliged for the tip. Are you here most afternoons?"

"Pretty much. I help pick up the slack in the summer when the boys are guiding."

"We'll make a point of coming back. And you can be sure we'll never mention that tributary in mixed company."

"What tributary?" Frank asked.

I insisted on paying for the flies and line. It came to just over a hundred bucks. I figured it was a small price to pay for great information.

James decided to head to the Green first, and then come back later to check out the secret spot. I was eager to give it a shot right away and not backtrack, but he insisted I wasn't ready for a gem like that, that I had to earn another stripe on a challenging river like the upper Green and prove I could handle the wind. "Besides," he said, "it's always best to let these things percolate a while, that way they gain flavor."

I knew better than to argue with him. As long as we were heading to new water, I could live with the delay, but there was no way I wasn't going to find out about that secret spot. I had a feeling we'd been given special information, and to disregard it would be sacrilegious to all that true fly fishermen held sacred. This belief came on my own accord, and I felt its validity as if it were a creed.

Sixty miles south of Jackson, not far past the town of Bondurant, the Green River crosses over Highway 191. This is the northern stretch of a river that eventually traverses south across Wyoming through three dams until it finally crosses into Utah some seven hundred river miles away. Almost all of that water is good trout fishing, but it would take a lifetime for a man to fish it all. If nothing else, the West is breathtakingly vast, a geography of possibility. The toughest choice to make is often where to start.

For our part, we decided to take our stand on the upper section of the Green, a winding stretch of pocket water tumbling from its source some twenty-five miles up in the Wind River mountains. The river was accessible by following a dirt road across Bureau of Land Management land, and for the first eight miles above 191, there were a number of primitive campsites along the river. James, of course, drove past these and parked the truck at the end of the road. "Here's where we start hiking," he announced.

I looked out at the water. It was wide and wadable, with enough boulders and eddies to keep three fishermen happy. "How far you plan on hiking?" I asked. I wasn't opposed to the work, but it didn't seem worth the effort to move.

"Not sure," he said. "Never been up there. Let's explore. We can take enough stuff for a few days."

"Sure," I said, with my eye still on the tempting water. "Looks good here, though."

James laughed. "It is. Really good. Let's start packing."

We spent the better part of an hour organizing our packs and eliminating everything that wasn't absolutely necessary. I was willing to carry more weight, but I think James liked the challenge of travelling lean. He kept taking stuff out of my pack every time I turned around, but I

The Eddy

managed to sneak in a few extra goodies when he wasn't looking.

Turned out, I was grateful for the lighter load. James had it in his head to cover some serious miles. I wasn't sure if it was because he craved the solitude, or he wanted to see as much water as possible. Either way, it was a haul. Fortunately, the terrain wasn't difficult to traverse, mainly high plains sage and river willow. Occasionally, we'd come across a stand of red pine next to the river, an odd sort of geographical punctuation mark in this wide-open country.

As we walked along the river, we watched a storm develop from out of the mountains in the Bridger Teton Wilderness Area. The clouds seemed to bunch up in the northwest and sit there as if gathering power. We didn't know if the storm would come our way, but the air had cooled, and we watched as lightning crackled in the far distance. We could not hear the thunder.

After nearly four hours of hiking, we set up camp near the river underneath a scraggly cedar tree. It wasn't exactly a postcard spot, but with a storm on the horizon, we figured it was best to settle in. We staked the tent down, secured the rain fly and vestibule, and made sure all the security lines were weighted down with rocks. Afterwards, we gathered some driftwood and sage for a fire and settled down to watch the storm, which clearly was moving our way. Against the backdrop of the black clouds, the lightning appeared more beautiful than ominous. "Let's sit out here as long as we can," I said.

James rolled over, arched his back, and put his arms above his head. "Sure," he said. He took a few sprigs of sage and tossed them on the fire to kick up the flames. The smell was pleasant, almost medicinal. "I'd guess we have an hour before it hits, maybe more. Should happen close to sunset. This one could be nasty."

We watched the sky for a while, not saying anything. It felt nice to be sitting with our packs off watching the drama out to the west take shape. After a while, I dug through my pack for my water bottle and went down to the river to refill it with cold water. Even though it didn't feel like it, we were at seven thousand feet, and at that altitude, it was easy to get dehydrated. When I came back, I sat across from James, who was still on his back, reading a book in the low light. Every now and then, he'd look up at the sky.

"What are we reading now?" I asked. James had eclectic tastes. Sometimes he'd start a book, and the next time I looked, he was reading something different.

"A history. An account of the Korean War."

"Oh," I said, a bit surprised. "Interested in the topic?"

He stopped reading and looked at me. "No, not especially. My dad served over there but didn't say much about it." He turned back to the book.

"What did he do?'

James shook his head and closed the book. "He was a marine, Toby. He was at the Chosin Reservoir, a particularly brutal place. He was awarded a Silver Star for valor. Didn't know about any of it until after he died."

I leaned back against the cedar and made myself comfortable. "Really? How'd you find out?"

James yawned and sat up. "Military funeral. Some of the vets told me. When I went to the bank, I found Dad's medal underneath some papers in a safety deposit box. That and nearly forty thousand dollars he'd managed to squirrel away for Jan and me. Money for college."

"Wow," I said. "How come he never told you anything?"

James opened the book again. He seemed eager to end the conversation. "The guy never said much, Toby. It wasn't his way."

"Oh," I said. I wanted to know more but wasn't going to push it. I didn't feel like watching him read, so I went down to the river for the last hour of sunlight and sat on a rock, watching the storm. I thought about my father, wondering if it really was best that I knew nothing about him, or at least anything about him that was good. I couldn't help but wonder, though, if there were things about him that I'd inherited, things I was powerless to change. Maybe

The Eddy

some of my anger came from him. Maybe James' anger came from his father. Maybe it didn't matter how much we tried. There was no way to disinherit blood.

When I came back to camp, James had his headlamp on and was pouring some scotch into a tin cup. Apparently, his packing wasn't as light as he led on. "Man," I said, "that storm's coming, and we're way out here like Huck Finn on a raft, vulnerable as can be, just waiting for it to hit." The weather always made me a little nervous, but it didn't seem to bother him.

James added a little water to his cup and took a sip. "Funny how often that book creeps into conversation," he said. "Something about Huck on a raft that doesn't quite let go."

I sat down next to James, away from the fire's smoke. "Is that what you like best about the book?" I asked. "Huck on the raft with Jim? Cause that's *my* favorite part."

"I don't know," James said. "I get something different out of it every time I read it. Twain's funny. He makes me laugh. He's also kind of dark."

I nodded. "Yeah, he is. I listened to you talk about the book in class. It opened up some for me. But it's still mostly a running away story, Huck getting away from his shitty father and all. I don't know, maybe it's just me and I've been thinking about this stuff, but I don't think Huck ever got away from his pap and what he did to him."

James laughed softly and stared into the fire. "You didn't know your father, did you?"

"No," I said. "Apparently, I didn't miss much."

"Well, that's debatable. I'm sure he was more than what you remember. Fathers are..." James didn't finish the sentence. He looked up at me with a half-smile. "So that you know, I didn't really know my father either. I grew up on the Iron Range around a lot of Finns. A real stoic lot, and my father set the standard. I'm not sure he was always that way, but that's what I remember. People tell me he was different before my mom died. I really don't know, though. The thing is, Toby, my dad went to work every day to a shitty job in the mines and never once complained. In fact, I don't think I ever heard him complain about anything. People admired him for his toughness, which was legendary. But I never knew him. We never had a conversation about anything other than hunting or hockey. If that."

"Did he ever say he loved you?" I asked.

James laughed. "No. When I was a teen, I got into trouble a few times. Looking back, I think I did it to get some kind of reaction out of him. Didn't work, though. All I got was community service." He paused, then continued, "You know, it was my dad who bought me my first Chevelle. He got it for me my senior year. One day, he just handed me the keys and said he was tired of me taking his truck. When I left for college, my sister cried like a baby. My dad? He just shook my hand and filled my car with gas."

"Helluva send off," I said.

"Yup. And that was the last time I saw him. He died four months later." James took a swig of scotch and looked up at the sky. The storm was getting close.

"Did you love him?"

James gave me a puzzled look. "Love? I don't know… He was always there. He took care of us. I respected him. I'm not sure love was ever part of the equation."

"That's sad," I said.

James shrugged. "Not really. I had it good compared to a lot of people. I never thought of it as sad. Complicated maybe, but not sad." James put his palm out and looked up at the sky. "Here it comes, Toby. Ready or not."

It was just after sunset when the storm hit with a vengeance. The wind reminded me of Kansas in twister season. The only thing that kept our tent from blowing away was our weight inside it. The rain was equally furious. It pelted the tent so hard, I thought it might put holes in it. The storm lasted a good two hours before it settled into a steady rain. Neither of us slept until we were sure the worst had passed. It would have been impossible to sleep anyway.

The Eddy

Chapter 26

The next morning was bright and clear, with that crisp, dry air that often follows storms. It hit me as I crawled from the tent, promising a new kind of day. After a breakfast of granola cereal, powdered milk, and beef jerky, we decided to fish our way upriver until mid-evening and then make our way back down. It had been two days since we'd fished, and I was anxious to prove I could handle this water. James let me use the new rod again, so I was confident from the start.

For most of the morning, James fished terrestrials with soft hackle droppers, and I settled on caddis nymphs with tiny Copper John droppers. We both caught fish. The river in this stretch, for the most part, was uniform—fairly wide, maybe seventy feet across, with few distinguishing aspects. I had to look for the submerged rocks and subtle seams to find the holding spots. The fish could be anywhere. I was used to reading water where it was easy to see the fishy spots behind a rock, a submerged log, a bend pool. Here, it was important to slow down and read the water.

We caught three species of trout in this section—browns, cutts, and rainbows. Neither of us hooked anything bigger than sixteen inches, which was not surprising. This section of the river was generally colder since the water had yet to warm as it flowed from its source, some twelve thousand feet up near Whiskey Mountain.

It was nice having the river to ourselves. Most people who fished the Green fished it much lower, where there was greater potential for big fish. The most popular stretch was below Flaming Gorge near the Utah border. James had fished down there several times and had caught big fish, but it was clear, technically challenging water. That kind of fishing appealed to me, but neither James nor I was interested in a crowd. The solitary experience suited us both.

For three days, we fished this upper section hard, hiking as much as fifteen miles every day. The afternoons were generally windy, and I often had to sit it out for a few hours because my arm ached from trying to cast into the wind. James sometimes stopped fishing at these points and helped me modify my casting. He was of the belief that the best lessons were learned under duress and, if I pushed through the arm fatigue and learned how to use the wind to my advantage, I could pretty much conquer any fishing extreme. In the end, he was right. Although I wasn't exactly proficient under these conditions, I learned how to adjust and not give up. We found we could pretty much catch fish on anything if we modified our casting to fit the conditions.

On the evening of the third day, as we were walking back to camp, thoroughly exhausted, I decided to make a few casts at a spot that had looked promising earlier but had produced nothing. James was content to sit on the bank and rest. We were still a couple miles from camp.

I was fishing to a slick behind a submerged boulder. The distance and conflicting currents made it challenging, but I was certain there was a fish. On my fifth or sixth cast, I managed to mend my line and get a perfect drift on the seam of the slick. The fish took my nymph hard. The biggest fish we'd landed so far on this section was sixteen inches, but this fish was considerably bigger. It pulled line off my reel and bolted downstream. I had to chase after it with my arms held high to keep my line from flattening out. When a fish makes a long run, the angle of the fly in its mouth changes, and often, this results in a lost fish. It's why fishermen usually hold their rod high after hooking a fish. Naturally, I'd learned this the hard way.

I finally got control of the fish about fifty yards downstream, and I managed to get most of my line back. When the fish seemed like he was spent, I got downstream

The Eddy

of him and gently fed him into my net. It was a cutthroat that measured twenty-three inches. It was the biggest fish I had managed to land.

James had watched the battle, following me along shore, and was waiting with his camera when I lifted the net. He took four different shots of me and the fish. Later, after he'd had the film developed in Jackson, I was stunned by the pictures' clarity and color. In one photo, the water appeared to have jewels on the surface, and the cutthroat, thrust toward the camera, seemed to draw in the viewer's eye with its buttery yellow color. In all the photos, I was shocked at how different I looked. I somehow seemed older. I looked more confident, perhaps tougher than I thought I was. I liked what I saw.

"That is a *hell* of a fish," James said. He was standing in the water next to me, watching as I revived the fish. "You couldn't have done that any better. That was impressive."

The fish finally perked up and darted from my grasp. I stood up and wiped my hands on my vest. "That was my greatest fish," I said, hardly believing I'd actually landed him. "That was tough water."

"I watched that cast you made," James said. "Absolutely textbook."

I was beaming. We got out of the river and went back upstream to gather James' gear. "I might've gotten lucky," I said. "But that was a fish I'll never forget."

"Well, you gotta be good to be lucky. You did the hard work and it paid off. You deserve that fish. The thing is, next time you might do everything right and lose a fish like that, so don't go getting cocky." He slapped me on the back. "The good fly fishermen always remain humble."

The next morning, over a pot of river coffee, we decided to break camp and fish forty-five miles south near the town of Marbleton. The plan was to drop me off at a section of water with all the gear I'd need for an overnight, and James would start twenty miles below me and work his way upriver until we met. That way, we could cover more water and share our findings. It sounded fine with me. I was ready for another solo outing.

It was almost noon by the time we got back to the truck. The temperature was near ninety-five at mid-day, and I started to become concerned about another long hike. We decided to shorten the length between us to a little more than fifteen miles, which made sense. That way, we could move a bit slower and fish the evening more deliberately.

At Marbleton, James bought a twelve-pack of a local microbrew out of Jackson Hole, and we sat on the tailgate of the truck, dangling our feet, enjoying the sensation of cold beer on a hot day. We argued for a while about what day it was, and finally agreed it was either the ninth or tenth of July.

"Hey, guess what," I said. "I turned nineteen either two or three days ago. I completely forgot about it."

James let out a low whistle. "Wow, you actually forgot your own birthday. Impressive. Well, happy birthday to ya." James held out his beer and we made a toast.

I would have been happy, I think, if we had decided to abort this part of the trip and head back up to Jackson Hole where it was bound to be cooler. After a few cold beers, I felt more like taking a nap than going on an extended hike. But James seemed as fresh as ever, so I didn't protest. When he drove away, I considered walking down to the water to take a cool bath and lounge around for a while, but deep down, I was determined not to let him hike further than me. So I reluctantly saddled up and began the arduous march downriver, figuring I might as well make a few miles since the fishing would be lousy at the height of day.

I'm not sure why I didn't put my rod in its case when I began hiking; I guess I was just lazy or fatigued, but, whatever the reason, it cost me. I was only a half-mile into the hike, plodding along, mind wandering, when I tripped over a river rock and went sprawling. I should have thrown the rod as I lost balance. I should have been thinking about what I was doing. I should have picked my feet up. But I did none of those things. I took a header and put my hand out to brace myself, snapping the Sage rod in two. The sound was

The Eddy

sickening. Just a snap, and the five-hundred-dollar rod was worthless. I rolled over on my side and swore as loud as I could. My elbow was throbbing, my rod was shot, I was mildly overheated, and I had at least another seven or so miles to hike, with no reward of fishing ahead. I didn't know whether to laugh or cry, so I just lay there laughing insanely. If anyone had seen me, they would've assumed some poor bastard had succumbed to heat exhaustion.

Eventually, I picked myself up and, for the rest of the afternoon, I trudged on. It was a difficult hike with the challenging shoreline, but there was nothing to do but march. Naturally, as it began to cool and the shadows lengthened across the river, an amazing Gray Drake hatch came off the water. Fish began rising in earnest, and the river came alive. All I could do was watch and laugh. I decided it beat the hell out of getting boiling mad.

Just before nightfall, I found James. His camp had been set up near the river, and he was intently fishing to the hatch. He did not see me coming, so I sat on the bank, exhausted, and watched him fish. About every third cast, he hooked a fish, and I could tell by his posture he was having a blast. When he finally noticed me, he just waved and kept fishing. I stripped off my clothes and sat down in the cool water, naked, and let the river bring me back to life. I sat in the water for over an hour and never once considered asking James if he had a back-up rod.

That night around the fire, James made dinner and let me relax. He knew my afternoon had been miserable, and he hardly said a word about the rod, other than to say it was no big deal, that all things eventually break.

By the time the stars came out, it had cooled considerably, and I was grateful for the good rest it promised. As we settled around the fire for our nightly conversation, I asked James if he ever got lonely. I had been thinking about the question all day as I trudged on, wishing I had someone to bitch to.

"Lonely?" he asked. "Sometimes, I guess. The days can get long, the nights longer. Not hearing anyone's voice.

It's a trade-off, I guess."

"You ever wonder about those mountain men, how they managed?"

He kicked at the fire, turning the fresh side of the logs to the coals. The flames flared and we backed away from the heat. "There's a price to pay for every choice you make," he said. "Guess it all depends on the currency you give to loneliness. For me, it's more like chump change these days."

"Well, I think it might get pretty depressing after a while, being alone for so long."

"Yeah," James said. He was nodding. "I suppose—but you can also get pretty depressed and lonely around people. Maybe even more so."

I leaned back on the log and looked at the night sky. "Yeah, that's true. I think I was so depressed in Kansas, I didn't really see people. I mean, they were there all around me, but I didn't really *see* them."

James unwrapped a Hershey bar and tossed me half. "I'm guessing what you saw and felt back then was as real as it gets. To you, at least. But the truth is a bit larger than you, isn't it?"

I laughed. "Kind of makes you leery of absolutes."

He looked at me and smiled.

Before I went to bed that night, I drank a quart of cold river water and settled in. In the middle of the night, I had to pee, so I crawled out of my sleeping bag to do my duty. It was cool out, and I shivered as I walked away from camp. Again, the stars were bright, with the moon nowhere to be seen. I stood out there for a long time, staring at the sky and listening to the river. I was tired, but I wanted to enjoy the peace that came from the hard-earned solitude.

As I stood there, shivering around the last of the fire's embers, I found myself thinking about what James had said about the currency we give to loneliness. Out here, I often felt alone, but I never felt lonely, and I wondered why that was. Was I content because I had paid the price for finding peace? And if so, what would I have to pay in the future to keep loneliness at bay?

The Eddy

As I crawled back into my sleeping bag, I couldn't help but shake my head. This was the kind of late-night philosophical shit that could keep me awake for hours. I tried to put the questions aside by thinking about the next day, but I guess I never quite buried it, because during the night, I dreamt of being lost in the mountains, and no matter which way I traveled, I always ended up in the same place. I awoke the next morning with my face in the corner of the nylon tent with my pants wrapped around my head. Not exactly a promising way to start the day.

Joe Paatalo

The Eddy

Chapter 27

After breaking camp, we decided to skip the fishing and make our way back to Jackson Hole. The hike back was a trudge with the sun pounding on us. My feet hurt from the day before, and no matter how hard I tried, I couldn't stop thinking about them every step I took. To clear my head, I tried to engage James in a conversation, but he seemed perfectly comfortable marching along not saying anything. I found it annoying.

"C'mon. Who's your favorite writer, James?" This was the fifth random question I'd thrown at him. I was hiking behind him and couldn't see his reaction, but I got him with this one.

"All right, you win. Favorite writer?" he said and kept walking. "I don't know, why?"

I confessed. "Because my feet ache and I want to think of something else."

I heard him laugh. "Okay, Hemingway, I guess."

"Why him?"

"Because he pops into my head on fishing trips. Because he's all about sucking it up and toughing it out." He looked at me and shook his head. "I also like Mary Oliver, the poet."

"Really?" That surprised me.

James stopped and turned around. "Geez, I told you I'm not a misogynist, Toby. I like her stuff. It's, I don't know, got mojo."

"Mojo?"

"Mojo. Power. That's the beauty of poetry, of stories. They can heal. Indians say stories have medicine. I believe that." James turned back and started walking.

"Medicine?" I asked. I fell in behind him.

"Sure. But you have to listen to them. And that's different than reading."

"If I listen close enough, will they heal my feet?"

"Sure… As long as you listen to them while wearing a good pair of socks."

When we reached the truck around noon, I was shot. I stripped off my pack and clothes and went down to the river to cool off. My feet were on fire, and when I stepped barefoot into the water, I felt my breath catch. James soon came down to the river to join me with a few cold beers from the cooler, and we both plopped down into the water facing the current. Neither of us said anything. Every time I took a swallow of beer, I felt its coolness work its way down to my empty belly. I looked over at James, who was wearing a serene smile. I knew he was feeling the same thing. We sat there for some time in the cool current with the hot sun on our bare shoulders, enjoying the beer and squinting into the bright sky. I felt a pleasant, well-earned ache in my muscles, an ache I wouldn't have traded for anything. It felt good to be alive.

Chapter 28

"Hey, boys, how was fishing?" Frank was behind the counter ordering a three-day license for a customer when we strolled in. We looked a little rough. The guy at the counter did a double take when he saw us. I'm sure we didn't resemble anything he'd seen on the fly-fishing literature describing the area.

"Not bad," I said. "We fished above Pinedale for four days and then down around Marbleton for a day and a half. Water flow was good, mostly wade-able."

Frank finished with the customer, wished him good luck, and sent him away with the obligatory flies in a plastic cup. "Haven't fished that part of the Green in fifteen years," he said. "Time just kind of slips away. How are the fish over there? Anything big?"

James pointed at me and said, "Toby got a twenty-three-inch cutty up there. I got some nice browns, but nothing *that* big."

"Well, that's a damn fine fish, Toby. Pretty rare up there." Frank whistled. "So, you boys going to hit the secret spot?"

"Thought we might give it a go, but we wanted to see if you'd like to go with us," James said.

Frank laughed. "Oh, no, my guiding days are done. You boys don't need me."

"No, Frank, we don't want a guide," James said. "We want to know if you'd like to fish there with us, maybe spend the night around a good fire. We'd like you to be our guest... Realizing the company is suspect, of course."

Frank took off his ball cap and scratched his bald head. "You know, I bet it's been five years since I've been up there. It's a bit of a hike."

"You look like you could handle it, Frank," I said.

He looked at me for a long time. The difference between us must have seemed striking. And maybe that appealed to him.

"You boys serious about this?" He turned to James, who was grinning. "I might slow you down some."

"We don't wear watches, Frank," I said. "We're never in a rush."

Frank let out a dry chuckle and rubbed his eyes. "I knew there was a reason I liked you boys. You're a dying breed, you know that?"

"How's that?" James asked.

"I've known a few trout bums in my life, but most of the new breed think they're trout bums because they fish a lot. That's not what it means to be a trout bum. Trout bums are a couple of guys like you who drive a piece-of-shit truck, smell like you haven't showered in a week, and are ready to bust ass just so you can see a new piece of water."

"Does that mean you'll come with us?" I asked.

"Yeah, sure. Why not? I'm due for some fishing. Gotta be honest, though. I haven't fished much lately, and I am afraid I'll slow you down."

"Don't worry about it, Frank," James said. "We'd be honored if you came."

Frank put his cap back on and asked, "Where you boys staying tonight?"

James shrugged. "Not sure. A campground somewhere."

"Tell you what," Frank said. "If you boys aren't in a hurry, I'll close the shop down in a few hours and then you can spend the night with me. That way, you guys can shower, which I strongly suggest you do."

I laughed. James raised his arm and smelled his pit. "He's right, Toby, it's time you showered."

Frank went around back and came back with a six-pack of Coors. "Make yourselves at home. And, by the way," he looked out at the truck in the parking lot, "I'm driving."

The Eddy

Frank's place was not far out of Jackson Hole. It was an older log house built on ten acres, most of which was mountainside. It had a huge wraparound porch with Adirondack chairs and hanging baskets of flowers. Inside, the place was meticulous, with modest but nice furniture. It was evident Frank was an outdoorsman. There were pictures everywhere of hunting and fishing trips. But there were no mounts on the walls. Instead, he had a few pieces of original art, mostly by local artists. They were colorful, almost feminine, and it was a curious incongruity. It seemed to indicate a woman's presence.

The house's best feature was a large rock fireplace in the middle of the living room. It was surrounded by overstuffed chairs and rockers. A quarter cord of split wood was neatly stacked on wood holders. On the mantel were photographs going back for decades.

"This is a beautiful place, Frank," I said. "How long have you been here?"

Frank was pouring a few drinks in the kitchen. "Thirty-five years. Sally, my wife, we built it from scratch." He came back into the living room with three highballs. "How old are you, Toby?" he asked.

"Nineteen," I said.

"Hmm, I guess you get the weak one then." He handed me a glass of whiskey and soda water. "Here's a toast to fishing," he said.

We all sat down next to the fireplace. Two labs, one chocolate and one yellow, settled in at our feet.

"The chocolate's Brookie and the yellow's Greg," Frank said. "I know, Greg's a dumb name, but Sally named him after an old boyfriend to keep me on my toes."

"Is Sally around?" I asked.

Frank sipped his cocktail and smiled. "She passed three years ago next month. We were married for forty-one years."

"I'm sorry," James said.

"Yeah, me too. She was eight years younger than me. Always figured I'd go first. But it don't always work the way it's supposed to."

"Your Sally was beautiful," I said. I was looking at a series of photographs on the mantel, some from the late fifties or early sixties. "She looked like Audrey Hepburn."

Frank laughed. "She was a little curvier than that, but yeah, she was a looker. Always turned heads, even when she was older."

We took our drinks and sat out on the porch. The dogs came with us wherever we went. Frank asked questions about our trip and seemed genuinely interested in what we were doing. He paid particular attention to me, which threw me off. He was what I imagined a grandparent would be like. But I'd never known my grandparents, and it occurred to me I'd never really had a long conversation with an older person.

Sometime around eight that evening, Frank brought out the moose steaks and fired up the grill. He broke out a bottle of Cabernet, made a big salad with some wild rice, and James and I sat down to the best meal we'd had on the trip. Frank was a master cook, and we knew from the first bite we were in the presence of greatness. "Don't cook too much these days," he said. "Haven't had a lot of company. I forget how much fun it is."

The moose was exceptionally tender. I'd never had anything like it. "Did you shoot this, Frank? It's incredible," I said.

"No, but I butchered it for a friend. He gave me some of the loins. Always thought it was better than elk, but that's debatable, I suppose."

James and I both ate vigorously. Frank must have sensed he had a couple of hungry dudes on his hands, because he made enough to feed a squadron.

After dinner, we sat around the fireplace again and talked fishing. Frank knew his stuff. It seemed as if he'd fished all the water within a hundred-mile range. As he told stories, I noticed he was never at the center of them; he was just the narrator. There was no hyperbole, none of the one-upmanship that often permeates the conversations of men.

The Eddy

I liked that about him.

"Did Sally like to fish?" James asked.

We were sipping the last of the wine and Frank put his glass to the bridge of his nose and closed his eyes. "I think she was a better fisherman than I was. More intuitive. Maybe even a better caster. She loved dry flies, especially Wulf patterns. She thought they were silly and pretty and had no business catching fish. But she used them all the time. She didn't fish as much as I did, but she was really good, especially with dry flies. Best woman I ever saw with a fly rod—but I'm a little biased."

"Did you teach her?" I asked.

He laughed. "Hell, no. Her daddy did. And he was a helluva fisherman. The funny thing is, I didn't even know she fished until after we got married. She told me she was afraid I'd be intimidated, and I wouldn't want to marry her. Can you imagine that? My, the times have changed." He looked at me. "Toby, you find a woman who loves the outdoors like you do. Don't settle for anything less. Trust me, find a woman who likes to chop wood and you got a partner for life."

"I'll keep that in mind," I said. "It sounds like good advice."

"I'm envious of your relationship," James said. "I think it's a rare thing."

Frank knocked back the rest of his wine and laughed out loud. "Hell, Mitch, we used to fight like a couple of alley cats from time to time. I got the scars to prove it. She was a pistol. I come from a long line of proud Republicans, but she was one hard-headed liberal. I didn't much like her politics, but I loved her passion. She'd about kill herself over some threatened owl or the closing of the migratory elk passes. No one wanted to take her on because they knew they'd get a black eye."

"I think we would've been friends," James said.

Frank looked away, was silent for a while. "You know what I'm most proud of? We were married for forty-one years and never went more than a week without making love, even when she was sick. Sally used to say it was better than DiMaggio's streak. Sometimes we'd get to that sixth day and we'd be out in town, and she'd stop and hold up six fingers. Not say a word, just flash me those six fingers." He laughed and wiped at his eyes. "Used to get me so riled up, I'd damn near have an accident trying to get home." He looked up at the mantel. "I miss her something fierce… Three years, Mitch," he said softly. "The heart remembers what the body forgets."

Frank was quiet for a while, staring at the photos on the mantel. We said nothing. We were content to sit and pet the dogs. Every now and then, one of them would place his head in my lap and sigh loudly.

"You know what I hate most about getting old?" Frank asked, breaking away from the mantel. "Your Goddamn eyes start watering for no reason. Makes you look like a sap." He wiped his face with a napkin. "Sorry about that."

James got up. "We'll take care of the dishes, Frank. And then I reckon Toby and I need to shower and hit the hay."

Frank stood and stretched. "Much obliged. You boys can wrestle over the bunk beds in the guest room. Plenty of towels in the bathroom. Don't mind the dogs; they like to sleep on the bed. Just kick 'em off. I used to throw 'em off all the time, but I sort of got to liking their company at night. Spoiled 'em, I guess."

"What time should we get up?" I asked

"Don't know about you two," Frank said. "But I'll be up with the sun. Can't seem to sleep late anymore. You boys sleep long as you like. I'll pack some food in the morning."

Chapter 29

James and I were up by 6:30. Frank already had breakfast ready—hot coffee, eggs, elk sausage, tortillas, and salsa. I might've slept in more, but it smelled too good. After a hardy breakfast, we packed our gear for an overnight and put it in Frank's Suburban.

"Not sure what rod I should take," Frank said. "Let's go pick one out."

We followed him into his den where he kept his fly rods and guns. Most of the rods were cased, but he had a few beautiful bamboo rods in a rack next to a fly-tying desk.

"Pretty fine rods, Frank." James was holding an old Orvis seven-foot bamboo rod.

"Yeah, but to be honest, I can't cast them as well when it gets windy. They are pretty, though. Sally used 'em more than I did." He opened a cabinet that held at least fifty rods, from fiberglass to graphite to boron. "You can tell I owned a fly shop, eh. Pick one out for me, Mitch."

James started laughing. "Isn't that a little like picking out someone else's underwear? It's kind of personal, don't you think?"

Frank turned and looked at us sheepishly. "I'm a little embarrassed, but I haven't really fished in the last couple of years. Kind of lost the desire. I thought about going out again, but I just haven't. When you boys came around, I don't know, I guess I thought it was time."

James grabbed an Orvis five-weight and a Hardy six-weight and handed them to Frank. "Grab your favorite reels. I'll clean the lines on the drive."

Frank reached into one of the drawers on his tying desk and pulled out a high-end Abel reel along with a handsome Hardy. "Guess these'll do."

"Shit, Frank, those things are worth more than my truck."

"That's not saying much, Mitch." Frank handed the reels to James. "Guess we're ready."

The hike back into the tributary, which I'll refer to as Sally Creek since I've sworn to never divulge its name or location, took us almost three hours. We could've done it faster, but we fished a bit on the way and stopped to rest a few times. Frank did not put his rod together. He insisted on waiting until we got to Sally. The water was pretty—a bit fast due to the rapid decline. James and I cast behind the rocks into all the slower spots and picked up a few fish, but nothing remarkable. When we reached Sally Creek, it looked like an extension of the water we had already fished.

"Don't let her fool you, boys. Another twenty minutes upstream, and you'll see a different piece of water."

And he was right. The stream opened up into a high mountain meadow. The river slowed and widened, as if it had no relation to the rest of the river. We sat on the bank, the three of us, and marveled at the slow runs, the bend pools, the riffled water. It looked, in many ways, like a hidden sanctuary. Whether it held the fish Frank talked about hardly seemed to matter. It was the most beautiful piece of water I'd ever seen. Even James struggled to find the right words to describe it.

"Ain't she something?" Frank asked. "I was hoping she was as pretty as my memory held her out to be. Guess I was right. This here stretch lasts for a little under a mile. It doesn't show up like this on the topo maps, so hardly anyone ever bothers to go up here, unless they're on a nature hike."

We were at eighty-five hundred feet, surrounded by mountains capped with snow. In the meadow, the yellow blacktops were blooming, and we could see the signs of elk near the river where they had come down to drink.

Frank took out his Orvis rod and pieced it together. "I suggest we fish it slowly all the way until we see the

The Eddy

waterfall. After that, we can work our way back down and make camp. And, if you boys aren't too offended, I was thinking of a few trout for dinner. Hate to think I lugged this olive oil all the way up here for nothing."

To say the fishing was excellent would be a disservice to the river. Fish were pooled in this stretch in remarkable numbers, and they were big. As Frank had suggested, the fish had moved up from the big water to this stretch and, whether it was due to high temperatures below or the fact that they saw this place as a kind of trout Mecca, I have no idea. The river was clear up here and not easy to fish, but with longer leaders and a little finesse, we all caught fish. I actually lost more than I landed, but every other fish seemed to run and take me close to my backing. I probably landed only ten fish throughout the day, but it was the greatest afternoon and evening I've ever had.

It didn't take long to see that Frank was more than a good fisherman. Even at seventy-one, he could throw a line beautifully. At one point, I sat on the bank and watched him. His casts were effortless, and he had the habit of watching his back cast as his rod loaded. There was no need to do this, so I think it was either an old habit that had served him well or perhaps he just liked watching the line behind him, a reminder of his capacity for precision. There was no indication he had been away from the water, other than a youthful exuberance he displayed when he hooked a fish, which may have been another lifelong habit. I had as much fun watching him fish as I did fishing myself.

Toward evening, we all gathered at the meadow's midsection and set up our camp so we could fish the final hours of light. This was not a day to burn daylight unnecessarily. Since we had yet to keep a fish, we decided in the last hour and a half of daylight we'd each keep one for dinner. Secretly, I assumed, we all wanted to bring back the biggest fish.

The dusk fishing was like one of those video productions you occasionally see on a Saturday morning, fish jumping wildly, reels singing in the setting sun. It almost felt staged, it was so good. I ended up keeping a twenty-inch fish, while Frank and James kept fish a little over sixteen inches. Since I had won the big keeper contest, Frank said I got the honor of cooking dinner. I knew I'd been had, but I didn't mind one bit.

We stayed up late around the fire, telling stories. Frank said we should all sleep outside around the fire, and I was happy to do so. The tents were set, so if it rained, we'd have shelter. James was up for it as well, so we hunkered down and told stories around the fire all night long. Frank had brought some secret hooch to drink and allowed me a small cup. I don't know how to describe it other than to say it straightened out my pubic hair and added a fair amount of color to my stories.

That night was one of the most enjoyable of the trip. Three generations of men lying around a fire in a secret spot, telling fishing stories and staring at the moon. I doubted whether it could ever get any better than this.

The next morning was gray. We broke camp and fished the miracle mile again, with the same results. I was all for staying another day, but James said we had to be careful not to get greedy and to leave this place wanting more. It reminded me of what he had said earlier about the Big Horn and great songs. I could hardly argue with it since Frank agreed completely. And it was his spot.

We hiked out that afternoon, taking our time and making sure we didn't tax Frank. He handled the hike well and, perhaps, enjoyed the rigor as much as the fishing. When we were less than a mile from his truck, we stopped at a spot where the tributaries met. It was beginning to drizzle, and the three of us sat on a bank chewing elk sticks and talking about the last twenty-four hours. I was talking about whether or not this day could ever be matched when I turned to James to ask a question. He was staring intently across the rugged water at an undercut bank. He hadn't heard a word I said.

"I'm going to fish that spot over there," he said.

The Eddy

Frank and I saw the place he was pointing to, and we both just shook our heads.

"Damn, Mitch, you're going to have to hike a bit to get in position to fish that little spot," Frank said. "The current's a little rough."

James pointed to a little gravel island. "If I can make it to that spot, I should be fine."

I wasn't about to argue with him. "Go for it," I joked. "I'll be right here taking a nap."

Frank and I watched as he made his way upstream. He grabbed a stout stick for wading and crossed the river. It was difficult, and I thought he was going to get swept down to us, but he finally made it. He walked down to the gravel bar and stood there calculating his cast. What he saw in that spot to deserve the effort was beyond both Frank and me. But we watched curiously as he made several casts to the run, trying to get his hopper to drift under the bank.

On his fifth or sixth cast, we saw the fish take the fly and James set the hook hard. Within moments, his six-weight rod was bent into the shape of a "C." We could hardly believe it.

The fish immediately made a run upstream into heavy water, and James lifted his rod high in an attempt to keep the hook angle from flattening out. The fish ran with gusto, and James was forced to jump in the water and chase him upstream. At one point, he was into his backing, but he managed to get some control over the fish and gain back what he'd given. Each time James seemed to get the upper hand, the fish would bolt upstream and the battle to regain line would begin again.

Frank and I hopped off the bank and followed the fight from the other side of the river, shouting encouragement. After close to fifteen minutes, it looked as though James was starting to tire the fish. He was getting it closer when we heard him swear and start running downstream. The fish had had enough of fighting the current and decided to make a run downstream. What James knew, before we did, was that if the fish got a good enough run, it would get into the faster water and the battle would be over. His only option was to get downstream of the fish and force it back upstream. We watched as James pulled parallel to the fish and, without hesitation, he jumped into the deep water with rod held high to scare the fish back upstream. There was a moment where it looked like the fish would get by him, but somehow, he managed to turn its head upstream again. By this time, it was clear the fish was running out of gas. It made one more run upstream, but it had lost its energy. It had little left to fight with. In all, the contest lasted more than twenty minutes.

Throughout the whole struggle, I felt like I was watching something rare and beautiful. A fish that size had no reason to be there; it was a jewel in an overlooked and forgotten place. It was bigger than any fish we'd caught, lost, or seen, for that matter. When he lifted it up, I could see its crimson spots, large as quarters. I fought my way across the heavy current for a closer look, the camera ready to freeze the moment. As James was removing the hook, I noticed the fish's skin was light-colored on one side, almost opaque.

"Looks like it's lived most of its life under that bank," James said, comparing the brown's flanks.

"Hold her up; let's get some shots." I was adjusting the lens, but James stopped me.

"I prefer to remember this one differently." He held the fish high for Frank to see and then slipped the behemoth back into the current. It took a few minutes for the fish to recover, but when it did, it turned its head into the swift water and was gone. James watched it melt back into the current and then stood in the river surveying his surroundings, committing them to memory. After a while, he crossed back over and found a spot on the bank near Frank. He was wearing that distant smile that always confused me.

"Holy shit," I finally said. "That was the most amazing thing I've ever seen. That thing, it must have been nine pounds! How big was it?" I was stuttering, I was so excited."

Frank, on the other hand, was just shaking his head

The Eddy

slowly. "Thirty-three inches?"

"At least," James said.

I felt like jumping up and down in celebration. But Frank and James were so subdued, you would've thought he'd lost the fish.

"I've been fishing and guiding most of my life, Mitch. Can't say I've ever seen anything like that. Especially in a spot like that. He had no business being there."

James nodded slightly. Both men looked out over the river and said nothing. I was utterly confused. I finally shrugged my shoulders and went to fishing that stretch. Obviously, it was better than it appeared. I must have fished that spot for another twenty minutes before both men got up to leave. I reeled in and we all walked the last mile to the Suburban, hardly saying a word.

On the drive back, I asked James what he was thinking about.

"Baseball, I guess. Don Larsen. Hemingway's *The Snows of Kilimanjaro*."

"Oh," I said, "because I was a bit confused. Now I understand." I rolled my eyes.

Frank laughed. "I'd like you boys to stay one more night. I've got some more moose if you're interested. And, Mitch? I was thinking maybe you and I might tie one on. In celebration, of course."

The final night at Frank's was as pleasant as our first night. James and Frank knocked back a few cocktails and laughed and told stories late into the night. I knew I was welcome to join them, but somehow, I felt it was best to leave them alone. I cooked most of the dinner, poured the early drinks, and took Greg and Brookie on a long walk. I went to bed sometime around eleven, but, before I fell asleep, I heard part of a conversation that surprised me. James was talking.

"Not long after my divorce, I quit fishing, Frank. It wasn't fun anymore. I knew then that things were bad. I had a period of darkness that frightened me. I remember one night sitting on my couch staring at my gun case for hours.

At one point, I unlocked it and cleaned every shotgun and rifle I had. I mean, I spit-shined them. When I finished, I took a long drive and tossed the cabinet keys in the Mississippi. It was largely symbolic, but the next day, I went and got myself medicated."

I couldn't hear exactly how Frank responded, but I heard James say, "No, I quit taking them. Didn't like the side effects. They made me numb. Helped for a while, though."

A few minutes later, they were both laughing. I rolled over and went to sleep.

It wasn't until after two a.m. that James crawled into the lower bunk. Within minutes, he was snoring, and I knew it was a sign he had had too much to drink. I slept on the couch the rest of the evening, snuggled between the two large Labs who couldn't get enough of me.

Chapter 30

I didn't get up until nine the next morning. Frank was up and had taken the dogs out. James was still asleep. Frank poured me a cup of coffee and we sat on the porch and watched the dogs chase each other.

"I still don't quite get it, Frank. I don't get that melancholy stuff yesterday."

Frank sipped his coffee and smiled. "It wasn't really melancholy, Toby. It was a remarkable thing, a rare thing. Many of us can fish a lifetime and not have something play out that way."

I still didn't get it. "I must be missing something, Frank."

"It's okay. It might be an older person's thing. If I spelled it out to you, you probably still wouldn't get it, and I wouldn't blame you a bit." He paused. "I think you should let it drop. In time, you'll get it, but you need a few more rounds on the odometer."

I stared out at the dogs. They were wrestling over a bone. "Okay," I said. "I'll trust you, Frank."

"Hey, I got something for you, Toby. I almost forgot." He stood up. "Wait here, I'll be right back."

Frank disappeared for a few minutes and came back with a small neoprene case. "I want you to have this. I've only used it once, but I figure you'll take good care of it and use it the way it should be used." It was a beautiful Lamson reel. I had no idea what it was worth, but I knew it was expensive.

"I have no business with something like this, Frank. I'm just getting started. This is too much for me."

"Toby, I have more reels than I know what to do with,

and most of them haven't seen water in years. You take this and use it. It'll last a long, long time if you treat it right. Decades. Maybe more."

I fondled the reel. It was exceptionally light. "I can't possibly see what I did to deserve something like this."

Frank gave me that dry chuckle. "Who says *deserves* got anything to do with it? Enjoy it, Toby. Fishing ain't the most important thing in the world. Not even close. But fishing can make you a slightly better person if you do it right. And fishing can help you get through some tough times. I kind of forgot that myself. Even old shits like me need to be reminded of that now and again."

I accepted the gift, not sure what else to say. Frank sensed my awkwardness and said, "Hey, let's go dump some cold water on that hungover road tramp."

It was late afternoon when we pulled out of Jackson Hole. We promised Frank we'd keep in touch, and while I couldn't speak for James, I knew I'd make the attempt. Either way, it took the edge off saying goodbye, which was surprisingly hard.

Neither James nor I felt compelled to fish, so we decided to cover some ground in the general direction of southwest Montana by crossing through the northern pan of Idaho. We didn't talk much, just an occasional comment here and there about the scenery. Each of us, it seemed, had a lot to think about. When we neared the Bitterroot Range near the Montana border, James finally clued me in on where we were headed. "It's time for some four-weight fishing. I thought we'd start with the Ruby."

"Sounds good," I said, but I had no idea what he was referring to. And then I asked him what had been gnawing at me. "That fish yesterday. Have you ever seen a fish colored like that?"

"Nope. Never," James said without hesitation. "I imagine it took years to grow that big, especially in that water. Honestly, it had no business being there, which made me admire it all the more."

"I was just wondering how you account for a fish like

The Eddy

that. I mean, it has to be really rare."

"Sure is," James said. "I was thinking this morning about the reports I'd recently read of sharks in the Mississippi, as far upriver as St. Louis. Can you imagine a shark going all that way? In fresh water? Is that just an anomaly?" He paused a moment. "I think we sometimes assume we've got it all figured out, that there's a scientific explanation for everything. I'm not so sure. Guess that's why I was thinking about *The Snows of Kilimanjaro* yesterday."

"I'll have to read that," I said. "I have no idea what you're talking about."

"Yeah, read it some time. But don't forget that sometimes mystery is a good thing. Sometimes it's okay to not understand. Some people always want answers and, if they can't find one to their satisfaction, they'll create one. Anyway, maybe it's okay to not know. Maybe there simply is no reason."

I nodded and looked out the window. I'd heard this line of reasoning before. I still didn't completely buy it. Surely, I thought, there must be a reason. I thought about this for a long time as we descended through the Beartooths. I wasn't sure if I could ever take comfort in mystery.

About an hour out of Dillon, I finally gave up the heavy thinking and began to list all the rivers I had fished that summer. Surprisingly, it was not difficult to do. Each one stood out in some way. I asked James if he ever forgot a river.

"No, not really. I sometimes forget the name, but I don't forget the river."

"Have you ever felt like you completely figured one out?"

"Never. If I ever got close to figuring one out, some event changes it. That's the thing I love about rivers; they're always changing. I've always thought each river has its own personality, its own patterns of behavior. I'd never say one river is the same as another. It'd be like saying one woman is the same as another. Does an injustice to both. To fully *get* a river, as much as it's possible, you have to see it in all its seasons—when it roars during the runoff, when it sulks during the dog days of summer."

"You talk about them like they're people," I said.

"Yeah, I guess I do, but I like rivers a lot more than I like people. They do have some of the same qualities, though. For instance, some rivers make you pay attention; they're fast, rough, and loud. They may not be as big as others, but they make up for it by their brashness, daring you to underestimate them. Others are bold and broad, kind of authoritative, self-confident even. And then you have some that are quiet and mysterious, modest at first glance, almost secretive. They reveal themselves only after you've committed to them."

I considered this. "Okay, so if I'm a river, what kind am I?" I asked.

James rubbed his goatee in thought. "I guess you'd be more like the latter. You're the river that runs through the mountains unnoticed and then suddenly opens up in a fabulous meadow." He was grinning. I could see he liked his answer. It was uncharacteristically sweet.

"I think you're the first type, James, tough and fast. Except you've got some obnoxious parts in the middle, parts that are unfishable, parts you want to skip over."

"Nice," he said. "You get fabulous and I get obnoxious."

"Not all of you," I said. "You've got parts that are rough too."

"Thanks," he said. "I feel much better."

When we got to Dillon, we stopped at a local fly shop for information, and I took the opportunity to call Winiski. I'd promised to keep in touch over the summer but hadn't done a particularly good job. She sounded happy to hear me. She kept asking about Oregon and my plans, while I wanted to talk about what we'd been doing. There was a slight disconnect. Finally, she said, "Toby, you seem to be avoiding the issue. It's okay to have one foot planted in the moment—but you need to have the other foot moving toward the

The Eddy

future."

I laughed. "Doesn't that mean I'll have to do the splits?" The line went silent. "Look, just promise me when I'm enrolled, you'll do one of those dances for me." I felt the need to keep it light, to assure her I was okay with the next step, but I was anything but confident. I'm sure she sensed it and let it go.

"Has Mitch spoken of school?"

The question surprised me. "No... Should he?"

"No. I guess not. I was just wondering." There was a long pause. "Send him my best, okay?"

I was a little depressed after talking to her. I felt the summer slipping away and wondered how it had happened so fast. In high school, three months was an eternity. Out here, it was something else. Time seemed to have collapsed on me, as if letting go of calendars and watches somehow changed the way time was marked. I wondered if it was just me. Did James feel it too?

When we got back in the truck, I mentioned Winiski and sent along her best. He didn't say much. I guess he didn't want to talk about school either. The Ruby, however, was another story. As with all new water, he was bubbling with excitement. "Four-weight stuff, hopper heaven, delicate presentations!"

His enthusiasm, however, came to a screeching halt when we pulled up to a bridge, which was one of the few *public* access points for the Ruby. "Those assholes," he growled, and then lit into a chain of expletives. The river was blocked by a barbed wire fence from the bridge down to the water. James got out of the truck, slammed the door, and stood staring at the river, hands on hips.

I didn't understand it until later, but here was what infuriated him: Most of the lower Ruby ran through private land, and many of the owners considered the river their own. That didn't sit well with James. The problem went back to the old debate as to whether anyone could actually own the water running through their property. Montana law was less than clear on the issue.

As it stood, the water itself was in the public domain, but the Ruby, with so few access points, was nearly impossible to get on, unless you accessed it from a bridge, which was public. Ranchers, however, argued the bridge doesn't extend down to the actual water line; therefore, anyone accessing the water from the bridge was trespassing. Further complicating the matter were rich ranchers and recreationists who purchased the land along the Ruby and sold access to the water with rod fees, something James was adamantly opposed to. For James, it certainly was acceptable to own land as long as enough of it was still in the public domain. But no one had a right to own water, especially a river. To be honest, I thought it was much ado about nothing. There was plenty of water to fish in the region, so it wasn't worth getting worked up about it.

But James was another story. He thought it was the beginning of the end, and he would have no part in ignoring it. In fact, he swore he'd make a point to fish the Ruby every time he came through this region, and, in case I wasn't clear on his reasons, his language left no room for ambiguity. "Fuck those guys. Fuck the asshole ranchers. They siphon off the water, degrade the resource, and then have the audacity to say it belongs to them to do as they please. These guys aren't idiots. If they were, at least they'd have an excuse. No, they're just arrogant and greedy."

James stormed around to the back of the truck and rummaged around in the bed until he found what he wanted. "We're gonna fish this river because it's our right."

I stood there watching, dumbfounded, as he marched down to the fence near the water and started cutting away at the barb wire with a pair of wire cutters. For ten minutes, I watched him feverishly destroy a section of the fence. When he walked back up to the truck, he was sweating profusely. "There," he said. "I feel better. What do you say we wade wet today? I'm hot."

I looked down the gravel road and shook my head. "Hope we don't get shot," I mumbled.

Once I got past looking over my shoulder, I enjoyed

The Eddy

fishing this section of the Ruby. The banks were impossible to walk due to the thick brush, so we waded the river for miles. The river was narrow, so we took turns fishing. Each time one of us caught a fish or missed a hit, we'd give the river to the other guy to fish. It made for some fun competition, and it was nice to meander up the river, enjoying the cold water against our legs on a hot day. The fish we caught were on the small side of what we were used to, but the scenery and the challenge made it worthwhile. It reminded me of some of the water we fished in the Black Hills.

After that day, we did not fish that section of the Ruby again. I think it was enough for James to make his point, which seemed to me to be unnecessarily over the top. To some degree, I understood his anger, but I'm not sure what cutting up a fence was going to accomplish, other than piss a few people off.

We decided to camp in the state forest near the upper Ruby, not far from the Gravelly Mountains, a quiet scenic place with few people. Most of the traffic was down below near Dillon and Twin Bridges, where people fished the Jefferson, Beaverhead, and the Big Hole. Up here, the fish were smaller, but that didn't seem to matter. The fish were almost secondary to the scenery. We spent the early part of the days casting three- and four-weight rods, throwing mostly terrestrials and dry flies. In the afternoons, James would read or snooze and I'd go on long hikes, taking postcard pictures, admiring fields of Rosy Paintbrush and mountain slopes covered with purple Silky Lupine.

On our last evening, we kept a few fish and fried them up for dinner with mashed potatoes and canned corn. So far, we'd killed a total of eight fish, not including the whitefish we smoked. Each time we killed a fish, I felt a twinge of regret, but I soon got over it around the dinner table.

Before we left Montana for good, we fished the Jefferson and the Beaverhead, including Poindexter Slough. They were all impressive rivers. I caught a number of fish over twenty inches, including a rainbow that measured twenty-four inches, my biggest fish of the trip. Oddly, it didn't put up much of a fight, which made me wonder if it was recently hooked and was so spent, it had little to offer. I released it before James had a chance to see it or take a picture. As much as I wanted a photo, the fish needed to get back in the water right away or it would've died. I spent ten minutes reviving it before it was able to swim off on its own. I had to laugh, because I knew James would've wanted all the details of the catch, but, as it turned out, I never told him. I kept that one for myself.

I would've been content to hang around the area for weeks, but it was high season and the crowds got frustrating. It seemed as if everyone wanted to fish the same stretches at the same time. For the most part, people were courteous, but a few times on the Beaverhead, drift boats with guides cut into our space and started casting to our water. James didn't say much, but I could tell he was steamed.

Near the end of July, we had a long conversation around the fire one night about how we wanted to end the trip. I was up for fishing Idaho, but James thought it best to bypass it in favor of Oregon. Just the sound of the word *Oregon* made me sick to my stomach.

"Toby, we've been out for two months. The summer isn't endless. You need to get to campus so you can check in, secure a dorm, and look for a job."

I wanted to argue with him, but I knew he was right. We decided, as a last hurrah, to swing through Ketchum, Idaho to visit Hemingway's gravesite and then head north of Bend, Oregon to try our luck at steelhead. "It's a fitting way to end this thing," James said. "Steelhead are beautiful, hard-fighting, and tough to catch. We'll find out how much you've learned."

The Eddy

Chapter 31

It was the first week of August when we finally left Montana and crossed back over the Bitterroots into Idaho. The old truck seemed to labor in the passes, and I was convinced it would overheat. I was in no great hurry, so I watched the truck's gauges with keen interest, secretly hoping for catastrophe. For the life of me, I could not understand how that truck kept going. Other than changing the oil and checking the fluids, James never did anything to it. At one point, I was convinced he was just going to settle down wherever his truck crapped out.

But the old Ford survived another mountain pass, and we made our way to Ketchum. I was more interested in fishing and finding a place to camp than finding a cemetery, but James seemed excited about the prospect of seeing Hemingway's grave. I never cared much for graveyards, never understood people's fascination with them. I decided it was probably just an older person's thing and that perhaps, in time, I would take more interest in them.

It was late in the afternoon when we found the Ketchum Cemetery. It was situated in the foothills of the Lost River Mountains. It was a peaceful, quiet place that was easy to miss if you weren't looking for it. James and I were the only ones there, which surprised us. Hemingway's site was beneath two large spruce trees. There was a long piece of gray granite, flush with the ground, with the name Ernest Miller Hemingway and the date July 21, 1899 – July 2, 1961. Next to it was an identical marker belonging to his last wife, Mary. They were understated stones and, from what I knew of his writing, they seemed appropriate.

"He sure lived in a pretty place his last few years," I

said, looking out at the mountains.

James, hands thrust in his pockets, surveyed the landscape. "I think, in some ways, the guy came full circle. A lot of his youth was spent in upper Michigan when it was first being logged. It was a wild, rugged place. A lot like here, but without the mountains."

"Ah, so that's where *Big Two-Hearted River* comes from," I said, thinking back to the story he made me read. "You think that was his best work?"

James took a deep breath and thought about it. "Maybe. I didn't always think so, but I could be convinced now. It was written when he was young, not too much older than you, Toby. It was a part of an experimental novel, actually. A series of loosely connected stories assembled like photographs."

For some reason, I envisioned his wall back home, plastered with four decades of pictures. "Well, all I know is it's a great fishing story," I said.

"Yeah, it is. But it's really a story about healing, Toby. It's a story about recovery and learning how to feel again after you've been kicked around so much you've gone numb. It's kind of why I wanted you to read it."

"Oh," I said. "I might've missed that part. I guess I really didn't understand who Nick Adams was."

James walked over to one of the spruce trees and sat down. The shadows were starting to stretch across the cemetery and, in the shafts of light through the trees, I could see the pollen dance in slow motion. I sat down across from James and stretched my legs and watched the particles, waiting for him to explain. I could tell he was fixing to say something by the way he cocked his head. I'd grown accustomed to the mannerism. "Nick is just us, a guy carrying a heavy load." He looked at me and could see my confusion. "The weight of history, Toby. We carry the weight of what we've been taught and *not* taught from an early age, and sometimes we spend a lifetime trying to recover from it." He smiled slightly and closed his eyes.

I considered the story again. "I thought it was mostly

The Eddy

about a guy fishing for trout deliberately. I mean, I loved the description of the river and fish, but I didn't see anything more than that."

"It's okay to see it as a fishing story," James said, eyes still closed. "As a fishing story alone, it stands tall. But keep it close to your vest, Toby. Reread it now and then. You may come to see it differently."

I tried to recall more of the story, but it was more impressionistic to me. The details were fuzzy. "I remember the description of the trout. That struck me as truthful."

James opened his eyes. He reached down and picked a dandelion and plucked off its withered brown head. "Hemingway admired trout because they hold their own in the tough, conflicting currents. They always face the current head on. They don't get pushed back. In some ways, their existence is a draw." He looked out at the mountains. "No, you didn't miss the point, Toby. It is about fishing. But sometimes, with stories, you have to revisit them. It's crazy to think you get it all nailed one time through, because you seldom do. It's like history. You think you get it, the whole cause and effect scenario, all that bullshit, and you sit back smugly and think you've arrived at enlightenment. But it's a false pursuit."

"In what way?" I was getting more confused. James sat there, staring out at the mountains with that slight smile on his face. "How do you mean?" I insisted.

"It's not linear, Toby. The journey, it's circular. Not only *can* you go back, but you *need* to go back." He stood up and slowly brushed himself off. "Man, it's taken me a long time to understand that," he said softly. He shifted his gaze to the lengthening shadows across the foothills and took a deep breath. "A real long time." He thrust his hands back in his pockets, chuckled softly, and started walking toward the truck. "We still have some daylight. Let's burn some pavement."

Joe Paatalo

The Eddy

Chapter 32

When we crossed into Oregon later that day, I was asleep and didn't realize for some time we were in a new state. James pulled over in the dark alongside an old logging road near the Malheur River, and we ate a dinner of sandwiches washed down with warm sodas. We sat on the tailgate with our headlamps on, listening to the water rumbling in the distance. The place was more creepy than idyllic. It wasn't a good first impression of Oregon. We slept in the truck that night to save time, and I spent the majority of the evening rolling around trying to get comfortable. An owl perched in a tree near the truck wanted to hoot all night long. It was amusing at first, but by four in the morning, I was ready to shoot it.

    I awoke from a rough sleep, stiff and sore, feeling ornery. I wanted a hot breakfast and a shower in the worst way. I convinced James to pull over at a truck stop where we could eat and clean up. I considered calling home, since it had been almost two weeks from my last call, but I was starting to doubt my decision to attend school in Oregon. I was afraid hearing familiar voices might make me turn around. Instead of calling, I filled out four postcards and sent them off. On each one, I ended with *Wish you were here.* I was sure they'd never know how much I meant it. The act of sending them managed to make me feel better.

    Back on the road, I settled in to watch the landscape, which wasn't much in eastern Oregon. James was on a J.J. Cale kick and didn't feel like talking, so I finally got bored and reached into my book bag and took out *Zen and the Art of Motorcycle Maintenance*, which I'd been trying to get through the last few months without much luck. After reading for a while, I put it down in frustration. "Hey, James, you ever read this thing?"

James looked over and started laughing. He turned down the music. "I can't believe you're reading that. Good for you."

"Well, I loved the way it started, but I'm so lost, I have no idea what I'm reading. What the hell is it about?"

"It took me several tries to get through it, so hang in there. It's pretty esoteric, but from what I recall, it's about the balance between the romantic and the mechanical view of the world. Pirsig sees the necessity of both. They're not mutually exclusive." James thought about it for a minute and then added, "It's sorta like you being a really good mechanic and appreciating the inner workings of things, but at the same time, you also appreciate all the ambiguity and mystery the world has to offer. Or something like that."

"Oh," I said, and flipped through the yellowing pages of the paperback. "I didn't get that, but I'm starting to appreciate mystery. When I first picked it up, I saw this pink cover and thought, Hey, maybe it's about a gay biker."

James laughed. "Not exactly. But I like the idea of a gay biker book. Maybe you should write it?"

"Maybe," I said. "Why don't *you* write a book?"

"No, I don't think so. If I did write a book, though, it would have to be about fishing. It's about the only thing I'm sure of."

"You could write one on anger management," I said.

James rolled his eyes. "Funny. I'm laughing inside. In your next life, you should be a comedian."

"Sure," I said, "and who will you be in your next life?"

James looked out his window and didn't say anything. Finally, he reached over and put Cale back on. "Anonymous," he said.

For the next three hours, I went back to watching the landscape and listening to the music. We racked the miles, not saying much. I tried not to think too much about what lay ahead, instead preferring to watch the high desert as it gradually changed into the eastern slopes of the Cascades.

The Eddy

On the surface, there wasn't much memorable about the ride, but to this day, when I hear a J.J. Cale tune, I'm taken back to that time and place, and I feel a twinge of excitement and fear. Music is funny that way.

By late afternoon, we'd made our way north along the eastern Cascades up to White River Falls State Park, a campground near the Deschutes, where we checked into a park loaded with fishermen. After setting up camp, we drove into Maupin and arranged for a drift boat. Since James had never fished the river before, he bought a guide, but not before making sure we weren't spending four hundred bucks on a greenhorn.

We elected to let the river surprise us in the morning. Normally, we liked to do some scouting, but since we were running low on days, we decided to get a few steaks and a nice bottle of wine to enjoy around a fire. I prepared dinner that evening, remembering James' elk steaks back in South Dakota. I made sure to use a coffee rub on the meat and to smother everything with freshly sliced mushrooms and onions. We ate slowly, savoring each bite.

After dinner, we put our feet up and sipped the last of the wine, listening to the laughter emanating from the other sites. It felt good to be in the company of fishermen, even if they were only on the periphery. Despite a few ugly incidents, fly fishermen were some of the nicest people I had ever met. I lost track of the flies given to me by a stranger, or the advice passed on by an older fisherman. Throughout the trip, I was told on numerous occasions how nice it was to see a younger person on the stream. At first, that seemed counter-intuitive. I figured fishermen were secretive and protective of their spots. But, by and large, I think they understood that the future of coldwater and trout depended on people who loved rivers as much as they did.

As the evening wore on, James explained a little more about steelhead, which were essentially rainbows that moved from large bodies of water to rivers where they returned to spawn. I was surprised that many of them traveled to and from the ocean as well, and it gave me great appreciation for their tenacity. Anything that traveled that far, under all kinds of duress, deserved special attention.

"But they're tough to catch," James said. "Especially the big ones. They fight like hell and will take you into your backing in a heartbeat. Don't be upset if you don't get one, even on this great river."

The Eddy

Chapter 33

We were at the launch before our boat and guide arrived the next morning, so James took the opportunity to string up his seven- and eight-weight rods. He chose the lighter rod and had me practice casting the heavier one. It wasn't all that difficult, but I could see how the additional weight could wear you out. "Pace yourself," he said. "It's a long day."

And it was a long day. Gary, our guide, was an affable, middle-aged fellow who had been guiding on the Deschutes for years. He was knowledgeable and filled with stories. He set me up with a few colorful streamers, showed me where to cast, and essentially left me alone for the first few hours. He was an excellent boatman. We never had to ask him to put us on good water.

The lower Deschutes was a spectacularly scenic river. Framed by tall rim rock, it ran wide and deep as it tumbled its way down to the Colombia River. The canyon the river dropped through was immense, and I learned right away to keep my eyes on the river. There were some serious rapids that could knock a guy overboard if he weren't paying attention. In all, I was just as smitten by the wildlife in the canyon as I was with the water. Eagles, osprey, mule deer, and bighorn sheep seemed to appear out of nowhere in the lower stretch. I don't think we went a mile without seeing something.

Unfortunately, neither James nor I could land a fish. Gary said we were doing all the right things, that our casting was excellent, and he was thrilled to have such competent clients. But we couldn't get a bite. Not one.

By late afternoon, I could see Gary was getting a bit desperate. He was working hard at the oars, back-rowing in tough water, doing all he could to get us some fish. He became increasingly apologetic, but James told him not to worry about it. That it was just fishing and that's the way it went sometimes.

In hindsight, it might have been too hot. The lower Deschutes can warm up in the summer and put the fish down, but Gary swore they were hammering them a few days earlier.

Toward evening, James quit fishing and enjoyed the drift, talking to Gary about guiding. I, on the other hand, continued to fish hard. A half hour before we took out, I hooked a fish, a big one. I had him on for all of ten seconds before he threw the hook. I was despondent, but poor Gary was apoplectic.

When we got off the river, Gary shrugged his shoulders apologetically. "I'm sorry, boys. I didn't earn my keep today. Just give me two hundred bucks and we'll call it even."

"Aw, bullshit," James said. He handed Gary four hundred fifty bucks. "You did a fine job. You're a good guide."

Gary reluctantly took the money, but not before promising to take us again, for free, when the weather was better. James didn't say anything, but I promised to take him up on it.

Around camp that evening, James broke out a good bottle of scotch. We had the last of the stew for dinner, and we were content to watch the flames and listen to the other fishermen laugh around their campfires. I felt like asking some of them how they did, but James insisted that few, if any, caught fish. It didn't seem to stop their laughter, though. In truth, I wasn't disappointed. Not really. The river was reluctant to give up fish, but it gave other things in compensation.

We stayed up late that evening but didn't talk much. The sun had left me dehydrated, and I drank a half-dozen Cokes. We decided it didn't make much sense to fish the river in these conditions and that, in the morning, we'd

The Eddy

make our way to the coast. It wasn't how I had anticipated our last day of fishing, but again, there were no guarantees.

In the morning, we broke camp, each of us going through the routines silently. Before we left, James went to use the bathroom and I took out my pocketknife and carved *T. Casper was here* into the picnic table. It was the only physical mark I'd left behind on the whole trip. I considered cutting it deeply into the soft wood, but decided a few scratches were best. It would be gone within a year.

On the road, we took our time heading south out of Portland and then hooked up with Highway 18 West to the coast. I was eager to see the ocean, but I felt oddly nauseated thinking about all the upcoming changes. As we were driving, I started thinking of how my whole life had been restricted to the interior of the country. And I guess, in some ways, it was a fitting metaphor for the way I'd been living—afraid of exposure, afraid of where the road might end, afraid to look anywhere but inward.

When the ocean came into view for the first time as we were coming over a mountain pass near Rose Lodge, I could feel my breath catch. I leaned forward and stared at the open expanse of water. There was nowhere to look *but* outward. And here it was, the dramatic line of demarcation between the end of the continent and the vast beginning of a new kind of world. This was it, I thought, a beginning *and* an end.

Sensing I was a bit out of sorts, James pulled into a scenic overlook so I could take a deep breath and take a few pictures. I got out, and for the first time, breathed in the hint of salt and brine. From up high, the ocean looked endless. I watched as the breakers came in, capped in white, ferocious and powerful. It seemed fitting that the continent ended here in such dramatic fashion. It seemed fitting that our trip would end somewhere near here. As I looked out over the Pacific, I felt both exhilarated and melancholic, an emotional cocktail that sat funny in my stomach. I looked over at James to gauge *his* reaction, but he was surprisingly stoic. He had been quiet since leaving the Deschutes.

We stayed there for half an hour, leaning against the truck, scanning the horizon, absorbing the new world. Finally, James got back in the truck and I joined him without saying anything. We drove down to Lincoln City, and from there followed Pacific Coast Highway 101 all the way to the Siuslaw National Forest, not far from Newport. I sat quietly, watching the scenery while listening to Charlie Parker. It was a sunny day with few clouds. Lost in thought, I sat back in my seat with the window rolled down, soaking in the scenic shoreline.

By late afternoon, we took a campsite not far from Stonefield Beach. We pitched our tent just off a ledge where we could see the ocean and then drove into the coastal town of Waldport, where James said he wanted to meet a friend. We purchased a few days' worth of groceries and, after we loaded them into the back of the truck, James threw me his keys.

"Here. You take the truck and head back. I'm just heading up the hill a ways."

I was under the assumption I'd go with him, so I was surprised. "You sure?"

"Yeah, take the truck. If I'm not back by tomorrow, don't worry. I'll be there the following morning at the latest."

"Do you want me to get you?"

"No. I'm fine. I'll get a ride. Cruise the coast if you want. Do a little exploring. Be sure to walk the beach at low tide and check out the tide pools. They're amazing."

I didn't ask anything further, figuring he knew what he was doing. I hopped in the truck and headed back to the campground.

I made dinner that evening, burgers and macaroni and cheese. I took my dinner to the ledge so I could eat while looking at the ocean. While the inland temperature was in the upper 80s, down by the ocean, it felt cool, almost sweatshirt weather. When I finished eating, I put a light jacket on, grabbed a few sodas from the cooler, and took them down to the beach. I sipped them while sitting against

The Eddy

a large piece of driftwood. When it started to get dark, I gathered some dry wood, made a fire, and watched a spectacular sunset. It would be my first of many ocean sunsets, and each time I experienced them, I felt I was seeing something new.

Before I went to bed that evening, I started to get a funny feeling about James. I started to wonder if he was going black again. I couldn't recall anything that might have triggered it, but I knew from experience it could come without warning. And then I remembered he hadn't told me anything about the friend he was visiting, which seemed odd. It might have been the dark, or the fact that it had been a while since I'd had a night alone, but with all that time to myself, I started entertaining dark thoughts. Old pieces of conversations started swimming in my head, stuff he'd said about school or his father or some book, things that hadn't made sense to me at the time. James had always liked his alone time, but for me, alone time could be hard time. As much as I tried that night to keep the dark thoughts at bay, they kept surfacing. Not able to sleep, I walked the beach for a long time in the moonlight, trying to let the crashing waves drown out my restless thoughts.

In the morning, I woke tired. I made some coffee and bagel sandwiches, but I wasn't hungry enough to eat them. Instead, I wrapped them up and took a long walk on the beach. It was near low tide, so I took James' advice and went tide pooling. I didn't know the names of all the creatures I encountered, other than the starfish and a few small squids, but I was mesmerized by the diversity of life in the pools. The colors—purples, oranges, and electric greens—were riotous. I spent hours climbing the rocks and taking pictures.

In the afternoon, I encountered a gentleman on the beach with a fly rod, casting for ocean perch. From the distance, there was something odd about his motion. I didn't notice until I got closer that he had only one hand. His left arm ended with a prosthetic clamp, and while it made for an odd-looking cast, he was able to throw the line with remarkable distance. I watched him for a long time, amazed at his proficiency. He had a long rod, and he would take a step backward as he loaded it, and then he would lunge forward and haul the line with his artificial hand, sending it far beyond anything I could do on my best day. After a while, I couldn't help myself. I had to talk to him.

His name was Ken. He was in his mid-twenties and had lived near the ocean most of his life. He fished inland steelhead and salmon, but his favorite kind of fishing was done in the surf. "I like the drama of the ocean," he said. "You never know what you might get."

He saw me looking at his missing hand. "I lost it when I was five," he said. "Never stopped me from doing anything."

"You cast beautifully," I said. "Better than I could with both hands."

"Thanks." He laughed. "You want to give it a try? I'll show you." He put out two more lovely casts and stripped his line back in. "It takes a little practice, but it's not as hard as it looks."

Yes, it was. The first time I tried it, I almost pierced my ear. The second time, I barely got the line out twenty-five feet. I tried to give the rod back to him, but he wouldn't take it until I had thrown at least two good casts. It took a while, but I finally managed.

"Trust me, it really grows on you. It's all about the challenge," he said.

"Yeah," I said. "I hear you there. You're awfully good at this. You ever wonder how good you could be if you had two hands?" I hoped the question wasn't insensitive.

He looked at me and smiled. "Not too often. Sometimes the absence of something makes you better. Who knows, with two hands, I might waste my life shooting pool or something." He took the rod from me and clipped off the fly. "I remember what it was like having two hands, though. I don't miss it that much. But sometimes, even after all these years, I still get ghost pains." He sat down on a rock, opened his cooler, and offered me a Pepsi. "I'm glad I was

The Eddy

born with two, but I'll take what I got."

Ken took a bottle of soda from the cooler and twisted the cap off with his good hand. He took a long swig and then looked at me. He was handsome, with long unkempt hair and sharp features. "So, tell me what you're about," he said.

We talked about fly fishing for quite a while, about the coastal rivers and the movement of fish. Like James, Ken seemed to draw something from water that was both primal and sacred. For him, fishing wasn't about the catching. It was about something else. But he had trouble articulating why he *loved* it so much. "I mean, it's great," he said, "Really great. But it pisses me off too." He scratched his head with his good hand. "Makes me wonder why I keep coming back sometimes—crazy love, I guess." He pondered the phrase and smiled. "Yeah, that's about right. Or as close to it as I can get."

"I think I know what you mean," I said. "When you're talking love and hate, words often fall short on both ends."

"Yeah," he said, nodding and looking out at the ocean. "You got that right. But it doesn't stop you from trying to figure it out."

Before leaving, I took his number and we promised to meet again to ocean fish. I knew for sure I would call. I was starting to like the idea of new challenges, and for the first time since the trip began, I started to think favorably about the next four years. As I walked back to camp, it dawned on me how odd that was. I wasn't used to thinking beyond the next day.

When I got back to camp, James still hadn't returned, so I took the truck up the coast and checked out some of the rivers that flowed into the ocean. I imagined myself on a Harley, cruising down 101 or following the rivers up into the mountains with my fly rods in tow. On the way back, on an impulse, I stopped at a barber shop and had my hair shorn to a nub. I asked the barber to put my ponytail in a plastic bag.

That night, as I sat around the fire thinking about James, I braided my hair into two long ropes. I figured I would send one to Takeita and keep the other. When I was done, I threw the remaining hair in the fire and watched it burn. I assumed it would stink, but I smelled nothing, other than a slight acrid aroma mingled with the dried cedar and pine.

The Eddy

Chapter 34

The next morning, James pulled up in an old faded red Toyota truck, blaring some old Dylan highway song. I was terribly relieved. I had almost convinced myself something had happened to him. "Geez," I said, "I was beginning to worry about you. You hungry?"

"Sure," he said, and sat down to a cheese and egg bagel. "I didn't recognize you at first. Thought I was in the wrong camp. I like the new look."

"Thanks," I said, and rubbed the top of my head. "Did you accomplish what you needed to?"

"Yeah, I took care of business, made a few phone calls. You have fun?"

I told him what I'd been up to, and he seemed to listen intently. "Say, whose truck is that?" I asked.

James didn't say anything. He walked back to the truck and grabbed an envelope. "Let's go down to the beach. I got something for you."

We found the spot where I'd had the fire the night before and sat down. There was still some coastal fog that had yet to blow off. James took a deep breath of ocean air and seemed to hold it for a while. He then looked at me and sighed. "I got a call from Jackson a while ago. He said he was being moved, but that I had my job back. I think he was surprised."

"Well, that's good," I said.

"I turned it down, Toby. I quit—I'm not going back. Deep down, I was hoping I'd be fired."

"Okay," I said, not sure where he was heading. "So you'll teach somewhere else. That's good."

"No," he said, shaking his head. "I'm done. I'm quitting and never going back."

I still wasn't sure what he meant. "Never going back to Minnesota or never going back to teaching?"

"Both." He handed me the envelope. "Inside, you'll find the title to the truck, signed over to you, the warranty on the Winston rod, and the letter I had faxed to Maggie. The letter says that I want you to have the Chevelle and all my tying stuff. Everything else Maggie can have, other than my gear."

I was at a loss for words. "I don't understand."

He smiled. "Well, I like gear, that's all."

I didn't think it was funny. "I don't want your stuff. I don't—what about the promise you made? Aren't you coming to Eugene?"

James looked at me and shook his head. "No, I'm not. You're on your own."

I felt like crying. "I don't want your fucking stuff, James. Why are you doing this?"

He took another deep breath and looked out at the ocean. He seemed to be searching for the right words. "Look, I don't expect you to understand this, but I've been in the eddy too long, Toby. Things have passed me by. For a long time now, I've been a pretender. I pretend to teach; I pretend at relationships; I even pretend to care." He looked down and kicked the driftwood at his feet. "But I don't really, at least not enough to work at it. So, I watch as stuff comes at me, and I end up angry. I end up mean. And worst of all, I hurt people... I guess I've known that for some time. It just took a while to see it." He looked at me, his eyes gray and tired. "I'm not going back because there's nothing to go back to."

I started to tear up. "But the promise. What about the promise to yourself?" I had come to see it as an albatross, but I couldn't help but admire it.

He rubbed his eyes. I could tell he was exhausted. "I'm breaking it. I'm letting go. I'm through with making promises."

The Eddy

Suddenly, I felt sick. "James, you'd never do anything to hurt yourself, would you?" He didn't answer right away. "Don't mess with me—promise." I felt myself getting angry.

"No, of course not." James paused. "So that you know, I started this trip with good intentions. I thought maybe I still had something in the tank, that I just needed a break and then I could go back and be of some use. Soldier on, right? Suck it up like the old man." He gave me a weary smile. "But I'm not him. I guess I'm at that portage again."

I looked at him, trying to read his face. I wanted to trust him. "Then why give me your stuff? I don't like what that means."

He laughed. "Don't read into it, okay. I want you to have it because I'm leaving everything behind. I don't want anything to do with that life anymore."

I sat there staring at him, still trying to comprehend. "Mr. James, you're the closest thing to a father I ever had. Maybe that's not saying much, but it's true." I could see him cringe as I said this. He stood up and starting walking toward the water. I followed behind him, trying to get my head around what all this meant.

Near the ocean, in the surf-packed sand, James took his shoes off and rolled his pants up. He dug his toes in the wet sand and smiled. "Feels good. Try it."

I took off my shoes and walked ahead of him to where the waves receded. I stood there and let the next wave wash up on me, soaking me to the knees. James joined me and we stood there getting wet, watching the waves erase our footsteps.

After a while, James said, "When I went off to school years ago, I wanted to believe it was all about hockey and new opportunities, but that wasn't really true. Looking back, I think, more than anything, I was trying to get away from my father—from all the things he was, from all the things he wasn't. After he died, the mystery of who he was got sealed. Bit by bit, without really thinking about it, I wiped him away completely. I mean, I sold the car he gave me, smashed his canoe, gave all the money he left me to my sister... But he never left, Toby. Not really." James looked at me. "Maybe I never really wanted him all gone. Just enough of him so I wouldn't be haunted. Doesn't work that way, though." He put his hands in his pockets and squinted up at the sky. "I'm not a father, Toby. I'm your friend. That's the best I got."

I looked over at him and studied his face. He was tan and fit but looked older than he was. I did not understand him. To me, he was a walking sack of contradictions. It would be a long time before much of what he said made sense to me. I just nodded and looked out across the ocean. There were no words for what I was feeling. "I'll miss you," I finally said.

James reached over and put his arm around my shoulder and gave me a half hug. It was the most physical act of affection I'd ever seen him make. It made me cry. "I'm sorry I wasn't always worthy of your company," he said. "Or your friendship. I hope you'll forgive me for that." I looked away and wiped my eyes.

"Let's walk," he said.

We spent the next several hours hiking the beach, watching the morning clouds dissipate and give way to another bright August day. James wanted to talk about my future, about what school would be like, the challenges ahead.

I was more concerned for him than for me, and I wanted to change the subject, but he insisted he would be fine, that Maggie had agreed to buy the carriage house and there was enough money to get by. But that was as much as he would say.

We eventually got around to talking about the Chevelle, and I promised to take care of the car and garage it in the winter, but he didn't seem that interested. I guess he knew I'd care for it better than he would.

In the end, we drifted back to the stories of our summer, reminiscing about the rivers, the fish, the people we'd met. I told him that he had made me a fly fisher for life, and he laughed. I guess he already knew that.

The Eddy

When we finally got back to camp, we took all of his gear and put it in the Toyota and sat down at the picnic table for a final drink. He poured two cups of Dalmore scotch and asked me to make a toast. It took me a minute, because I was close to tears again, and there was so much I wanted to say. But finally, I raised the cup and said, "Here's to friends. Thank you, Mitch."

We drank and raised the cups again. This time, he made the toast. "Here's to the pursuit of joy. May you find it in the toughest places."

We finished our drinks, and I reluctantly walked him to the truck. "So where are you heading?" I asked.

He looked to the north. "Guess I'll just follow the coast until I run out of room. After that, I don't know. I'm thinking Alaska. And then maybe Canada."

"Canada?" I was surprised.

"Sure. Why not? Beautiful country, lots of water, humane politics. Who knows, maybe I'll take up skating again." He climbed into the truck and started the engine.

"And what will you do?"

He looked out at the road and shrugged. "Reinvent myself, I guess. As far as that's possible."

I looked off down the highway to where the road curved. I wondered if it *was* possible. I wanted to believe it. "Before you go, I have something for you," I said. From my back pocket, I pulled out one of the braided ponytails. "Figured you could put it on your mirror."

He started laughing and then rummaged around the truck until he found a bobby pin left over from the previous owner. He clipped the hair to the rearview mirror and then admired it. "It's perfect for holding flies," he said.

"You know," I leaned in towards his window, "I remember you said you once had a truck like this, maybe about the same year. What's up with that?"

He grinned, looked around the inside of the cab, and pointed to the new stereo. "Not quite. But I guess you're right. As much as you may not like it, the past always seems to make its presence known." He hit "Play" on the deck and

Joe Paatalo

Dylan's "Tangled up in Blue" began. He was laughing as he drove away. Neither of us said goodbye.

The Eddy

Epilogue

I never saw James again after that, although I heard from him from time to time. Sometimes it was a postcard, sometimes a message left late at night on my phone from an unknown place. Usually, it was a quick note to say he was well and to report on the fishing he was experiencing. But never more than that, and never anything that I could trace. I don't know whether that was intentional, but it doesn't really matter.

As for me, my days in Oregon passed quickly. Looking back now, it's funny how some things seem to race by, while others, like that summer with James, stretch out in my memory, unconstricted by time. I continued to fish in those years at the university, especially when things got difficult and I felt myself sliding. There was something about standing in the current with the river pushing against me and a fly line singing above my head that always restored my balance.

In time, though, without my complete awareness, fly fishing and the rivers I sought became less about healing and more about possibility. I'd like to think now that James, too, finally arrived at this place. But I can't be sure.

When I graduated from Oregon, I received a package in the mail from James. It came from Nova Scotia, of all places. In it was an eight-by-ten of a long strand of braided hair, filled with perhaps a hundred flies. Below the picture in the box, surrounded by Canadian newspapers, was a lovely six-weight bamboo rod he had built. My name was etched above the grip. It said The Toby Twister, Edition # 1.

Eventually, I did return to the Midwest, to Michigan of all places, to teach at a reservation school near the shores of Lake Superior. And it was there, alongside the great lake, I finally began to understand what James meant about the *necessity of going back. As I sit here now, putting the final touches on this story, I am reminded of a conversation he and I had not long before we parted. He told me that, as I got older, the memories of these days would soften, lose their hard edges, become more like impressionistic paintings. And maybe, to some degree, that's true. But as I return to that time, almost fifteen years ago, I see that I have stretched the canvas, painted with circular strokes, played with light and shadow—all in the pursuit of understanding. I have tried to be truthful, but I suspect James would accuse me of spin. He would not, however, argue against my truth, because he, as much as anyone, always understood that memory remains a work in progress.*

www.ingramcontent.com/pod-product-compliance
Lightning Source LLC
Chambersburg PA
CBHW070913030426
42336CB00014BA/2400